Outsmarting the Smart Money

Understand How Markets Really Work and Win the Wealth Game

Lawrence A. Cunningham

McGraw-Hill

New York   Chicago   San Francisco
Lisbon   London   Madrid   Mexico City
Milan   New Delhi   San Juan   Seoul
Singapore   Sydney   Toronto

McGraw-Hill

A Division of The McGraw-Hill Companies

1 2 3 4 5 6 7 8 9 0 AGM/AGM 0 9 8 7 6 5 4 3 2

ISBN 0-07-138699-8

Printed and bound by Quebecor/Martinsburg.

Contents

Part III

Preface and Acknowledgments

A joy of writing and publishing is expanding one's circle of friends. After I self-published *The Essays of Warren Buffett: Lessons for Corporate America*, hundreds of people from around the world contacted me. Many friendships arose, some nurtured in person, but most sustained by the exchange of ideas in writing and e-mail. When McGraw-Hill published my book, *How to Think Like Benjamin Graham and Invest Like Warren Buffett*, the group grew. These friends and many others of longer standing motivated me to write this book on behavioral finance, and I thank them all for making *Outsmarting the Smart Money* a reality.

One of these new friends observed that my work and investment philosophy, developed by Warren Buffett and Benjamin Graham, drew on a deeper economic tradition born in Austria. Giancarlo Ibarguen, professor and secretary general of the Universidad Francisco Marroquin, Guatemala, inspired Chapter 1 of this book. Called "Crossroads," the chapter shows the link between these traditions and explains why investors haven't heard of the profound ideas concerning investment psychology.

Friends from the world of journalism include David Henry, formerly a columnist at *USA Today* and now Associate Editor of *Business Week*. David's support has been invaluable to me. He helped me locate a very capable editor for this book, Ira Breskin, whose thoughtful comments hit the ideal between suggestion and critique. I met the publishing team at McGraw-Hill through previous books, and they deserve thanks as well, especially Kelli Christiansen, Jeffrey Krames, and Lydia Rinaldi.

My colleague at Cardozo Law School, Chuck Yablon, co-teaches an annual summer program with me at Oxford University on comparative corporate governance. We and our students learn a lot from the chance to look at the United States from a different perspective.

Last year Chuck pointed out to me that some managers use market volatility and loose U.S. disclosure rules to boost the value of their stock options. This book's discussion of how they do so in Chapter 6 draws on his work, co-authored with Australian scholar Jenny Hill, and I thank them both for allowing me to adapt it. Thanks also to my student, Martin Beeler, for helping with the adaptation, and to another student, Colette Reiner, for her research and writing assistance in other parts of this book, and to Justin Belair for proofreading it.

Though I was born and raised in Wilmington, Delaware, New York City has been my home for 15 years, the last five with a perfect skyline view of the World Trade Center from one mile due north. I've spent time living in other great cities—four years of high school in Philadelphia, a year each living in Boston, London, and Washington, D.C.—but there is no city like New York. A book about investing by a New York author owes deep gratitude to the people who make New York the world's financial capital. My thanks to New Yorkers such as Ace Greenberg of Bear Stearns, Sandy Gottesman of First Manhattan, and Howard Lutnick of Cantor Fitzgerald, and to non-New Yorkers whose leadership and acumen in global investing sustain New York—friends such as Warren Buffett of Omaha, Charlie Munger of Los Angeles, and Jack Bogle of Valley Forge, Pennsylvania.

New York remains the citadel of financial freedom despite the staggering losses caused by terrorist assaults on it. Everyone remembers where they were when they learned that New York and Washington were attacked on September 11, 2001. I was riding my bicycle from Boston's Back Bay neighborhood to Boston College's Newton campus, where I was spending the year as a visiting professor. The news was being reported over the radio in the deli where I stopped to buy iced coffee. At school, my students and I skipped our accounting class to watch television reports.

In succeeding days, it was hard to work on this book, then in its final stages. It wasn't so much distraction as that the work seemed trivial compared to the suffering and apprehension. At Ground Zero were many of my former students, now lawyers: a veteran New York City police officer who helped evacuate his office building, Joseph Inzerillo kept fellow workers calm and safe; a former New York City Emergency Medical technician who rescued the rescuers, Andrew Leftt, took them out of harm's way; a candidate for New York City

Council District 1, the neighborhood that included the World Trade Center, Elana Waksal Posner consoled her constituents that primary election day. My personal nightmare culminated in learning that my schoolmate and friend, the respected author and commentator Barbara Olson, died in the hijacked jet that hit the Pentagon, after cell-phoning her husband, Solicitor General Ted Olson, to warn him of the imminent horror.

Finishing the book would not have been possible without the support of people like these, students, colleagues, neighbors, leaders, friends old and new, in person and by mail. The list includes benefactors of Cardozo Law School, Sam and Ronnie Heyman, Eric and Margereta Javits, and Earle and Carol Mack among them, and colleagues there such as Arthur Jacobson and John McGinnis. At the top of the list is my wife, JoAnna Cuningham, who edited the manuscript, and my Mother, Anne Cunningham Brown of Chadds Ford, Pennsylvania, an endless source of strength in good times and bad.

In the days after September 11, I received hundreds of e-mails, checking to see if my family and I were okay, from friends in every part of the United States and a dozen other countries, including this one from Professor Ibarguen in Guatemala:

> I hope you and your loved ones are in good health. My thoughts and prayers have been with you and the American people during the last week. I am deeply saddened and concerned by the monstrous attack on America. The loss of precious, innocent life is unbearable. I have been trying to find the words to express my sympathy but there are none. The principles expounded by your founding fathers shine, for me, like the bright light at the end of the tunnel we are all trying to get our own countries out of. In thinking about the spirit of America there is hope. Yet after this ghastly event I fear for the loss of freedom in the U.S. all in the name of national security and the war against terrorism. Terrorism is evil and justice must be done but not at the expense of freedom. Americans must be as vigilant as ever to guard liberty at home.

This book is written against the background this vision paints, a background threatened but not undermined by terrorism's violation of staples of capitalism and democracy, rights that include the

American finance theorists say that even if these biases afflict the lesser among us, the star traders are immune. This proposition is examined and refuted, explaining that some financial pros have incentives to avoid making corrections, others find the task too risky, and all suffer from the same cognitive biases everyone faces.

Readers of financial newspapers are aware of the numerous debacles encountered by "smart money," ranging from the derivatives room at Barings in Singapore, to the mortgage desk at Kidder Peabody, to the geniuses at Long Term Capital Management and the fiends at Enron. The upshot is sustained price-value differences that undermine the efficiency story taught in the fanciest U.S. business schools. The discussion shifts to horse-race betting, where the setting of odds is remarkably efficient and contrasts this with closed-end mutual fund trading, where the setting of price is clearly not.

Completing this part of the book is an account of market action drawing on the cognitive biases to explain the kind of behavior markets exhibit. It is impossible to predict market behavior, yet the psychology that produces inefficiencies tempts people to do so using charts and other mysticism. Flags, pennants, and tea cups—staples of the chartist's stock in trade—are for the birds, this part shows, debunking these technical approaches to trading as no more than voodoo.

Among the valuable points from Part I are:

- How a commonsense finance philosophy was nearly lost in the dustbins of history, and how drawing on it now can improve investment performance (Chapter 1)
- How mental shortcuts lead investors off the path, and how to get back on (Chapter 2)
- How even the fanciest hedge funds boasting the most sophisticated money managers go astray (Chapter 3)
- How the market actually works, warts and all, and what to make of claims to predict market movements (Chapter 4)

Part II zooms in on ways corporate management can take advantage of the inefficiencies. Discussion focuses the behavioral-finance lens on managers. They can take advantage of market inefficiency in ways that both benefit and harm stockholders. Smart investors need to understand which side their managers are on.

Key practices start with the timing of public offerings and share repurchases. Public offerings are invariably made at times when the offering prices paid are greater than the business value delivered. Yet investors are repeatedly seduced by the prospect of getting in on hot offerings to make their fortunes. The only fortunes being made are for the peddlers and promoters in these high-priced deals. Share repurchases should operate in reverse, to take advantage of prices below values, but they do not always work that way.

Spin is not limited to Washington, D.C., but affects corporate disclosure as well. Many investors do not recognize the broad discretion corporate managers have over the timing and content of corporate disclosure, particularly as it relates to management's ability to influence a company's stock price to increase the value of stock options.

Two surprises stand out. One is also true of Washington. To paraphrase columnist Michael Kinsley's quip about Washington: the disgrace isn't in what's done that is illegal, but what is legal. The other is unique to corporate America. People understand that managers may bend the numbers and truth to show better results than they achieved. The surprise is that they also have incentives to show bad results on other occasions. The interplay affects stock-option value.

Biases affect management. The most costly context is takeovers, explained in a chapter called "The Winner's Curse." This refers to the tendency of bidders at auction to overpay. In the corporate context it concerns managers using shareholder resources to overpay for takeovers, the most costly consequence of absentee ownership.

Among the things you will take away from this part of the book:

- How nearly $30 billion was shifted from investors to entrepreneurs and their backers in the late-1990s IPO shuffle, and how to profit from the fallout (Chapter 5)

- How share buybacks went from obscure to wise to foolish in the past three decades, and how to spot red flags that distinguish the wise from the fools (Chapter 5)

- How managers lawfully condition corporate disclosure, the controversial role analysts play, and how to take advantage of information (Chapter 6)

- How to use new accounting rules to identify managers who habitually use shareholder wealth to overpay for corporate takeovers (Chapter 7)

- How managers use "*pro forma*" and other novel gimmicks to play games with accounting numbers, and areas to look out for (Chapter 8)

Turning from ways managers play the market to help or hurt you, the final part of the book explains how you can help yourself. Even the most experienced and sophisticated investors have been stung by Ponzi schemes and other financial scams. It considers what those financial scams teach us about ways an investor's mind-set can fail in doing investment analysis.

The book's final part provides solutions to the investor's dilemma. It presents critical habits of mind that investors can develop to deflect cognitive biases, along with strategies to improve investment decision making. These range from promoting objective patterns of thought to assessing loss aversion to enhancing the ability to calibrate probabilities.

The lessons point in one direction: a long-term, value-oriented investment philosophy. It operates with the least interference from psychological biases that afflict other investment approaches. The book explores what this means, as well as the role group decision making in investment clubs can play in promoting bias-free investment decisions.

The final chapter draws the stark contrast to the agony of urgency that arises from day trading and margin use, the crashes that follow related excesses, and how intelligent investors steer clear of "smart money" in these escapades.

Among the lessons in this part are:

- How to recognize mental errors in assessing financial opportunities (Chapter 9)
- How to think clearly about investment alternatives (Chapter 10)
- How to define your value function, a new risk assessment tool (Chapter 10)
- How long-term, value-oriented investing resembles evolutionary adaptations of the species (Chapter 11)
- How to become a millionaire: start as a billionaire and then day trade using borrowed money[2] (Chapter 12)

The book draws and reports on excellent academic research. It develops original lines of thought by extending the lessons from this work to the ways investors and managers behave and what this means for how markets operate. It identifies the practical lessons from these links. Readers emerge much better informed about investment theory and practice, what works, and how to combine intelligence and discipline to generate superior investment decisions.

Part
I

1

Crossroads

The United States is richer than ever, yet also more financially illiterate. We devote more resources to examining how abstract economic actors behave than to studying how people behave. In business schools nationwide, more teaching is done about economic models than about how to improve investment behavior.

The gap between the models and reality is illustrated by retelling the story of *Other People's Money*, an off-Broadway play turned into the popular 1991 film starring Danny DeVito and Gregory Peck, and affectionately known as *OPM*. DeVito plays a corporate raider named Lawrence Garfinkle ("Larry the Liquidator"). He wants to take over and liquidate the struggling New England Wire and Cable, an old-line manufacturer led by Peck's character, Andrew Jorgenson, who resists Larry's hostile bid.

The climax is a proxy contest for control of the corporation's board, pitting the young and brash Larry the Liquidator against the old and seasoned Jorgenson. The most dramatic scene is a shareholders' meeting where the Liquidator and Jorgenson debate.

Jorgenson speaks first, greeted by his shareholders with a standing ovation. On money matters he defers to printed material sent earlier to stockholders. He rises instead to discuss other issues: the company's history, its employees, and its hometown. These are the company's foundation that will sustain it through turbulent times.

Jorgenson points a finger at Larry the Liquidator, accusing him of "playing God with other people's money." Jorgenson says corporate raiders create no value, build nothing, and run nothing. Larry's claim that the company is better off dead than alive is both painful and shortsighted. He will kill the company if he gets control, tear it down, and sell it off.

As America reinvests in infrastructure, Jorgenson argues, New England Wire will resume its prosperous course. Investment in production is a better long-run strategy than the one Larry the Liquidator offers, he says.

The Liquidator takes the stage next. The shareholders are hostile, greeting him with hisses and boos. "Amen, amen, amen," he begins. "Where I come from, that's what we say when we hear a prayer."

"But all the prayers in the world won't help this doomed company," he argues, "because technology has passed it by—the cable industry has been killed by fiber optics. The capital invested in this company should be invested elsewhere. Liquidation is the best way."

Despite the initial applause for Jorgenson and boos for Larry, the shareholders vote for the Liquidator. Why? Before the big meeting, they received proxy materials and phone calls from both sides, soliciting their votes. At the meeting, they expressed a clear preference to stick it out for the long run.

Following the speeches, they do an about-face. Were they merely responding to rational arguments that had been made before? Perhaps it was the drama of the delivery, the vividness of what Larry said? But then, they had just heard Jorgenson's loyalty speech as well.

Looking at the economics, it could have been the ready cash that Larry offered. The alternative was an uncertain future. All Jorgenson could promise was that ultimately, we'll get there. The path to that goal was fraught with contingencies. In contrast, Larry pays cash today, end of story.

To put some numbers on it, suppose that Larry's offer of an immediate cash payment upon the company's liquidation was $50 per share, and the best Jorgenson promised was the equivalent of $8 per share, annually, for the next 30 years. Which is better?

Take a shareholder who owns 1000 shares. He is looking at either cash today of $50,000 or an annuity of $8000 for 30 years. How does he compare these offers? Standard economics says the choice should be the one that is worth more after discounting the payment stream to determine the present value of the annuity.

Doing the math is simple and doesn't need to detain us. What could be tricky is picking the right discount rate. This is the interest rate that reflects the difference between the value of today's dollar compared to what a dollar will be worth a year from now. The adage says that a bird in hand is worth two in the bush. But the tough question is how much more is the lone bird worth?

The discount rate is the answer. A reasonable benchmark is the average interest rate paid on money market accounts. Suppose that is 7 percent. Discounting a 30-year annuity of $8000 at 7 percent indicates that the total present value of that payment stream is about $100,000. Even if you used a tougher test of say, 10 percent (the long-run historical average rate charged on American mortgages), the present value of that deal is about $75,000. Based on these numbers, New England Wire holders were wrong to opt for Larry's bid.

Maybe these are not the numbers *OPM*'s author (the late Jerry Sterner) and director (Norman Jewison) had in mind. But I've chosen these numbers because these are the real numbers that the Pentagon offered some retiring military personnel in its early 1990s downsizing.

The retirees were given a pamphlet explaining the discounting just discussed and invited to choose between two alternative severance packages.[1] More than half the officers and nearly all the enlisted personnel chose the $50,000 cash today instead of the more-valuable but longer-term payout options.

These men and women are not stupid. They represent a cross-section of ordinary Americans and are not a statistical aberration given their sufficiently large number. Their dilemma reflects the one facing the shareholders in *OPM* and many Americans handling financial decisions.

The story epitomizes a widespread preference for cash today rather than returns tomorrow. It is an old story, something the British economist John Maynard Keynes mentioned in the 1930s: "there is a speculative zeal in making money quickly, and remoter gains are discounted by the average man at a very high rate."[2] This financial impatience is shared by employees and investors alike.

Standard economic textbooks used by most American business schools tell the opposite story. In them, people described as "rational" always make accurate financial calculations and act on them to maximize wealth. Chapters on investment theory in these textbooks go further, acknowledging that some people behave differently, but that "rational" ones correct their errors.

The gap between how people behave and how economists presume they behave may help to explain most Americans' financial illiteracy.

Where We Stand

Longevity and leisure have increased in the past few decades, but so has the misunderstanding of how investors and markets operate.[3] This mix is a recipe for disaster. The longer we live and the more leisure we take, the more financial savvy we need to grow investment resources. Wealth is on the rise and must be husbanded to meet the demands of longer and more leisurely lives.

The country is prosperous. Real net worth of U.S. households grew by about 50 percent between 1990 and 2000.[4] Real earnings of American workers grow steadily. Average income of the top 1 percent of gross income earners hit $1 million in 2000, up from $420,000 in constant dollars in the last generation alone. Among the top fifth of gross earners, the average is $167,500, up from $109,500. Average income for all households soared nearly 30 percent in the decade from less than $40,000 to well over $60,000. There is a lot of new money around.

Earnings of middle-income families quintupled in real terms during the last century. The portion of income spent on vital needs, such as safety, food, and shelter shrank, while more was spent on lesser needs, such as communication and transportation.

Two-thirds of American families own their homes and more than three-fourths own or lease cars; virtually everyone has a television and telephone, 60 percent of households own computers, and 40 percent own cell phones and camcorders.[5] Park use is up, spectator-sports attendance is up, and domestic and intercontinental travel are up. Vacation homes, dining out, and expensive leisure toys are *de rigueur* for greater numbers of families from the middle class on up.

At the same time, the gap between rich and poor widened. Poverty declined, but not evenly. The top fifth of gross earners received more than half the total earned income, up nearly 10 percent from a generation earlier. The bottom fifth has always gotten slim pickings, and their share has fallen further in the past generation. Their average annual pretax income remains under $12,000, slightly less than a generation ago.

Even so, at all income levels the workforce in the past century went from one of extracting material to processing it, farming shrank, and people flocked to cities and suburbs. Workplaces are generally cleaner, more "user friendly," and safer than ever. People are better educated, with huge rises in the percentage of high-school and college graduates and those with graduate degrees in the last two generations.

Life expectancy is up substantially. The country is healthy, safe, and well housed. Annual traffic-death rates fell substantially. Infectious diseases that plagued the nineteenth century largely were brought under control, including the ravaging scare of acquired immune deficiency syndrome (AIDS).

Business has boomed. Per-capita gross domestic product (GDP) grew eightfold in the last century; corporations proliferated, winning more patents than were awarded to individuals. Stock activity exploded, with billions of shares now changing hands daily on the New York Stock Exchange alone. The Dow Jones Industrial Average grew 2.5 times in the first half of the last century, and 47 times in the second.

The country became a nation of stockholders. Before the 1970s, few individuals held stocks. Employees enjoyed old-fashioned pension plans, created in the years following World War II. The early plans were defined-benefit plans, obligating employers to make pension payments to employees during their retirement. The employer would fund those future payments by periodic investment of resources in a pension fund. The employee did not become an owner of anything other than a claim against the employer.

In more recent years, many corporations redesigned their pension plans as defined-contribution plans. Largely driven by tax considerations, these plans usually require or allow employees to make specified contributions to a retirement fund during the time they are employed, and some of them also obligate the employer to make matching contributions to the fund, also during the time of employment. Payments made to retirees are drawn from that fund, and the employer has no separate obligation to make payments during retirement. An employee under such a plan assumes the role of account owner, with much of the funds invested in corporate equity.

In the early 2000s, nearly 100 million Americans are now stockholders. That figure represents an increase of over 60 percent in the past decade alone. They hold several trillion dollars in equity securities, directly, or through mutual funds and retirement vehicles. Millionaires are now so numerous they are being called the "mass wealthy" by private banking firms, which aggressively campaign to recruit as clients the country's approximately 2 million "high-net-worth" individuals (those with liquid assets exceeding $500,000); the half million or so "extremely wealthy" ones ($5 million plus in liquid assets); and the tens of thousands of "superrich" ($35 million plus).[6]

Despite this rise of the American stockholder, the quality of knowledge concerning savings, investments, and markets is low. A lot of the extra money can best be described as "dumb money"—investment capital held by people who are financially illiterate.[7] Half of Americans who own stock cannot tell you what happened on Black Monday in October 1987 (global stock markets crashed by nearly 25 percent). One-third of Americans who characterize themselves as experienced investors do not know what a "blue chip" stock is (a stock issued by an established company, the term derives from the premium chip in poker games). One-quarter of Americans don't know the meaning of basic economic terms, such as recession, depression, or inflation (consult a dictionary).

Many self-described investors do not know what the Federal Reserve does. (It sets monetary policy through adjustments to various target interest rates and administers the national banking system.) People blame or credit the president for the performance of the national economy (undeserved, except in rare circumstances). People do not know the average rate of return on stocks in the past 50 years (about 11 percent). Even self-described experienced investors have a tough time explaining the relationship between interest rates and bond prices (inverse).

Our educational system poorly prepares students for the unprecedented growth in income and net worth. There is limited high-school training in economics, required college finance courses are unheard of except for finance majors, and there is a perverse cultural delight in expressing a fear of numbers. ("I'm not a math person" is treated as a reasonable excuse for an inability to make basic computations, such as calculating 20 percent tips on restaurant bills.)

The national savings rate (roughly, aggregate income minus aggregate consumption) fell during the 1990s. It has teetered at negative, with total spending exceeding total earnings and the difference funded with credit cards and other debt. During the 1990s' bubble boom, consumption grew more rapidly (about 4.4 percent) than did the rate of growth of income (about 3.3 percent).

The rate of savings for retirement has fallen, with as many as one-fifth of workers reporting that they have saved nothing for retirement.[8] Half of American workers have no employee pension plan, and among those within a decade of retirement the median asset value of retirement savings is well under $100,000.[9]

Personal bankruptcies under Chapter 7 of the U.S. Bankruptcy Code reached record high levels.[10] Congress responded with a five-year reexamination of this escape hatch from credit card, auto-finance, and other consumer debt, that included contemplation of mandatory credit counseling as a condition of filing.

As wrenching as the move from manual and extractive labor to service and technological labor was—with mass dislocation, reeling communities, and frustrated families—the country made the transition and now boasts one of the most technologically savvy work-forces globally. The fallout from prosperity has been tougher in many ways, with a more sedentary lifestyle yielding increases in adult and child obesity. But ever vigilant, Americans are out to conquer these side effects with regimens of diet and exercise.

As a nation, Americans are behind the eight ball in learning how to invest the prodigious wealth they have rapidly accumulated. Most Americans have been baptized at the alter of investment by a plunge. People with no experience in equity markets leapt in, starting with the involuntarily leaps taken with the demise of the old-fashioned pension plan in favor of direct investment by employees in defined-contribution plans, such as 401(k)s.

Immersion continued with the steadily expanding availability of self-directed retirement vehicles, such as individual retirement accounts (IRAs). It spread to the dividend re-investment plans (DRIPs). It expanded with discount brokers. It multiplied with on-line trading. It proceeds with ever-expanding investment opportunities, such as direct-access trading, a computer-based technique enabling investors to place trade orders that are executed directly on exchanges without the help of any intermediaries along the way.

A newfound commitment to investor education is arising in response, but it is shockingly late. Economists for centuries devoted substantial resources to studying the principles relating scarcity to satisfaction of needs. One might have thought that the current generation of finance professors would have educated new investors. Alas, during this rise of the American investor, leading investment theorists were holding their heads high in the reaches of abstract theory.

American Finance

Leading professors at America's top universities—and almost all others—are devotees of efficient market theory, a story of perfect stock markets where the value of a stock is exactly equal to its price. The result of this story is generations of Americans not thinking hard about investment. This is the case because, according to this school, that hard thinking is already done by others. Large, sophisticated investment firms and institutions with far greater knowledge of financial information have already figured everything out about every company and priced the value. The best everyone else can do is pick stocks out of a hat or throw darts at the stock tables.

Efficiency theory is based on standard economics that assumes rational human actors. This means two things. First, people are motivated by self-interest, and second, they accurately appraise trade-offs. They would know, for example, the difference between $50,000 in cash paid today and the promise of $8,000 paid annually for 30 years, and always prefer whichever is higher. Unrealistic as this is, the plot gets more ridiculous.

Economists develop market models based on the assumed behavior of better-trained actors. In the efficient market model, prices of publicly traded stocks are the best estimate of their value. This price-equal-to-value idea results from rational investors studying reliable information about the cash flows companies are expected to generate, and investing accordingly.

Any time someone makes a mistake in this calculation, another investor corrects it. Even if some investors are not rational, the process operates as if everyone is. When new information becomes available, investors interpret it and act on it, keeping the market in perfect harmony. In the efficient world, price always equals value.

Investors only make money by bearing risk, this American finance story says. A related model tells you the relationship between risk and return. The most famous one is called the "capital asset pricing model." It says the risk of each stock is based on the volatility of its price changes compared to overall market-price fluctuations. Underlying this risk model is market efficiency: so long as price equals value, then the risk of value fluctuation matches the price change.

These efficiency and risk models are supported by bulletproof mathematical formulas. Price histories are statistically "regressed" against one another to see if there is any "correlation." Risk based on price fluctuations is broken into an "alpha" function that captures "firm-specific risk," and a "beta" function that shows how "market risk" works on a particular stock. The mathematical virtuosity of these elegant proofs is unmatched in economics history.

Proponents of efficiency theory used these models to create the biggest academic success story of all time. Those who developed the proofs got tenure at the fanciest business schools, including Chicago, Harvard, and Wharton. Many won Nobel Prizes. The models spawned an entire field of American academic finance. It's the birthright of the economics department at the University of Chicago, and spread like wildfire to economics departments at every university in the country. It later penetrated trading rooms, board rooms, court rooms, classrooms, and chat rooms worldwide.

A chief reason for the success is that these models helped prove the possibility of yet another model dear to the heart of American economists—the perfect market. It is a theoretical construct used to study all sorts of economic behavior and problems.

Stock-market-pricing and risk models are alluring because, out of all the places where economic actors interact, stock markets offer the best chance of meeting most requirements of a perfect market. There are lots of people; so no one acting alone can have a direct impact; items traded are homogenous; a tremendous amount of information is available; and the costs of trade are low. In most cases, economists have to make these unrealistic assumptions, but not so in the stock market.

For ordinary investors, the big lesson provided by this modeling is that it is a waste of time to think about individual stocks. There is no point in figuring out what a share of stock is worth by studying a company. Just check the stock price in *The Wall Street Journal* for its value. Then expect your return to be solely a function of risk, measured by how volatile that price is. That's what three generations of American university students were erroneously taught.

The efficient-market idea's dominance emerged in the 1960s as the handmaiden of Eugene Fama, a young doctoral student at the

University of Chicago who shot to fame for his uproar-creating assertion that financial analysis for stock-picking purposes was not worth a nickel. Another of the pioneers, Michael Jensen of Harvard University, triumphantly announced in the early 1980s that the efficiency story was the "best-established fact" in economics.[11] Efficiency theory thoroughly dominated thought through the late 1980s. The zeal abated as market behavior persistently varied from what the model predicted, raising the question of whether the declarations of its champions said more about the state of economics than efficiency.

Telling investors not to think is a travesty, particularly when so much wealth is at stake, while poverty lingers. It is difficult to assign requisite blame, but academics and finance professionals across the country bear responsibility. Academics are paid to search for truth, objectively determined. Most devotees of market efficiency undoubtedly believe they do. Skeptics might invoke Samuel Johnson's famous line—"No one but a blockhead writes, except for money"—to observe that academics also seek tenure and fame. These goals can conflict and create scholarship beset with subtle, involuntary biases.

Wall Street professionals benefit from the efficiency story in two ways. Contributing research and knowledge, the engines behind the marvelous dance that leads prices to reflect value, is a useful social role. They also benefit from others believing there is no use joining the effort. The more people who believe in the efficiency story's lesson not to think about companies, the fewer competitors professionals face in finding attractive investments.

Whoever is to blame, it is shameful that efficiency theory has held sway for so long. Today more skeptics voice doubt about the validity of the efficiency story, including to a modest extent, Fama. Fama's first relevant published paper is "The Behavior of Stock Market Prices."[12] The title gives away the weakness, for prices are inanimate abstractions created by human behavior. To recast the National Rifle Association's (NRA's) quip, stock prices do not behave; people do.

Behavioral economics—how people behave—is emerging as the leading disciplinary approach to investment analysis. It is led by a group of economists who were once mavericks but now assume mainstream prominence. These principally include Richard H. Thaler, formerly of the University of Rochester and now of the

University of Chicago; Lawrence H. Summers, once a U.S. Treasury Secretary and now President of Harvard University; and Robert Shiller, the Yale University professor who wrote the best-selling book *Irrational Exuberance.*

Behavioral economics emphasizes two things. First, a substantial amount of stock pricing is based on trading by investors who do not accurately perceive underlying business values, and hence produce prices that do not equal those values. So investor sentiment, rather than rational economic calculation, contributes significantly to establishing stock prices.

Second, even investors who accurately perceive underlying business values do not always step in to offset those who do not, because they believe risks are too great to compensate for such an undertaking. This limited arbitrage, when coupled with investor sentiment, yields pricing that does not equate to value.

Nor can risk be measured by price volatility, as the efficiency story would have it. If price truly equals value, price volatility would be a good measure of business risk. But with mispricing, price gyrations reveal nothing about business risk. They are price risk. Determining business risk requires thinking about business, not about prices. Individual investors lose millions of dollars ignoring this point.

In the real world, investors who think about individual businesses will be rewarded. Why? Because while price-value discrepancies arise, they also disappear. Over time, prices converge on value, so returns go to the investors who are best able to identify shares whose prices are below value and hold them until the price is at least equal to value.

Death of the efficient-market idea is imminent, but it has held onto its last breath even as research steadily reveals its fatal infirmities. The efficient-market idea is a goal worth pursuing, but one not likely to be realized. It will remain the exception rather than the rule.

Displacing efficiency models will be a pricing theory that accounts for trading by investors, not abstract rational players. Here, decision making is not perfect. Choices are hard to explain. Information is incomplete, complex, or misunderstood. People act with limited cognition. Prices and values differ. This is how the stock market really works.

To apostles of efficiency, behavioral finance is heresy. In the context of economic thought, it is not. It may be alien to the efficiency models and to much of post-World War II American finance theory, but it is an integral pillar of a school of economic thought that, mostly due to historical accidents, has been muted.

The Austrians[13]

The most valuable economic lessons unknown to most of today's investors were developed by the Austrian school of economics. Proponents of this school said the principal task of economics is to examine how people achieve their goals. Any aggregate economic activity—whether of a nation or a stock market—simply is the sum of individual action. Understanding activity requires a grasp of individual behavior.

Behavioral studies show that people first address vital needs, such as food and shelter. Once the vital needs are satisfied, new ones arise, making what once were luxuries into needs. In a primitive society, providing shelter and food were enough; in an advanced one, travel or sport gain importance.

Needs are endless. The value of goods and services that meet those needs is subjective. This theory of subjective value relates to all commodities traded—from meat, to cars, to World Series tickets, to stocks. Since value is subjective, explanations of economic behavior must first address the mental state of those participating, as manifested by their actions.

Studying people's actions in economic markets reveals uncertainty, limited knowledge, the inevitable passage of time, and an unknowable future. People tend to make decisions based on tacit rather than complete information; they estimate relative weights not according to precise scientific calculation of probabilities, but using rules of thumb, tradition, and rote.

These methods are rational, though less pristine than the rational behavior emphasized in American finance's efficiency story. The Austrian school considers all economic behavior as rational. This is the case whether or not the behavior is appropriate in light of the goals sought. Actions may be contrary to goals and may fail to meet expectations, but they remain rational as long as they follow reasonable deliberation.

American finance and Austrian economics differ over the roles economic models serve. American finance regards models as forecasting tools. The only test of a model's value is its ability to make accurate predictions. Even a model filled with ridiculous fictional assumptions is successful if it makes more accurate predictions than rival models, a claim the efficiency theorists assert for their model.

The Austrians regard prediction as dubious, and the demise of the efficiency story supports that position. Austrians therefore prefer to judge the value of economic models not by their predictive capacities, but by whether they offer satisfying explanations. Making realistic assumptions is central to that test.

The major tenets of the two schools are quite different. Take the role of uncertainty. The American models ignore it, giving clean models with crisp predictions, such as the idea that rationally determined prices equal risk-adjusted values. The Austrians try to deal with uncertainty, simply because it is a fact of life.

Obviously, American simplifications make analysis easier. But the Austrians say that simplicity defeats the exercise, which is to understand real-world events (such as market prices overcompensating for changes in business values).

The Austrians account for the fact that things change over time. Individual preferences constantly evolve throughout life. Individuals have access to incomplete knowledge and information and face changing expectations about the future. To assume otherwise—time standing still, uniform preferences, perfect information, and knowledge of the future—would obscure what many consider the critical insight Austrians emphasize.

That insight is that market behavior is best viewed as a discovery process. The markets continually generate opportunities that can be seized by astute individuals. The process involves trial and error, where creative people with fluid views and expectations and limited knowledge continually grow. The marketplace is not static, or complete with order and balance, but a dynamic process. It is not a place where prices are likely to equal values, and it is not a place accurately described as "efficient."

It is neither necessary nor possible for anyone to know or understand the full complexity of the market. Nor is it possible to predict its future. The perpetual disequilibrium created by ignorance and limited cognition begets an endless stream of opportunities for new knowledge, new technology, and new discovery. It also leads to altering preferences and evolving expectations. The cycle feeds itself in an ongoing learning exercise. Models that do not capture this terrific complexity of market and human interaction simply will not explain much that is true about the financial world.

Some proponents of the Austrian view of economic decision-making compare market actors to chess players. In choosing chess moves, players must consider their opponents' responses, what options those leave, their opponents' options following each of these moves, and so on, until the end game. Chess players who consider all of these multiple possibilities always win. But the scenarios are infinite. Almost no one beats the computer unless the computer is programmed to let them.

Devotees of American finance respond with a different image of economic actors: billiards players. Expert pool shooters may not know the laws of physics, geometry, and mathematics that explain the relationship between force, angle, and spin that leads to sinking balls. Even so, the shooters play as if they understand these things, and it is this intuition that matters.

Many game metaphors are invoked to contrast these competing views of investors. The games vary widely in the relative importance of skill versus luck in determining the outcome. Chess and billiards are pure skill games. Roulette and dice are games of pure chance. Games of mixed skill and chance include backgammon, Scrabble, and bridge. What is the combination in investing?

While skill is an essential factor in stock-picking success, luck also plays a role. So a better metaphor for investment markets than either chess or billiards may be backgammon, bridge, or Scrabble. No player knows everything or controls the hand that's dealt—the roll of the dice, the deal of the deck, the letters on the squares. Skill relates to how one handles the circumstances.

Under this common-sense view, the Austrians tell the more convincing story. Consider which of these images best describes stock market investors. Are they like chess players in lacking perfect knowledge that leads to making occasional mistakes? Are they like billiards players since they make decisions with imperfect information, but often get things correct? The Austrian school has the better of it once you recognize that even Minnesota Fats missed some big shots.

Why then have the Austrian school's ideas had modest influence on American finance? It cannot simply be that the American approach is cleaner and more elegant, leaving the messy details behind. There are also accidents of history to consider.

Lost in History

By the 1930s, the Austrian school was a major European intellectual force full of renowned thinkers. The first dean of the Austrian school was Carl Menger (1840–1921), a law and political economy professor at the University of Vienna and chief architect of the subjective theory of value. His numerous disciples included Ludwig von Mises (1881–1973), who emphasized that the purpose of economics was to study human action, and Freidrich von Hayek (1899–1992), an expert on human behavior and a leading champion of individual freedom.

In the throes of World War II, members of the Austrian school fled Vienna to scattered places around the world. Without an intellectual center from which to operate, the exchange of ideas diminished.

Amid the turmoil, a major forum remained to sharpen the ideas of Menger and his decedents. This was a great debate, pitting Mises and Hayek against leading socialist economists, such as Oskar Lange. The topic was whether a centrally planned economy could prosper, an urgent issue as totalitarianism proliferated in Germany, Italy, Spain, Russia, and Japan. Battlefield engagements matched equivalent intellectual firepower summoned in the debate.

Drawing on the Austrian school's understanding of the complexity of economic decision making, Hayek argued that the problem was too big for central planning to address. No committee could dictate the relationships between supply and demand of all goods and services in society. This practical argument was suffused with an emotional appeal to individual autonomy. While Hayek argued forcibly, the absence of a home base led to declining interest in the Austrian school.

The Austrian school did not die, since numerous scholars continued to toil. Hayek went to the United States, where he met up with Aaron Director, an economist associated with the University of Chicago. In 1944, Director persuaded the University of Chicago Press to publish Hayek's now-classic work, *The Road to Serfdom*, a meticulous argument for individual freedom against central planning. Hayek later helped develop a center to promote private enterprise at Chicago. He won the Nobel Prize in economics in 1974, along with Gunnas Myrdal, for his analysis of economic fluctuations and of the complex interdependence of economic, social, and institutional phenomena.

Yet the major strain of Hayek's work eventually embraced by American finance had nothing to do with economic actors and the complexity of their decision making. Instead, they seized on his apology for individual freedom. The Chicago school took from Hayek and his colleagues the mantle of *laissez-faire* capitalism, ignoring his principles of human behavior.

This loss may be a natural result of the fact that the debate Hayek was waging was primarily about whether government or individuals should direct economic affairs. It was not a debate about behavior. The strongest grounds for the Austrian position were based on morality and philosophy. Backers did not argue that people make the right decisions, only that government decisions would be worse, the position later championed by American economists such as 1976 Nobel Prize winner Milton Friedman.

The Austrian school was neglected immediately after World War II due to its lack of interest in mathematical modeling, which had become the rage among economists elsewhere. Math was in vogue among economists because it helped explain how market prices worked to match supply and demand (called equilibrium theory). It also boosted the standing of economics, promising to render the dismal science a more forward-looking enterprise.

Pictures of market equilibrium have no place in the Austrian view because markets are endlessly in flux. People hold subjective values with changing preferences. As a result, the elegant mathematical equations that describe these pictures are useless. The Austrian school is skeptical that mathematical models can capture the complexity of economic behavior. Mises put it this way in his classic work, *Human Action*, responding to math zealots as well as to critics of economics as a discipline:

> The impracticability of measurement is not due to the lack of technical methods for the establishment of measure. It is due to the absence of constant relations. If it were only caused by technical insufficiency, at least an approximate estimation would be possible in some cases. But the main fact is that there

are no constant relations. Economics is not, as ignorant positivists repeat again and again, backward because it is not "quantitative." It is not quantitative and does not measure because there are no constants.[14]

Hayek expressed similar concerns in his 1974 Nobel Memorial Lecture. He thought that while math may be useful in the physical sciences where variables are observable and measurable, neither is true with markets. This position led mathematical economists simply to disregard data that could not be quantified, even though it was highly relevant to how a market operated. As Hayek put it, "they thereupon happily proceed on the fiction that the factors which they can measure are the only ones that are relevant."[15]

These Austrian economists were not math-phobes. They were cautious to recognize its limitations and averse to being carried away with its seductiveness. A virtuous side-effect of this stance is that Austrian methodology is easily accessible to intelligent people, unburdened by the required technical know-how that shackles American finance and its efficiency models.

Also putting the Austrians on the back burner as the twentieth century drove forward was the extraordinary rise of Keynesian economics and the overshadowing debate on the proper role of government in democratic capitalist societies. While Hayek and the Allies may have defeated totalitarianism, Hayek was less successful in debates with Keynes.

John Maynard Keynes was already a prominent figure, as well as a successful investor, by the time of the stock market crash of 1929 and the ensuing Great Depression. When no one seemed to have any answers to the economic challenges facing the world, Keynes offered some. They involved using fiscal policy, including deficit spending by governments, to stimulate sluggish economies. Politicians, especially Franklin Roosevelt, embraced the principles. Keynesian fiscal policy has been in the economic artillery of all capitalist societies since.

Mises and Hayek developed the theory of business cycles to dispute Keynes. They argued that central banks create business cycles through interest-rate policy. Unregulated interest rates enable profitable investments to be made and unprofitable ones to be avoided. When central banks lower interest rates to stimulate an economy, it encourages investment that would otherwise be unprofitable. The investments eventually falter and bring on economic contractions. Credit is tightened, interest rates rise again, and in the economic downturn, the bad investments wash away. And so the cycle goes. Keynes agreed that there were market-induced business cycles, but argued that the fix was government deficit spending. This view carried the day.

Keynes also offered convincing explanations for the 1929 crash and Great Depression which he attributed to excessive speculation and crowd psychology. This became the popular political position, furnishing the philosophical underpinnings for the intricate securities laws Congress initially enacted in the 1930s and since expanded.

American economists, led by Milton Friedman, argued instead that the most immediate cause of the Great Depression was the tight contraction of the money supply during the late 1920s and early 1930s. The problem was not a lack of government spending, but a lack of liquidity. There was no need to increase government spending. So long as correct monetary policy was in place, private-market forces would take care of the spending and savings decisions.

The Austrian school recognizes that crowd psychology plays a role in many market gyrations, particularly crashes. However, members would not consider that explanation adequate for the 1929 crash. This episode is better explained by a story more like the one Friedman told. The supply of credit expanded greatly during the 1920s, fomenting a speculative expansion and bubble that eventually burst.

Apart from the 1929 crash, Austrians sympathize with psychological accounts of the causes of stock-market spasms. However, they disagreed with Keynes that government was the cure. They believed instead that individuals are better than government in making economic decisions, even if those decisions are beset by psychological error. Market fluctuations and business cycles should run their courses.

Once again, the Austrian's behavioral contributions were lost in the battle between the likes of Keynes and Friedman. The Austrians in effect staked out a middle ground, agreeing with Keynes's diagnosis and with Friedman's cure. Psychology is a major factor in stock-market pricing, and investors must be taught to deal with that.

Friedman is a Hayek fan and wrote the introduction to a special edition of *The Road to Serfdom*. What unites the two is a shared preference to allow markets to allocate resources, free of governmental intervention or regulation. Hayek recognized that individuals are best to make personal economic decisions because of the incompetence of others to do so. Friedman believes in free markets because he thinks people are perfectly rational, or at least act as if they are.

Had World War II not dispersed the Austrians from their center of learning in Vienna, the tragedy of American finance's preoccupation with efficient markets may have been mitigated. There would be far less emphasis on abstract modeling. The role of investor behavior would figure more boldly.

The Road to Recovery

As American economists meld psychology into their work, American business-school professors are beginning to appreciate human behavior as a factor in market activity. Interestingly, the new learning does not consciously draw on Austrian economics, but contemporary American psychology departments.

American psychologists have uncovered a rainbow of cognitive biases that play a crucial role in influencing stock-market prices. Scores of research articles chronicle a bewildering number of biases, at least 50, though they arise from a few core characteristics of human behavior. Together, they contradict much of traditional American economic theory.

Traditional theory would find it strange, for example, that the shareholders in *Other People's Money* even attended the shareholder meeting where Larry the Liquidator pressed his case. Only a handful of individual investors attend meetings, a fact that economic theory explains by noting that for small shareholders, the time and effort required to read relevant information (like proxy materials) and attend a meeting to become informed is not worth the effort. Better to free-ride on the efforts of, say, mutual funds and other institutional investors, whose investment levels warrant such investigations.

In the film, of course, these holders investigated for themselves. Does that make them irrational? According to those economists, apparently so. It may just exhibit a zest for control, a well-documented desire so strong that people even create illusions of control—something documented by psychologists but alien to American finance. Maybe that also explains why they voted the way they did.

If so, Hollywood reflects a better understanding of economic life than the University of Chicago.

How does the role of individual behavior influence the action? The stories Larry and Jorgenson tell are polar opposites. Even if the economics were reversed, so that the cash today was greater than the present value of the annuity, the holders did not follow the script of economics textbooks. They came to the meeting cheering Jorgenson and booing Larry and, solely on the basis of their respective speeches, reversed themselves.

The switch may be due to vividness, a tendency of people to act on information that is instantly available or within memory, as we will see in the next chapter. Cognitive biases such as vividness are not unhealthy. But they can produce undesirable results. In the case of investing, the biases often operate to make trade-offs between increased wealth and increased self-control. Bringing the biases to the surface is a first step to deciding whether the trade is worth making, the subject of the next chapter.

2

Investor Sentiment

Economists who understand behavioral psychology know that traders act on hunches as well as information. Markets treat such ill-informed trading and well-informed trading the same.[1] Both types affect prices. Smart investors are aware of the role sentiment plays in stock-market pricing and work to get their own sentiment under control. This chapter introduces the major behavioral tendencies of investor sentiment.

To understand the role of psychology in stock-market trading requires drawing on the work of Daniel Kahneman and the late Amos Tversky, cognitive psychologists and economists who in the early 1980s began to question the rationality assumption in American finance. Their innovative, systematic testing documented a range of psychological forces that lead to decisions inconsistent with the predictions of pure economic models. While their work is described as pioneering, the key findings have been known for a long time. A principal finding they formalized, and christened the *endowment effect*, was described by Oliver Wendell Holmes, Jr. over a century ago:

> It is in the nature of a man's mind. A thing which you enjoyed and used as your own for a long time, whether property or opinion, takes root in your being and cannot be torn away without your resenting the act and trying to defend yourself, however you came by it. The law can ask no better justification than the deepest instincts of man.[2]

Standard economics has no room for psychology such as this, where people act on instinct and hold subjective, idiosyncratic values that influence their decisions. Standard economics constructs instead use fictional economic characters and objective values, embracing the view that people maximize expected value, are fully informed using unbiased information, and are cognizant and free of emotional bias. Anybody out there like that?

Standard economics goes on to define a method of decision making that these rational economic actors use. Called "rational choice theory," it advises that to select from among uncertain prospects, figure the probability that each will happen, and assign a value to each possible outcome. Multiply the two and pick the greatest one.

This approach to decision making sounds great in theory, but this is not how people make decisions. People do not constantly try to maximize utility, they are rarely fully informed, and are prone to biases. Some behavioral researchers usefully describe this world as inhabited by "cognition misers," people who don't want to spend too much brain power making decisions.[3]

Behavioral finance does not reject rationality. It certainly does not assume irrationality, randomness, or stupidity. Rather, it is more like the Austrian school, redefining rationality as any reasonable human action. Actions are often biased by social factors, perception, and rules of thumb. While all this may still be rational, it can lead to poor decision making.

It is common for wine lovers to buy good bottles and hold them while their prices appreciate. Such connoisseurs often drink these highly valuable bottles after they appreciate, but refuse either to sell them or buy more at the appreciated prices. Their actions are not explained by standard economics, though Holmes would be able to explain them. They are easily explained by the following behavioral insights, starting with the endowment effect:

- People place higher values on things they own than on identical things they don't own, leading them to name selling prices higher than buying prices.
- People prefer the status quo, a bias against change that leads people to prefer what they have.
- People are averse to loss, giving greater weight to the downside than the upside, reinforcing the status-quo bias.

Psychological explanations have been developed for a wide range of behavior that isn't well explained by standard economics. The bewildering array of documented biases and other shortcuts ultimately arise from a few roots. Focusing on these roots, the intelligent investor can learn to conquer the major behavioral tricks.

Loss Aversion

A retiring military officer's preference for cash today instead of an annuity with a higher present value might be explained in terms of an aversion to the uncertainty of the payout stream. This aversion to loss explains why rational choice theory doesn't describe how most people make decisions.

The classic extreme example is the St. Petersburg paradox, named for the Academy of Sciences to which its discoverer, the Swiss mathematician Daniel Bernoulli (1700–1782), submitted his work. It offers the choice of $1000 cash or the right to play a coin-flipping game with an infinite expected value.

Most of us take the thousand, preferring that sure thing to the vagaries of the game (the expected value is infinite because the game continues to pay doubling amounts every time a heads comes up, though it ends if a tail comes up). Most people would take $100 instead of playing.

Why? Because money value (expected value) differs from psychological utility (peace of mind). In psychological terms, loss aversion is a more useful way to think about behavior than the expected-value approach.

Take an up-to-date, routine example: why are annual stock returns 6 percent higher on average than bond returns? Part of this bonus for stock investing is that stocks are riskier than bonds. But they are not that much riskier, and standard economics cannot explain the excess, though hundreds of research articles were devoted to the effort.

Using loss aversion, the puzzle dissolves. Investors have risk appetites that differ from those postulated by the efficiency story.[4] The 6-percent spread is attributed to investors' loss aversion, which gives greater weight to losses than to gains. The weight is greater in this case by about 2.5 times. This is why, for example, to induce people to bet on a coin toss where they must pay $100 if it comes up tails, people routinely require a payoff of $250 for them if it comes up heads.[5]

Loss aversion implies that people prefer to stand still. A classic study informed players they had just inherited millions from a great uncle. They then were divided into two groups and asked to give instructions concerning how to allocate the funds for investment. One group was told that the uncle had a significant portion of these funds invested in a moderate-risk fund while the others were not told how the funds had been invested. Both were told to specify allocations among a range of portfolios (from high risk, moderate risk, U.S. Treasury bills, and municipal bonds).[6]

How would you allocate the respective inheritances (assuming taxes and transaction costs are of no significance)? The portfolios chosen by players when the uncle's allocation hadn't been specified was pretty evenly distributed across portfolio types. For players who were told how the uncle had allocated the funds, there was a substantial inclination towards leaving things the way he had it. Love and respect do not explain the difference; conservatism does.

Loss aversion can be explained in terms of *cognitive dissonance*. This is behavior arising from a conflict between two choices where there are pros and cons associated with each. It occurs when decision makers think they made the right choices but also perceive evidence showing the opposite. The perception is the cognitive, the discord the dissonance, and if things had instead agreed, we would call it cognitive consonance (or resonance).

People invariably work to overcome cognitive dissonance when it arises. Of the variety of strategies used, the most common is the forcible tactic of restating the merits of the choice, what some people call *rationalizing* the decision or putting it in the best possible light.

Let's say two people each buy a different pharmaceutical stock, Pfizer and Merck. Subsequently, they downgrade their assessments of the stocks they didn't pick. Another version is an adaptation of the old Groucho Marx line about not wishing to be a member of any club that would accept him as a member. People tend to like private associations more when they are difficult to join.[7]

Loss aversion means people prefer predictability to uncertainty. This leads investors to prefer companies with stable earnings rather than erratic earnings, even when the value of the stable earnings is lower than the value of the erratic earnings. Thus people prefer a growth rate over three years of 15 percent + 15 percent + 15 percent rather than 28 percent + 5 percent + 32 percent, even though economically these unstable figures provide superior long-term results.

A favorite Wall Street maxim advises investors "to let profits run, but to stop the losses." Do investors usually heed such advice? Consider this example. An investor has stock in Microsoft now priced at $10,000 that she bought for $5000, and also stock in IBM trading at $10,000 that she bought for $20,000. She needs $10,000 to pay her son's college tuition bill, and these are her only resources. Which should she sell?

Applying the Wall Street maxim, the correct answer is to sell IBM, to cut the losses and keep the winner, letting the profits run. But most people choose to sell Microsoft. (The best bet might be to sell half of each, hedging the prospects and producing offsetting tax effects.)[8] Selling the winners and holding the losers is the norm, so most people violate the Wall Street maxim most of the time.[9]

Preferring not to change anything, people hold the losers because selling them is (a) an admission of error plus (b) a potentially incorrect decision (again!). The stakes are high. People may nevertheless be willing to discard the winners because that enables them to claim the success of being correct (with no further risk of price deterioration that would instead prove them wrong). Cognitive consonance.

Investor inclination to cling to losing stocks and unload winning stocks illustrates the sort of loss aversion known as the *disposition effect*. Consider this hypothetical situation. Highball and Lowball bought Home Depot shares at $200 and $100, respectively, and today's closing Home Depot price was $150, down $10 for no identifiable business reason. Who is more unhappy about today's $10 decline?

Most people concur that Highball is unhappier with the $10 decline because he is suffering further losses, whereas Lowball is still ahead of his purchase price by a substantial amount. For the same reason, it would be harder for Highball than Lowball to sell Home Depot, even given the same fundamental picture of that company's prospects. Yet the financial effect of today's events is identical to each of them.

Explanations for the behavior of wine connoisseurs and investors is found by relating a classic study of the variation of loss aversion Holmes mentioned, known as the *endowment effect*. Half the people in a study group are given mugs selling in the bookstore for $6.[10]

They and the other half are told that, after everyone has examined the mugs, mug owners would be asked to name the price at which they would sell the mug and the others to name the price at which they would buy it. They are also told that the experimenters would use the quotes to figure a market clearing price and that all trades that satisfied the clearing price would be executed.

Standard economics predicts that after effecting all trades at the clearing price, mugs would be owned by those who like mugs better than the others. Since the mugs were distributed to half the group randomly, then it should be the case that half the mugs trade. That is, trading volume should be 50 percent. Actual results? Trading volume was far lower, about half that expected. The reason was in the reservation prices: the median seller price was about twice the median buyer bid.

The open question was whether low trading volume was due to reluctance to buy or to sell. To test that, a study group was divided into three subgroups:

Sellers were given mugs and asked whether they would sell at designated prices, ranging from a quarter to $9.25;

Buyers were asked whether they would be willing to buy at those designated prices; and

Choosers were asked whether they would rather have a mug or the like amount of cash.

Set up this way, sellers and choosers are in the objectively identical spot of deciding to choose cash or the mug at designated prices. So standard economics would predict that the price named by the choosers would be like the price named by the sellers. Surprise. The choosers acted like buyers. The median reservation prices of sellers was about $7, while that of buyers was just under $3 and choosers just over $3. This justified concluding that low trading volume is due to sellers' reluctance to sell.[11]

The results of experiments like this, as well as actual field data, show that contrary to standard economics and rational choice theory, people are averse to loss and to chance. Just because a stock is underpriced doesn't mean they'll buy it, and just because it is overpriced doesn't mean they'll sell it. These are not people who will guarantee prices in stock markets that are equal to underlying values.

Mental Accounts[12]

People approach their income and investment preferences in a way that is at odds with standard economics as well. The income question asks why income levels rise with age in most labor markets, even though productivity levels usually decline beyond a certain age. The simple-minded explanations of standard economics are not very good (that employers want to encourage people to stick around long enough to recover investments made in their training or to discourage employee shirking by increasing the stakes of dismissal).

Survey evidence reveals a more satisfactory answer. Employees prefer wages that increase over future time. This is true even though getting paid the higher amounts now and lower amounts later would give an employee greater financial value than the other way around.

Players were asked to choose between identical jobs with identical total nominal pay but structured differently: flat, rising, declining. Three-fourths of the players took rising, even though the present value of the declining pay option would be greatest (not to mention less would be left on the table if employment terminated early). Virtually all people repeated that choice even after this was explained to them.

Why? Self-control. Workers want a rising income profile because they don't trust themselves to be able to save enough from flat or falling income to sustain the higher, desired future consumption they expect to have.

Similar reasoning explains why so many people have more tax payments withheld from their paychecks than is required. They do not trust themselves to sock away enough money to pay the Treasury on April 15. Better to get a refund, even at a cost.

These are examples of *mental accounts*. People do not always elect the economically "rational" course, in an American finance sense, but instead use strategies designed to assure a minimum level or type of performance. Rising wages to pay for rising desired consumption; excess withholding to guarantee meeting the tax burden.

Mental accounts are more powerful in the context of savings and investment. For example, a tough question is how much to save and invest. More is probably better, but it takes discipline to save and invest anything at all. And discipline can be expensive.

The question of the right or optimal level of savings/investment compared to consumption confounded economists for years. The

1985 Nobel Prize in economics was awarded to Franco Modigliani
for purporting to solve it. He proposed the following method
steeped in the tradition of abstraction favored by modern American
finance theorists. It is called the life-cycle method:

- Figure the present value of your total wealth (consisting of current income, net assets, and future income).
- Figure what principal amount of annuity you could buy with that
  amount.
- Annual consumption should be the amount you'd be paid annually on that annuity.

Again, do you know any people who operate this way or act as
if they do? Forget about the life-cycle story if you think about
bequests. The method says nothing about building resources to
leave for your children, grandchildren, and others. Forget about the
story also if your propensity to consume as compared to your
propensity to save changes over the course of time.

As common sense would tell you, consumption levels are closely
related to income levels. The young and the old, who on average
are lower earners, consume less than the elegant model commands;
those in between, on average higher earners, consume more than
that.

Also as common sense would tell you, but again contrary to the
model, not all wealth sources are equal. The life-cycle model doesn't
care where money comes from. But most people do.

People treat $1000 differently depending on whether (a) their
brothers gave it to them as a gift; (b) they won it in Atlantic City; (c)
their neighbors paid them for hauling firewood; or (d) it arises from
stock-price appreciation. They would also treat each circumstance
differently if the amount were $5 instead of $1000.

Why? Because most people use mental accounts. People treat
claims in the life-cycle model differently. People generally consume
most of their current income, less of their future income, and varying amounts of their savings from time to time.

A major reason for the mental accounts is to impose self-
discipline. Consumption is easier than savings. People want things
now. Yet they know they will need resources later. They save for the
rainy day, but often need some help. Mental accounts provide it.

Folklore developed around these mental accounting devices. The old adage implores that one must "never invade principal." Interest is akin to current income, so spending interest for current consumption is permissible. But never spend the savings—that is a different type of wealth, something more like "permanent" wealth. Less grandiose are slogans such as, "live within your means," and Benjamin Franklin's, "neither a borrower nor lender be."

The more people make, the more they spend (consistent with Austrian economic philosophy). Things go the other way too. People who reasonably expect high incomes in the coming decade (or lifetime) nevertheless husband resources today based on today's budgets—law and medical students spring rapidly to mind.

Mental accounts impose self-control that otherwise would be absent. They are particularly useful—maybe urgent—for that vast majority of Americans for whom savings, whether out of discretionary income or in general, is simply alien. Better for them, as well as anyone with limited liquid assets, to keep their assets in hard-to-reach places, such as certificates of deposit (CDs), pensions, 401(k)s, IRAs, and home equity.

Self-control helps explain the way 401(k) plans are used by people earning less than $50,000 annually. For many in this category, it is "irrational" (in an American-finance sense) to invest funds in these vehicles. Funds paid from the accounts during retirement are taxable. At certain break points for income before and during retirement and with certain assumed levels of return on invested balances, depositing the maximum amount exposes them to higher tax rates when withdrawing funds than they would be exposed to otherwise.

The investment payoff and tax advantages before retirement are outweighed by greater tax burdens during retirement. This is quite an anomaly in the design of the tax and retirement-planning system, something cured by the so-called Roth IRAs that are not taxed at withdrawal. The lack of apparent concern about the anomaly among many who lose this way suggests that something like behavioral self-control rather than pure wealth-maximization drives them.[13]

These sorts of "untouchable" ways to store and build wealth generate greater savings. The life-cycle theory, of course, would say that these are simply alternatives or substitutes, that the identical copy of a person with $100,000 in a 401(k) would have $100,000 saved elsewhere. Evidence shows this simply isn't so, and that these tax-advantaged vehicles do encourage greater savings levels.[14]

Similar results operate concerning home-equity wealth. If that wealth were the same as savings-account wealth, then homeowners would be seen to save less than others. The facts show the opposite. Homeowners generally save more than tenants.[15] On top of that, they enjoy additional savings from the deductibility for income-tax purposes of mortgage-interest payments and certain real-property taxes.

Reference Points

Mental accounting is related to other techniques people use to simplify decision making. In terms of assessing investment risk, investors often look not at levels of final wealth attainable, but at gains or losses *relative to a reference point*, such as a stock's purchase price.[16] The path can be more relevant than the end. Take a classic example where alternative end states are identical, but the routes there differ, and people systematically express a preference. (See Figure 2-1.)

A and B are identical in terms of their ending positions. Consider the calculations.

The value of (1) in both cases is a place $25,000 richer than you are. In A, that is the $20,000 richer you are plus $5,000 won. In B it is the $30,000 richer you are minus $5,000 lost.

The value of (2) in both cases is $25,000. In A, add the $20,000 richer you are to the $5,000 value of a 50-50 chance of winning $10,000 (i.e, 50 percent of it). In B, subtract from the $30,000 richer you are the $5,000 value of a 50-50 chance of losing $10,000 (again 50 percent of it).

Despite being identical, people prefer option (1) in A but option (2) in B. The reason people fail to see these as identical has noth-

A	B
You are richer by $20,000	You are richer by $30,000
Choose between	*Choose between*
(1) winning $5,000 and	(1) losing $5,000 and
(2) a 50-50 chance of winning $10,000	(2) a 50-50 chance of losing $10,000

Figure 2-1   Identical end states with different reference points produce different choices.

ing to do with the different enrichments A and B start out with. Rather, the difference is in the course of getting to those identical end states.

A is written in positive terms. Both choices are upsides (winning, winning). People like the sure thing when it comes to upside. They opt for the $5,000 cash now (military retirees again). The bird in hand is worth two in the bush, given loss aversion.

B is written in negative terms. Both choices are downsides (losing, losing). The surprise is that people prefer the risky thing in B. They opt for the 50-50 chance in option B that includes the possibility of losing nothing, even though they know it also carries the chance of losing much more. This is risk seeking—they are willing to take the risk in order to have the chance of losing nothing.

This insight has significant implications for how investors make trading decisions when stocks are priced above or below their value or above or below the prices at which they were purchased. Gains are going to be sought and protected due to loss aversion (sure things are better than uncertain ones). Losses are going to be cut only after effort is put into eliminating them altogether.

Think of how this asymmetry explains "get-even" impulses. A gambler ahead in the game by $100 does not feel joy equivalent to the despair he feels when he is behind in the game by $100. When ahead by $100, that may be fine, and he may even go home; being behind by $100 hurts, and the urge to come back, to overcome that loss, to get back to even, is more powerful than any feeling when $100 ahead. Hence the long lines at automated teller machines (ATMs) in casinos.

Different decisions are made depending on how a problem is framed. Examples of *frame dependence* are all around us. Ever wonder why the regular price is always listed on the ticket right along with the sale price or why the salesperson makes a point of telling shoppers this? Or why the suggested retail price and "your" price are both featured on e-tailer Web sites? It is the same reason why gas stations describe the difference between the cash and credit-card price as "lower with cash" rather than "higher with credit card," and why vendors offer "volume discounts" rather than "single-item surcharges."

These things matter and matter very much, yet you won't see this stuff in the standard economic models. Take a fun and famous illustration of frame dependence in this theatergoer comparative.[17] (See Figure 2-2.)

A	B
You are going to a play but don't have a ticket. They cost $100. At the box office you notice you lost the $100 bill you had planned to use. Buy a ticket?	You are going to a play that you bought your $100 ticket for last week. At the turnstile you notice you lost your ticket. Buy another?

Figure 2-2   Equivalent choices framed differently produce different selections.

These situations are identical in most ways: analytically, financially, cost-benefit wise, and so on. But they are treated differently by most people. The vast majority of people still go to the play when they lost the cash and hadn't yet bought the ticket, but do not go if they had a ticket and lost it. All other things being the same between the two, the difference is in the way things came up. Or in the survey, how they are framed.

How things are described or pictured to investors has significant effects on their decisions. Surveys ask prospective investors to make asset-allocation decisions between stocks and bonds. They are shown graphs depicting the performance of stocks over various time periods, such as those portrayed in Figure 2-3. One graph depicts yearly data, say from 1950–2000, yielding pictures of smooth-looking, upward marches with infrequent, periodic blips. The other graph shows monthly data, say for 1999–2001, which are quite different, filled with jagged, spiking, violent-looking lines.

How do these images influence your stock-bond allocation? Would it surprise you to learn that investors shown the long-term graphs are far more likely to allocate far greater percentages of their assets to stocks than were investors shown the short-term data?[18]

Likewise, traders who focus on the short-term horizon generally feel more risk (and they are right to do so if they trade on that basis using that time horizon) than investors who focus on the long term (equally correct). But these viewpoints also influence decision making. The results of that decision making include results that have nothing to do with causing prices to align with values in stock-market trading.

Some view this sort of frame dependence as an additional explanation for the premium return on stocks compared to bonds. They emphasize that the record of stocks delivering much higher rates

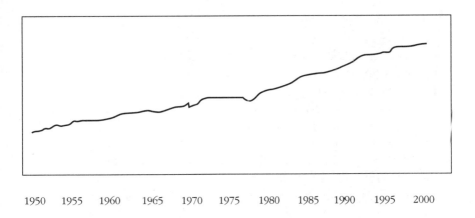

1950   1955   1960   1965   1970   1975   1980   1985   1990   1995   2000

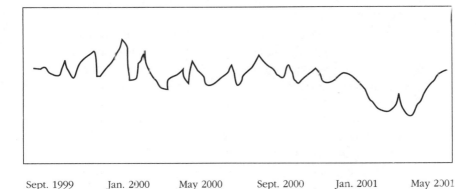

Sept. 1999   Jan. 2000   May 2000   Sept. 2000   Jan. 2001   May 2001

Figure 2-3   Investors considering long-term annual equity returns (top image) allocate more to equities compared to bonds than investors considering short-term monthly equity returns (bottom image).

than bonds occurs over a particular time frame. Under narrow framing, investors look at returns on an annual or quarterly basis.

Given that loss aversion is on average 2.5 times as intense as gain seeking, the premium on stocks simply compensates for the risk of loss over relatively short time periods. If the time frame were extended, this theory predicts, the premium would eventually vanish.[19] (Whether this is the case will only be known if or when American investors adopt a long-term investment perspective.)

Another aspect of frame dependence concerns how broadly or narrowly a decision is drawn in relation to others. Decisions are often presented in apparent isolation of each other, though they may be about related subjects. Rational choice theory prescribes choosing options in particular decisions that produce the best cumulative state of affairs (in investing terms, the highest net financial value from all investment decisions).

To do so, all components of that cumulative state must simultaneously be evaluated rather than judged on discrete terms. Yet across a whole range of investment decisions, investors habitually isolate and make individual decisions rather than develop a comprehensive investment policy.

Suppose, for example, two goals are to produce an aggregate amount of savings to fund a child's college tuition ten years from now, and to own a new car now. It is common for people with these two goals to establish a college fund to meet the educational goal and to take a bank loan to buy the car.

Generations have been reared to think this way. But from a financial viewpoint, this narrow framing by separating the goals is not maximizing and is inconsistent with rational choice theory. The car loan will invariably cost more (say 14 percent) than the college fund pays (say 8 percent, minus say 2 percent allocable to income taxes on the interest).

Subject to the benefits from self-control that mental accounting like this can generate, a superior strategy would frame the question in broad terms, combining rather than separating the goals. Using cash to buy the car saves paying the 14 percent price of the loan and cedes only the 6 percent after-tax return. The college fund won't get started today, but it will get going tomorrow, with an ultimate balance higher than under the narrow-frame strategy.

A narrow framing of risk-related decisions obscures the variability of risk that occurs when a series of related decisions are made together rather than one-by-one. When, as is common, the relative risk of a series of gambles is lower than the sum of the risk of each of them because some offset, each particular bet should be made in the context of the whole.

Yet there is evidence that investors take decisions, say on the stocks in their portfolios, one at a time.[20] It is another symptom of loss aversion. People ask whether they should buy Dell or sell Cisco, for example. Even assuming that the underlying, fundamental values of these stocks are identifiable, the answers may be different for different people, depending on what other investments are in the mix.

They may also be different depending on the person's loss averseness. Failure to integrate these decisions by adopting a broad frame helps to explain the undue amount of both buying and selling of individual securities and the substantial, excessive stock-price volatility on major stock markets.

Rules of Thumb

Estimating probabilities from vague variables takes time and effort. To enhance speed and minimize effort, people use rules of thumb. Without knowing it, they rely on attention and memory as if these are infallible, yet they are not. People frequently violate probability theory, including basic principles of logic and statistics. The rules of thumb used to take these shortcuts ultimately boil down to a few roots.

The first is the *availability bias*. This describes the propensity to judge the frequency or likelihood of things based on memory or imagination. Events that are easy to recall are believed to happen more often than they do. Images most recently or vividly remembered hold greater power over judgments than those from the dimmer past.

While often accurate, factors uncorrelated with frequency affect availability and can lead to biased judgments. Thus people think, wrongly, that car accidents and homicides are more common causes of death than diabetes or stomach cancer because our culture depicts them in more-memorable ways. The stockholders in OPM may have been wrongly persuaded to follow Larry the Liquidator in that proxy battle due to the drama of his speech. This is why debaters, trial lawyers, and other persuasion experts like to have "the last word."

In investing, impressionistic behavior fuels trends and "hot stocks." If all the media buzz surrounds the Internet, people start believing the Internet is the place to be, as so many investors realized to their chagrin in early 2001 after paying inflated prices for companies whose names ended in "dot-com." Likewise, in the 1960s when all the talk was of electronics, people started to invest in any company whose name ended in the suffix "tronics."

The availability bias helps to explain investor fixation with earnings data, earnings estimates, and how they compare. Earnings are the source of business value, but what earnings mean is crucial. And the meaning becomes cloudier the more companies employ accounting tactics to massage earnings, whether exploiting those that permit no accounting at all for stock options or making adjustments to reserves of various kinds to smooth earnings over multiple reporting periods. Worse, as a later chapter will explore, is the effect of the availability bias in interpreting earnings reports based not on generally accepted accounting principles but on accounting principles companies are increasingly making up out of whole cloth.[21]

Two commonly cited symptoms of the availability bias might be explained on more intelligent grounds. One is the tendency of employees to buy a disproportionately greater share of their employers' stocks than others, particularly in tax-benefited accounts, such as 401(k) plans. The other is the similar tendency of investors to buy disproportionately more stock of companies organized in their home countries than of foreign companies.

These examples may simply be functions of superior knowledge and self-control. In the case of home-country bias, currency translation and income-tax matters contribute; and in the case of employer bias, many plans match employee contributions with company stock and otherwise limit an employee's ability to diversify.[22]

Occasional loathsome conduct by corporate higher-ups, such as occurred in the Enron accounting debacle in the late 1990s and early 2000s, is not a compelling argument on its own to reverse a decision to concentrate 401(k) funds in an employer's stock.

While diversifying investments beyond employer stock is profoundly wise if other investments are sound and superior, crooks can operate anywhere, and the risk of being taken by a stranger is no easier to assess than the risk of being taken by one's own senior management. These points notwithstanding, members of Congress rushed after the Enron meltdown in 2002 to propose legislation limiting the portion of a 401(k) plan in an employer's stock to 20% of the total investment.[23]

The *overconfidence bias* refers to the pervasive proclivity of people to think they know more than they do and otherwise to overrate their own abilities. Common examples are that 80 percent of drivers think they are better drivers than average, and despite a divorce rate of 50 percent, newly married couples invariably believe they will beat the odds. Most people also believe that bad things (like ill health and divorce) are more likely to happen to other people than to themselves, and good things (like staying healthy and married) are more likely their own fates.[24]

For investors, overconfidence bias is seen in the habit of construing investing success as confirmation of their abilities, even where the results are not due to any particular research, insight, or skill. It includes a propensity to underestimate the role that chance or luck played. Notably, these biases are asymmetric: positive events are seen as being the product of one's skill and ability, while negative ones are seen as being due to external forces.

Another major rule of thumb is *pattern seeking*. This is an inclination to predict by projecting a long, future pattern based on a short, recent history, rather than understanding that the recent events could be due to chance, not an emerging pattern.

The human mind searches for patterns in all sorts of events, including random ones. For example, contrary to the beliefs of many basketball fans, just because a player has been making lots of 3-pointers from 20 feet, that doesn't mean he or she is more likely to hit the next one (or less likely, for that matter).[25] For the nonfan, just because the series of letters AAAABBBB looks less random than the series of letters ABBBAABA, each series is equally likely to have been the product of random configuration according to the tosses of a coin.

Pattern seeking uses the shortcut of superficial benchmarks rather than taking a hard look at probabilities.[26] The shortcuts produce causal judgments based on the degree of similarity between cause and outcome, such as linking the size of a cause with the size of its effect. That is why many doubt that small viruses can cause fatal disease. It also produces judgments of similarity from sample sizes that are too small to be statistically meaningful. Market watchers extrapolate a few price-change episodes as an indication that a pattern is afoot and will recur.

Seeking patterns where there are none is symptomatic of people's need to *perceive* themselves as the originators of changes. This is why a commonly successful negotiating tactic is to "make it seem like it was their idea." Feelings of control, in turn, promote feelings of competence and self-esteem; loss of them carries negative side effects, like fear and depression.

For investors, there is no way to control the trading price of stocks in a portfolio. But control isn't necessary. Perceived control can be gained by believing in patterns that one can detect. A good example in the late 1990s was the habit of market participants ranging from high-paid analysts to small-stakes day traders to predict high-revenue growth rates of high-tech start-ups several years ahead in light of recent performance.

Variations often appear in investing. One variation is a tendency of people who have chosen a voluntary course of action to resist evidence that it was ill chosen. This *commitment bias* is an unconscious shift in attitudes to preserve consistency with an earlier decision. It helps explain why people cling to stocks whose fundamentals have deteriorated.

A prevalent variation is *social proof.* People adopt existing opinions formed by others rather than form their own. Instead of exercising independent judgment, people often follow the leader with lemming-like instinct.

People often await action by others before acting themselves. This is why it is far better for an accident victim to be seen only by one person than to be crowded by dozens—the odds are higher that a lone bystander will offer help than 1 in a group of 12 will. To address this problem, lifeguards and emergency medical teams are trained to point directly at a single bystander when asking for help from a group and order, "*You*—call 911!"

The power of *authority* is related to the pull of social proof. This is the point that people are persuaded by arguments based on the identities of the authors as much as the substance of their claims. It is the saying, "they should know." For example, it is sensible to accept advice from dentists to floss teeth, since this is a subject within their professional expertise. Dentists' advice that it is okay to keep smoking, on the other hand, deserves no special weight due to their positions as dentists, but their authority positions lead patients to respect their judgments in areas outside the scope of their authority.

The last variation to consider is the *self-serving beliefs* bias. This means making inferences from new information that enable the news to confirm what one already believes. Sometimes called the Peter Pan effect, it is the simple reflex of believing what you want to believe.

These biases wreak havoc on the efficiency story, but create opportunities for smart investors who recognize and control them, raising the related question of whether such investors actually populate the market today, a question the next chapter considers.

3
Limited Arbitrage

People rightly consider Sir Isaac Newton a pretty smart fellow. Tradition has it that amid a speculative run-up in stocks during the 1720s known as the South Sea Bubble, Sir Isaac observed the overpricing and chose to sell all his holdings at a 100 percent profit. As the bubble continued to grow, however, he changed his mind and reentered the market.

Alas, Newton's emotions got the better of his genius. When the market crashed, Newton lost six times what he had made. He is quoted as saying, 'I can calculate the motions of the heavenly bodies, but not the madness of people;" he might have lamented, "When the whole world is crazy, it does not pay to be sane."[1]

Experience shows that no investors perform the Herculean tasks assigned to them by efficiency models. Errors persist. Even investors with towering genius make mistakes in stock-market investing. And no investor is free from bias. The evidence continuously shows substantial and sustained deviations of price and value that go uncorrected.

Efficiency theory pioneers originally treated these as anomalies because there were few, but they are now so numerous they have become the rule rather than the exception. The latest one is simply the huge gyrations in all market indexes in the late 1990s and early 2000s, which cannot be explained in terms of fundamental changes. We encounter other anomalies in this chapter, but let's start with an explanation of why the so-called smart money ain't so smart.

Arbs Mired

You might expect mutual- and pension-fund managers and stock-brokers exercising discretion over client accounts to correct market inefficiencies. Don't, for they are unlikely to. This is not only because they share cognitive biases, which evidence shows they do.[2] It is also because investors who manage other people's money have incentives not to correct market inefficiencies.

Agent investors have other goals besides trying to do "rational" things with their client's resources. Chief among these is to look good amongst their peers, for that is how their performance is measured. To achieve that goal, institutional investors often choose portfolios close to the benchmark of evaluation like the S&P 500 index. They often pick the same stocks to avoid falling behind one another. Such herding is particularly common among young mutual-fund managers. Many opt for popular market sectors with conventional weighting of portfolios.[3]

Another reason agent investors may not close price-value gaps has to do with client psychology. Clients criticize investment advisors who lose money by pursuing unconventional strategies, yet easily forgive those who lose money the same way everyone else does. This creates incentives for investment advisors to follow the crowd, rather than to think independently.[4]

Investment advisers add window dressing right before quarterly and annual reports are issued, buying stocks that gained during the period and dumping those that lagged. These efforts to spruce up portfolios widen discrepancies between price and value even more than ordinary trading based on cognitive biases. Portfolio pumping, as it is also called, exaggerates trends and may cause pricing anomalies that occur at the end of each trading cycle (year, month, week, day), natural times to window dress portfolios.

Portfolio pumping is illegal if done with intent to manipulate the price of a stock or value of client accounts. Yet it remains widespread. The Securities and Exchange Commission prosecuted two high-profile enforcement cases involving window dressing in mid-2001, one against ABN Ambro of the Netherlands and one against Oechsle International Advisors of Boston.[5] Routine tape recordings of telephone conversations between traders at these firms revealed their intention to manipulate the prices of stocks, including

Volkswagen and Banca di Roma, though they were unsuccessful in those efforts. The firms were fined $200,000 each for failing to supervise managers; the managers were suspended from money management for one year apiece and fined $75,000.

Many institutional investors are obliged to adjust portfolios by virtue of a company being added to or removed from an index the institution owns.[6] One result is that when stocks are added to the S&P 500 index, for example, their prices immediately rise about 3 percent. The fact that a stock is added or removed from such an index does not indicate its value. At most, it signifies a judgment by the index-keeper about whether the stock is a measure of the sector the index is trying to track. The price change is due almost entirely to demand for that stock by investors who are mimicking the index. These skewed effects are amplified as more institutional investors index and benchmark.

Institutional investors must manage cash inflows and outflows, without regard to fundamental changes. Pension and mutual funds receive investment dollars on regular and periodic dates. This capital must be invested. It may be parked in money market accounts for some time, but there is pressure to buy securities that match the fund's advertised focus. That pressure skews asset allocation and encourages purchases with diminished consideration for price-value relationships.

Financial pros face incentives to keep the dumb money dumb. Consider how seldom security analysts issue "sell" recommendations for stocks they follow. Putting stocks in the sell category is particularly rare among "sell-side" analysts at big firms (major investment-banking houses in the underwriting business). While there are times when analysts downgrade stocks to a sell rating, the norm is to give favorable recommendations.

One study showed that during the raging bull market of the late 1990s, an investor managing a portfolio based solely on changes in analyst recommendations would have enjoyed a 7.6 percent return following the highest-performing firm's record, and a loss of 36 percent following the worst.[7] The investor would have lost money by obeying the advice of all but four of the scores of analysts surveyed. (Intelligent investors using analyst recommendations read the underlying report rather than rely solely on the conclusory advice, as Chapter 6 will discuss.)

Another study of nearly 90,000 big-firm analyst recommendations showed that stocks with "buy" and "strong buy" ratings bore greater risk but generated lower returns than those graded "hold."[8] The superior investment strategy would have been to sell stocks that the analysts tout and buy those on which they were lukewarm.

Analysts attribute this strange result to pressure they face to pick stocks that will deliver big returns. The models they use tell them the only way to do so is to "swing for the fences," and take on big risks. It may equally be due to the fact that, like the rest of us, analysts become overconfident based on past success.[9] Either way, so much for the pros' leveling market inefficiencies.

Nor can markets count on arbitrageurs' using personal funds to neutralize the price-value differences that ordinary stock-market trading creates. Arbitrage is a risky business. Suppose an arb knows that the dumb money has overreacted to some wonderful news at a sketchy Internet company, so the price of that stock is some substantial multiple of its value.

To correct for that, the arb could take a short position in that stock. That is, he would sell borrowed shares at today's high price and await the eventual correction to buy them back and repay his lender. But suppose the dumb money is also stubborn and holds that price above value for a period longer than the arb has available to close the short position (buy that stock). The arb is stuck.

Arbs do not always read the market better than others. Leaders in finance can issue diametrically opposite financial prognostications. Perennially cautious Federal Reserve Board chairman Alan Greenspan can warn of a slowdown in the overall economy on the same day that noted bull-market strategist Abby Joseph Cohen of Goldman Sachs & Co. is talking about an imminent rebound. What is an arb to do?[10]

Arbitrage has other limits. While scores of arbitrageurs acting symphonically may nudge prices towards value, there is no way each acting alone can do so. Hardly any institution, no matter how large or skilled, can itself affect market price. Even central banks in many countries are powerless to affect currency prices despite tremendous resources and powers of intervention.

These structural and risk-related factors put limits on arbitrage as a device to assure market efficiency. Coupled with ordinary cognitive biases, such as overconfidence and loss aversion, investors can count on enduring inefficiencies.

Worse, people described as "smart money" become quite stupid when they start believing the label fits. That belief usually signifies someone thinking they are smarter than they are. A more apt label for these hyperconfident money managers than smart money is smarty-pants. These pros can cause disasters.

The Anxiety of Rationality

Overconfidence plagues even the clearest-thinking arbs in whom efficiency theory places its confidence to keep markets efficient. Take the case of Long Term Capital Management, the fancy hedge fund run by finance's brightest, which ran into havoc in the embroiled markets of the late 1990s.[11]

The enigmatic John Meriwether, a veteran of the once-venerable trading powerhouse Salomon Brothers, founded Long Term in 1994. He made Salomon's arbitrage practice famous by staffing it with geniuses. He tried to do the same at Long Term. It would become famous for other reasons.

Long Term's top arbs were luminaries from academia. They included Robert C. Merton and Myron S. Scholes, two fathers of the efficient market story who won the 1997 Nobel Prize in economics for their work developing a new way to value financial hedging instruments known as derivatives.

These Nobelists along with David W. Mullins Jr., former Harvard University economics professor and retired vice chairman of the Federal Reserve Board, joined Meriwether and a dozen other impeccably credentialed arbs. Launched with $1 billion in equity, the group borrowed more than $100 billion from the world's most sophisticated commercial and investment banks.

Their plan was to discover temporary pricing differences between equivalent securities. To illustrate the plan's simplicity, imagine that a corporation issues two separate series of bonds that are identical in all respects except they were issued in different seasons of the year, say spring and fall, and are owned by different sorts of investors, say individuals and institutions. Each bond promises to pay $1 in present value three years from now.

Due to sentiment about spring and fall or to the biases of individuals versus institutions, however, the fall bonds are trading at

$0.95 and the spring bonds at $1.05. The arbitrage play on these identical but mispriced bonds is to buy fall bonds and sell spring bonds short (borrow the $1.05 bonds promising to repay with bonds bought later, for $1.00). The arb pockets a nickel on each position when eventually the prices converge to $1.

In the words of Myron Scholes, the strategy at Long Term was this simple—they were "vacuuming up nickels others couldn't see." This is precisely the arbitrage activity that efficiency fans applaud—picking up cash from the market floor to drive away inefficient pricing.

Long Term vacuumed up lots of nickels in its first few years. One dollar invested in Long Term at its 1994 founding grew to four dollars by early 1998. Apparently this success went to the traders' heads. Brimming with bravado, the firm neglected to take precautions that it must have felt only less-successful competitors needed to take.

The firm conducted no independent risk assessment and failed to establish any internal control. All 16 of the principals did whatever trading they chose, without oversight. Most companies require two supervisors to sign off on matters as simple as issuing a check for more than $5000. But the ethos at Long Term saw no need to micromanage its shining stars.

The firm borrowed an enormous amount of money to boost returns on the bets it made. After all, it is hard to make a lot of money vacuuming up nickels one at a time, but picking them up 20 at a time turns them into dollars. The firm's leverage ratio (borrowed funds listed on its balance sheet compared to funds of its principals that were at risk) was huge, regularly around 33 to 1. So for every $100 of borrowed money, the firm's owners had about $3 at stake. With lenders being paid first in the event of insolvency, this meant that if the fund's value fell 3 percent the owners would be wiped out, a margin for error only the highly confident can bear.

The firm carried an additional layer of debt not listed on its balance sheet. It engaged in numerous "derivative" transactions, the hedging instruments at the center of the Nobel Prize awarded to Merton and Scholes. They were side-bets not reported on Long Term's financial statements. Instead of buying a bond outright, for example, the arrangement calls for one party to pay another a certain amount if the bond's market price rises, and the other party agrees to pay a proportional amount if the bond's price falls.

When Long Term's derivative positions are counted as part of its borrowing, its leverage ratio rose to as much as 60 to 1. Operating with this much leverage meant that if the value of the fund fell by 1.66 percent, the firm would own nothing, lenders taking all. That basically meant the firm was operating with no margin for error and stupendous self-confidence—the slightest bump in the road would bring disaster. To put that in perspective, industrial corporations simply cannot operate with that amount of debt, and are considered too aggressive when leverage is greater than 7 to 1.

Efficiency devotees, including those at Long Term, would not recognize a leverage ratio as measuring risk.[12] For them, risk is about price volatility. In the case of a hedge fund, risk is measured by how much net assets rise and fall. A leverage ratio of 5 could be highly risky if invested in erratically priced securities, while one of 100 could be conservative if invested in securities with narrow price fluctuations. For that matter, many Wall Street investment banks operate with leverage ratios well above the levels typical of industrial corporations, sometimes as much as 25.

Common sense suggests that this approach to measuring risk overlooks significant exposure to losses. The commonsense definition of investment risk is the possibility of loss. When the capital structure of an investment fund is so laden with debt that tiny vacillations in portfolio value can wipe the entire equity out of the firm, risk is high, even if invested in the most price-insensitive securities.

In Long Term's case, the risk from this commonsense view was even greater, for the sums involved were staggering. About $100 billion was borrowed and a mere $3 to $4 billion invested as equity. At times, the firm also held positions in derivatives that exposed it to bets as high as $1 trillion. This sounds like wildly irrational behavior from members of the school of American finance so keen on rationality.

The firm committed the fundamental error of pattern seeking. Bets were made as if the experience of the recent past guaranteed a similar environment a few years later. The computer models Long Term created to help detect price discrepancies were all predicated on the direction of past price movements of securities. But past patterns are not reliable guides, given the randomness of the future.

In early 1998, Long Term viewed U.S. Treasury bonds as overpriced, and a host of others—junk bonds, European government bonds, and mortgage-backed securities—as underpriced. So the firm sold short the U.S. Treasuries and loaded up on mortgage backs, Euros, and junk.

Past patterns were disrupted in mid-1998. A financial crisis broke out in Asia. Stock markets fell worldwide. The Russian government defaulted on its debt and devalued its currency. Sellers flooded the market for the defaulted Russian debt. Buyers were scarce.

In a global "flight to quality," investors dumped the junk and Euro bonds Long Term held, buying U.S. Treasuries. This led the price of Treasuries to rise, and their yield, which moves in the opposite direction, to fall. The decline in yields, in turn, led to a decline in the interest rate on mortgages, depressing the value of the mortgage-backed securities that Long Term owned.

To recall the spring-fall bond example, in this berserk market it was as if the spring bonds suddenly traded at $3.00 and the fall bonds suddenly traded at $0.25. Long Term's nickel-sucking vacuum cleaner now worked as a pump. It lost nickels as fellow investors sold junk bonds and European issues, more as the price of the U.S. Treasuries it had been compelled to buy rose, and even more as the value of its mortgage-backed securities fell.

Long Term could have absorbed much of this nickel regurgitation if it was not so leveraged. But the downside to leverage is proportional to its upside. As these nickels disappeared with the asset value, lenders started to make margin calls, demanding more nickels than Long Term had. The debacle wiped it out.

Genius and money, buoyed by past successes, led to a stupefying hubris. Long Term's strategists saw patterns that did not exist. By the fall of 1998, panic and fear set in. The geniuses sought to be rescued. The Federal Reserve brokered a bailout by 15 large financial institutions, mostly former lenders to the firm. At that time, for every dollar invested in Long Term in 1994, an investor had about five nickels left.

How could such geniuses and finance masters have been so irrational? Maybe they weren't. Maybe everyone else in the market was acting irrationally while they were acting hyperrationally.[13] The odds of the pricing going the way it did—spring bonds up to $3.00 and fall bonds down to $0.25—were around 1 in 50 million. The likes of experienced men of affairs such as Alan Greenspan and then-Treasury Secretary Robert E. Rubin admitted they had never seen such a financial crisis.

In this view, Long Term's positions were not the product of over-confidence, pattern seeking, or other cognitive bias. The real irrationality in this story is the failure by other professional money managers to exploit the arbitrage opportunities. They should not have allowed the price gaps to widen so much in the first place. They certainly should not have allowed them to persist.

Whichever view you take—Long Term strategists as superstar paragons of rationality, or as overconfident, pattern-blinded human beings—the moral of Long Term's saga is the same. Arbs are not immune to cognitive bias, and arbitrage is a risky business. The nickels and dollars lying around the market are not always seen and are never free.

Rogues

Long Term is not an isolated instance of financial sophisticates doing dumb things. Consider the dozen examples depicted in Table 3-1. In each case the story is analytically similar. Traders noticed inefficiencies in market pricing between two or more very similar assets. They bought one priced too low and sold another priced too high. Doing this should have enabled them to reap the differences when each price-value gap closed. But sometimes it takes too long for convergence to occur.

"Never jam today," says the White Queen in *Alice in Wonderland*, and the same is sometimes true of arbitrage. Mispriced securities may never converge. When a trader must settle his position before prices converge, he loses. A desire to get even can tempt him to try his hand again. Sometimes it works. Other times it does not, as the cases listed in the table illustrate.

In each of these incidents, a powerful and overconfident figure, scantily supervised, made mistakes and tried to cover his tracks. That aggravates the situation. Losses multiply, often exponentially, until it becomes financially impossible to continue. Nearly every major financial institution has been rocked by a major arb trading scandal, many of which are chronicled in books or on film.[14]

Adherents of efficiency theory dismiss these instances of major market disruptions as anomalies, believing these are isolated and unusual. They argue that rational people refrain from rogue trading because the costs outweigh the gains.

Table 3-1 A Dozen Rogues, a Dozen Billion Dollars

Sumitomo Corp. (Japan)	1996	$2.6 billion	copper trades	Yasuo Hamanaka, trader (convicted)
Orange County, California	1994	$1.7 billion	interest-rate derivatives	Robert Citron, treasurer (settled)
Metallgesellschaft AG (Germany)	1994	$1.5 billion	oil futures	U.S. refining and marketing operation (settled)
Barings PLC (Britain)	1995	$1.4 billion	Japanese equity index futures	Nick Leeson, trader (convicted)
Daiwa Bank (Japan)	1995	$1.1 billion	U.S. Treasury bonds	Toshihide Iguchi, trader (convicted)
Showa Shell Sekiyu (Japanese subsidiary of Royal Dutch/Shell)	1993	$1.1 billion	foreign currency	Yukihusa Fujita, general manager of the finance department
Merrill Lynch	1987	$377 million	mortgage-backed derivatives	Howard Rubin, mortgage trader (denied charges)
Salomon Brothers	1991	$290 billion	U.S. Treasury bonds	Paul Mozer, bond trader (plea bargained)
Kidder, Peabody (General Electric)	1994	$210 million	allegedly unauthorized "phantom profit"	Joseph Jett, head government-bond trader (denied charges)
Colelco (Chile's state-owned copper company)	1996	$170 million	fraudulent trades	Juan Pablo Davila, futures trader
ABN Amro Bank (Netherlands)	1993	$70 million	foreign currency options	James Martignoni (convicted)
Chemical Bank	1996	$70 million	Mexican pesos	Victor Gomez, vice president

The catalogue of rogue traders suggests that periodic disruptions by financial pros are inevitable. It may even be that these are not aberrations, but natural products of the culture in which traders operate. Efficiency devotees may have the cost-benefit calculus backwards.

The aggressive trading behavior demonstrated in these financial escapades may inspire awe and respect, raising the expected value of the payoff incommensurably.[15] The prospect of earning millions of dollars and enjoying the adulation of one's peers may tempt high-profile traders.

Big-time traders engaged in high-stakes financial gambles become Wall Street superstars. And to the superstars go the spoils. On Wall Street, as in Hollywood, music, and sports, a disproportionate share of the winnings go to a handful of the biggest stars. It may be sensible to want to be one of them. Yet becoming a star in finance isn't necessarily connected to trading that benefits from narrowing gaps between price and value.

The trading rooms of major financial powerhouses should, according to efficiency theory, teem with efficiency-promoting arbs. It is a picture of dutiful researchers carefully studying market movements, much as rocket scientists chart the courses of space probes. The raucous nature of actual trading rooms shows a far different group, more like spectators at a rugby match, or characters from the film *Animal House*. They are not looking to promote market efficiency, but to win. Trading firms pay traders to make money, not to make efficient markets.

Traders are among the most overconfident of occupational groups. They have to be. Theirs is an intensely competitive, astoundingly lucrative, high-risk, fast-paced, change-charged work environment. Wallflowers need not apply. Firms bargain on these individuals' pushing the limits of risk to make more money. That means more for the trader and more for the firm.

Even the most successful arbs stumble. The most famous examples include George Soros and many of his associates, such as Victor Niederhoffer. These men have a sharp sense of market pricing and timing and generated billions of dollars in profit by arbitraging small price differences between similar financial instruments. Yet even these giants are imperfect, as was shown when the funds Soros managed tumbled substantially in 2000 and when Niederhoffer closed his fund and lost his personal fortune in 1997 after bad bets on the S&P 500 and foreign-currency miscues.

Fabled mutual fund manager and index fund popularizer John C. Bogle rattled off a long list of hedge fund failures to refute the argument that Long Term was an isolated example.[16] Arbs lost billions in hedge funds throughout the 1990s due to adverse market movements, interest-rate changes, liquidity squeezes, and other ordinary conditions of adversity that make it impossible to count on arbs, or anyone else, to iron out all market mispricing. Bogle's roster is impressive: apart from Long Term, the Soros Fund, and Niderhoffer's fund, Askin Capital Management, 1994, $420 million; Argonaut Capital Management, 1994, $110 million; Vairocana Limited, 1994, $700 million; Manhattan Investment Fund (losses unspecified); Julian H. Robertson Jr.'s Tiger Management (losses unknown); and Ballybunion Capital Partners, 2000, $7 million (a lot of money to someone!).

Siamase Twins

Besides doing dumb things that produce spectacular debacles, financial pros fail to do smart things. A good example is not exploiting seemingly obvious arbitrage opportunities afforded by what are known as Siamese twins.

Siamese twins are businesses that are joined at the hip economically, but whose shares trade separately on different markets. The cash flows and control rights of each twin are allocated by agreement, so their respective share prices should move in lock step. If they are out of step, at least one of them is mispriced, and arbs should be able to profit from the difference.

They don't. Large price discrepancies between twins persist. The only explanation is market inefficiencies, providing textbook examples of price-value deviations seen across markets that go uncorrected by arbs.

Here are three corporate pairs whose stocks do not trade in accordance with their respective splits of economic and governance rights.[17]

■ *Unilever* is a 50-50 joint enterprise created in 1930 by Unilever N.V. of the Netherlands and Unilever PLC of Britain. The Dutch half is an S&P 500 member listed in the Netherlands, Switzerland, and the United States, owned mostly by Dutch and American investors. The British half trades on the London Stock Exchange, is part of the FTSE 100 (a *Financial Times* index akin to the S&P 500), and virtually all its stock is British owned.

The two Unilevers should be priced identically, but they are not.

- *Royal Dutch Shell* is a 60-40 joint venture since 1907 of Royal Dutch Petroleum of the Netherlands and Shell Transport and Trading PLC of Britain. Royal Dutch is an S&P 500 member traded mainly on the New York and Amsterdam Stock Exchanges and owned mostly by American and Dutch investors. Shell Transport trades on the London Stock Exchange and is part of the FTSE 100, with nearly all British owners.

  Royal Dutch and Shell Transport should be priced in the 60–40 ratio of their cash-flow and power sharing, but they are not.

- Until merging with GlaxoWellcome in 2000, *SmithKline Beecham* was a 50-50 split resulting from the 1989 merger of SmithKline Beckman, then a U.S. corporation, and Beecham Group, then a U.K. company. The respective shareholders received different equity instruments, with the old U.K. company's shares trading mainly in London by mostly British investors and the old U.S. company's shares trading mainly in New York with mainly American investors.

  SmithKline and Beecham traded unequally.

The pricing discrepancies between these three pairs of Siamese twins should produce easy money. If arbs actually correct mispricing as the efficiency story says, surely they would flex their corrective muscles on the Siamese twins. These are among the largest, most-liquid, and best-known stocks in the world. They trade on numerous major and regional exchanges globally. They can be bought and sold in local markets by local arbs at very low cost. They are perfect substitutes for one another.

Yet they remain mispriced. The price discrepancies correlate well with the relative performance of the stock-market indexes in the country in which each twin trades. For example, the price of Unilever traded in New York fluctuates in tandem with the U.S. S&P 500 rather than with the price of Unilever traded in London; the price of Unilever traded in London vacillates with the London's FTSE 100 rather than with Unilever's New York price.

No efficiency proponent has offered a good explanation for these differences. One possible explanation is differences in tax regimes and how one country treats gains and losses realized in another country, or how various countries treat withholding taxes on dividends, and so on. In these cases, however, the tax environment does not differ very much and certainly not enough to explain the discrepancies.

The behavioral explanation is simple. Prices are affected by the location of trade and the psychology of market participants at that location. Pricing discrepancies reflect the degree of inefficiency in the underlying markets where the stocks trade. When the New York Stock Exchange convulses but London remains calm, the price of Unilever traded in New York is rocked while Unilever stock traded in London holds steady.

It is not for a lack of trying that arbs have not eliminated the pricing discrepancies in the Siamese twins. Arbs at Long Term noticed that Royal Dutch was overpriced while Shell Transport was underpriced. So, following the standard arb play book, they bought Shell Transport shares and sold short Royal Dutch shares. Awaiting price convergence proved futile. Instead of converging, the price spread widened, with Royal Dutch shares rising as Shell Transport shares fell. Long Term lost the bet.

So here you have dollar bills (and pounds, gilders, and Euros), not nickels, lying on the ground, and no one scooping them up. Some may try, as did Long Term, but for others the risk is simply too great to bother. Staying on the sidelines is safer.

The opposite route is also taken: if you can't beat 'em, join 'em. Suppose the crowd is bidding up prices in a certain sector to substantial multiples of value. An arb can either go short in the expectation that the price-value relationship will be restored, stay on the sidelines for fearing that it won't happen soon enough, or join the party. Many join the party.

This turns an old Chicago-school-of-economics joke on its head. A naive economics student spots a dollar bill lying in the hallway and tells his professor so. The professor replies that this is impossible, for if there were a dollar bill lying in the hallway, someone would have already picked it up. There are dollar bills lying on the world's trading floors. Sometimes they stay there. Sometimes they multiply.

Horse Races and Closed-End Funds

To benefit from buying an underpriced stock or selling short an overpriced stock requires the price-value relationship to correct eventually. A chief reason arbitrage of this sort is limited is that it may take too long for that to occur. If arbs could be sure that the gap would close within a fixed time, we could expect more-effective arbitrage. Siamese twins would be accurately priced.

There is a market where mistakes are corrected in just this way and for just this reason—the race track. The contrast with stock markets is sufficiently great that it is worth taking a few minutes to consider how efficient this market is.

Handicappers of horses are quite good at making their betting market efficient.[18] They make it efficient not because they are smarter or less prone to sentiment than investors, but because there is closure at the track. A race is run and it is over. The bets are paid off. Track hounds are never exposed beyond the race. More than that, they can eliminate their exposure by waiting until the final minutes before post time to place bets.

For stock markets, short of liquidation and the like, there is no closure. Stocks have perpetual lives. There is no waiting until the last minute because there is none to wait for. The time between opening a trade and closing with a profit can stretch out to infinity, and the arb is at risk the entire time a position is open and may be forced to close at unfavorable moments.

As in investing, there are two ways to approach betting at the track. Fundamental handicapping calls for examining horse-performance data to gauge the probabilities of winning (value) and comparing these to the posted odds (price). Technical strategies look at ways in which betting is inconsistent with the probabilities of different outcomes (anomalies) offering money-making opportunities (arbitrage).

In horse betting, the market is the 20 to 30 minutes before a race (longer in the case of graded races, such as the Belmont Stakes and Kentucky Derby). Bets can be made for a horse to win, place (come in second), show (third), or any combination of these. Bets are winners if the horse comes in at or ahead of the bet (e.g., bets to show pay if the horse comes in first, second, or third).

There is a separate pool of money for each slot. Payoffs are determined on a *pari-mutuel* basis, so that winners divide spoils of losers, less about 15 to 25 percent for the track's take, plus breakage (costs due to rounding payoffs down to nickels and dimes per dollar bet). Payoffs are based on final odds, so bettors do not know actual payoffs when bets are made, though they become more apparent as post time nears.

Win-pool efficiency is strong. About one-third of all races are won by the horse bet most heavily to win (the favorite). On the other hand, compared to actual results, there is underbetting of favorites and overbetting of longshots (those bet most weakly to win).

Place and show pools are also remarkably efficient, with a minor exception. The odds implied for a horse to win should be consistent with the odds for it to place. So, for example, if 40 percent of all bets to win are on the seven horse, but only 15 percent of the bets to place are on that horse, there is an inefficiency to be corrected (the seven horse to place is a great bet). Mismatches in these proportions occur in 2 or 3 races out of 10.

Horse-betting pools are also efficient in more exotic betting formats. Daily doubles (picking the winner of two successive, predetermined races chosen by the track) generally pay the same as parlays (picking the winner of one of those races, then betting the winnings on the winner in the succeeding race). Similarly, in exacta betting (picking the first and second horse in a race), the win pool for a horse usually matches the exacta pool for that horse.

What explains the substantial efficiency at the track? Railbird wisdom is that smart money—at the track, someone with an insider's edge—bets late. This folklore is seen in action when there are substantial changes in the odds in late betting—betting in the last five or so minutes before post time.

Odds for horses that eventually win fall steadily until race time and fall rapidly in the final minutes before the race. For all horses "in-the-money" (those that win, place, or show), final odds are lower than "morning line" odds (those predicted in the morning by the track handicapper). For out-of-the-money horses, final odds are higher than morning line odds.

The final odds for winning horses fall to about 96 percent of the morning line. As to bets made in the last eight minutes of betting, final odds fall to about 82 percent of the morning line; and for money bet in the last five minutes before a race, the odds drop to below 80 percent of the morning line. For the losers in the race, the odds go the other way, 1.5 times the morning line.

These changes in the odds from those set early in the morning to those set at race time show that smart bettors wait. They seek inefficiencies, situations where too much or too little is bet on a particular horse in a particular pool. They bet to offset these, erasing most inefficiencies. In most cases, the only remaining inefficiencies are in the place and show pool (so a good tip for novices heading for Belmont is wagering to place and show favorites whose odds fall in the last minutes before a race).

In addition to there being no risk of adverse change beyond the final minutes before a race, another distinction between race tracks and stock markets matters. The spoils are split differently. *Parimutuel* betting is a zero-sum game. Net of the track take, every dollar won by someone is a dollar lost by someone else.

The system was invented by Pierre Oller in his native France in 1865 and called *parier mutuel*, French for "mutual stake" or "betting among ourselves." When exported to England, the British called this form of wagering "Paris mutuals," eventually evolving into the current form.[19]

The stock market is an open system. Winners do not make their money only, or even mostly, from losers. Substantial gains from investing come from fundamental business performance. When an investor buys General Electric stock at $40 per share and holds it as it appreciates over the years to $140 as GE's business generates profits and expands, the $100 increase is not taken from other investors.

Nor, in the stock market, does everything the losers lose go into the pockets of the winners. When someone buys a stock at $100 only to turn around and sell it at $75, for example, it is not the case that someone else pockets that $25. It can, and does, vanish. It can vanish due to business deterioration. When a company's profitability falls and its stock price is cut over a series of quarters, the losses one stockholder suffers are not gained by another. They are gone.

You can see how wealth vanishes in stock-market trading by noticing that stock pricing is discontinuous. Suppose a stock opens at $50 and closes at $45. This does not mean it could be bought or sold at $49, $48, $47, or any other increment between those points during the day. A stock opening at $50 and greeted with nothing but sell orders can quickly trade at $45. The $5-per-share reduction in price does not go into anyone's pocket.

The certainty that ill-informed bettors cannot hurt you when you place a bet a minute before post time is unparalleled in the stock market, with one exception: closed-end mutual funds. Closed-end mutual funds are publicly traded mutual funds that make an initial offering to raise capital, then invest that capital, and do no more investing. Equity investments are locked in.

As a result, the value of the fund is simply equal to the value of the securities it owns. The price of the fund's shares are set by their daily exchange trading. If this market is efficient, then the price of the fund should equal the value of its holdings. This is seldom the case.

Instead, most funds trade at prices that are substantial discounts compared to the value of the holdings and sometimes the price is a premium to the value. Why don't arbs fix these pricing errors? As with Siamese twins, it is often too risky given that mispricing may persist.

To overcome that risk, an arb could buy all shares of the entire fund. An arb who buys all shares of something at a price equal to 90 percent of its value, say, can pocket the 10 percent difference. That would seem even a surer thing than betting on heavy favorites to place in the last minute before a horse race.

A major difference between the track and the closed-end fund is that buying all the shares of a fund requires approval of the Securities and Exchange Commission, which regulates mutual funds. Approval is not guaranteed. Nothing in investing is risk-free, including arbitrage.

Why are closed-end funds priced at discounts in the first place? Efficiency devotees attribute the discounts to investors' not trusting fund managers to channel the full value of the investment securities to the holders. They can take fees, for example, greater than those justified by performance. This is not a good answer, of course, because sometimes funds trade at premiums to value. Also unexplained in the efficiency story is the great variability of discounts over time and across funds, ranging from as small as 3 percent to as much as 25 percent from the 1960s to the 1990s.

The answer to all these puzzles is investor sentiment and limited arbitrage. Closed-end mutual funds are the slice of the market most dominated by individual investors rather than by pros. So there is potentially more sentiment and certainly less arbitrage than in the broad market. The combination devastates the efficiency story, calling for a story of how markets really work, told in the next chapter.

4

Diagnosing Mr. Market

Why are some investors successful? Consider the style championed by Benjamin Graham. It seeks economically sound businesses that are underpriced. Evidence of underpricing includes stocks with low price-to-earnings ratios. If it is an attractive business, the underpricing may be due to unwarranted market pessimism about future earnings. If future earnings turn out better than the pessimists predicted, the price eventually will reflect that. The investor succeeds.

Pessimism and optimism are alternating characteristics reflected in market trading. The market each day and over successive short periods chugs along slowly, the product of conservatism and cautious changes in outlook (the status-quo bias). Then, at intervals separated by substantial lengths of time, comes a correction, a wake-up, a major change. Sometimes an upward march is sustained for so long and reaches such dizzying heights that the meeting with reality amounts to a market break, an astonishing overreaction. In these times, people see in everything all the great fears of the ages, a view that one bad thing is a sign of so much more.

Astute investors such as Graham recognized the moodiness of the market. He named the whole process Mr. Market. Its inefficiencies can be exploited. Graham didn't worry much about why, partly because no one had really given the question extensive thought. Now that the efficiency story is fading, the search is on.

One study shows strong correlations between weather and markets.[1] Glorious sunshine in major financial centers brings market rallies, torrential thunderstorms dampen market prices, and ordinary weather is linked with dull, sideways markets. The moodiness of Mr.

Market turns out to be a reflection of the moodiness of investors, which, in turn, is influenced by the weather. Market reality is more intricate than this correlation, but the study underscores the importance of psychology in financial markets. If markets are not efficient, what are they? How do they work?

It is not enough to document the many things efficiency theory fails to explain or show that investor sentiment and limited arbitrage impair it. Criticism requires building a better mouse trap.

Ups and Downs[2]

The late Fischer Black, an outsider to the economics profession who was trained instead in math and physics, developed a theory in the mid-1980s of ill-informed traders (called "noise" traders) populating the market.[3] This was a giant step, given the dominance of efficiency theory at the time. In the noise-trader model, ill-informed traders cause mispricing of stocks and risk for arbs who leave mispricing in place. The trouble with Black's model was that it reached too far, giving an explanation for any kind of trading imaginable, whether or not it occurred. A better model would explain only those things actually observed.

Researchers building on Black's insights developed a more refined model, called the positive feedback model. Markets experience momentum, they said, where new purchases are made based on recent purchases, and new sales are made based on recent sales. Price changes in one direction bring pressure in that direction. This model captures the psychological phenomenon of "extrapolating trends," believing things that have been going a certain way for a while will keep going that way a while longer.

While useful to describe extraordinary market phenomena such as bubbles and breaks, noise-trader and positive feedback models don't address the more-routine shifts between the continuation (and chasing) of trends and the correction. Financial markets are not like the "Energizer Bunny"—they don't just keep going and going. Instead, there are short-term continuations met by ultimate reversals.

More-dynamic accounts capture both the extraordinary bubble-break phenomena and the quotidian cycles. These models are built on the premise that investors hold mistaken beliefs and make bad judgments—the behavioral finance story.

Dynamic market accounts explain shifts between investor under-reaction and overreaction. They come in a couple of flavors and undoubtedly will be reshaped by the new generation of psychologically inclined American finance theorists. So far, this is the state of the art.

The main model begins by viewing investors as sharing mistaken beliefs and bad judgment. Behavioral baggage plagues everyone. The dominant psychological forces at play are the status-quo bias and the pattern-seeking bias, along with a hefty dose of overconfidence.

Investors learn about their performance and what they are capable of doing in biased, self-promoting ways. When they digest information to form their judgments, they are not entirely sure how precise their analyses are, but consider them good enough to act on. Subsequent news either confirms or refutes their judgments.

Investors pat themselves on the backs too much and kick themselves too little. News that confirms the judgments is seen as so rich that the people become more confident in their abilities than is justified. When news refutes the judgments, confidence is reduced, but less than is warranted. So there is conservatism as to bad news (*oops, got that one wrong*), and pattern seeking as to good news (*right again, as usual!*).

There are two versions of the shared-mistaken-beliefs model. In the first one, people digest company news as favorable, buy its stock, and see the price rise.[4] As new information arrives that seems to confirm the accuracy of the judgment, the price rises further (*yes, I am pretty good at this, aren't I?*).

Lots of folks do the same thing, pushing price ahead of what the news justified. Investors begin to see that (*well, the news wasn't quite that good now was it?*). A return to a more reasonable self-perception ensues. And the price settles back to a level more in line with the news. There is a smoothness to the process of this hump-shaped price evolution, yielding short-term positive price trends met by long-term reversals. Exactly what markets do.

This model's insight concerning the interplay of the status-quo bias with pattern seeking is corroborated by a standard experiment using the toss of a coin that is known to be loaded and therefore biased. The player is told the coin has either a 70-percent chance of heads or a 70-percent chance of tails, rather than the usual 50-50 chance of either.

A clear-thinking player would start off by assigning a 50-50 chance of either bias, heads or tails. As the coin is flipped and keeps coming up heads flip after flip, a cold-calculated updating would adjust the 50-50 chance incrementally, such as: 53-47, then 57-43 then, 61-39, then 67-33.

Players in this experiment adjust, but not in accordance with probabilities. Also, their errors are on the low side at the outset and move to the high side by the end. The first few adjustments are too small (51-49 then 55-45, say), showing conservatism and underreaction. Succeeding adjustments are too great (62-38 then 69-31, say), showing pattern seeking and overreaction.[5]

This model is also supported by the propensity of people to overlook basic lessons from statistics. When two variables are related, but imperfectly, extreme values on one tend to be matched by less extreme values on the other. As examples, tall parents on average have tall kids, but not as tall as they are; straight-A high-school students tend to do well in college but not quite as well (on average); and a company's low-profit years tend to be followed by better ones, and vice versa.[6]

In investing, people often get this last example backwards. Instead, they believe they see trends stretching into future quarters after witnessing steady profit increases in each of the prior three quarters. They fall prey to the well-documented gambler's fallacy.

It refers to the incorrect belief that a roulette wheel landing on double-digit numbers time-after-time is "due" to land on a single-digit number; or that a coin coming up heads several times in a row is "due" to come up tails the next time. While it is true that a coin tossed 100 times will come up heads and tails randomly, with about 50 of each, four tails or heads are likely to be tossed in a row quite a few times. This is also true with corporate earnings, though stock prices don't map this.

In the second version of the shared-mistaken-beliefs model, underreactions and overreactions are explained by a more involved story.[7] This one supposes that earnings of a particular company (or all companies) is random. Could be up this quarter, or down, just as the flipping of a coin could be heads or tails. But investors don't understand probability theory all that well and substitute rules of thumb.

If investors view the world this way, then it would be no surprise for them to believe (wrongly) that when earnings trends reverse—a series of 10-cent increases followed by a 5-cent decline—this signals a normal reality check (what statisticians call reversion to the mean). They thus underreact to the news. No big deal. They exhibit the status-quo bias (conservatism).

Nor would it be a surprise if instead, when investors see a sequence of growing earnings reports—a fourth quarter in a row enjoying a 10-cent increase—they interpret this (again wrongly) as a shift to a growth phrase. Big news. They now exhibit pattern seeking, see a trend, and believe that earnings will continue to grow in the future.

Another experiment supports the insight that investors mistake the randomness of corporate earnings and prices for predictable patterns alternating between trends and reversals. MBA students were asked to make predictions of the future direction of various series. Some series exhibited sequences of continuations in earnings or price (such as $1, $2, $4, $7, $8) and others sequences of reversals (such as $2, $1, $4, $8, $6). People underreacted to the reversals (seeing the shift from $2 to $1, for example, as a return to normalcy) and overreacted to the continuations (seeing them as a sign of things to come).[8]

The result is underreaction during short horizons and overreaction longer term. As with the hump-shaped picture in the first version of this model, the process can be quite smooth. It is also the case that the same misperceptions that drive momentum in one direction drive the longer-term reversal. That means stocks with the largest pricing momentum should get the largest pricing reversal, and that stocks of businesses facing greater uncertainty should register more mispricing. Empirical data support both points, as do experimental studies.

These two models are souped up by noting that different sorts of investors exhibit different sorts of mistaken beliefs or bad judgments.[9] A shorthand version of this story divides the world into two broad types of market participants: those who examine news relating to fundamental information (investors) and those who respond quickly to price changes (traders).

Investors tend to underreact to news, digest it, evaluate it, and eventually act on it. The resulting gradual price pressure in a particular direction is seen by the traders, who jump on it, thus accelerating its direction, hastening the reaction, but ultimately pushing too far, producing longer-run overreaction. The result is short-term underreaction to news and long-term overreaction to news.

For traders, an effect of this behavior is jittery trading decisions. A common example at the trader level is the selling of one stock deemed "cold," quickly followed by the purchase of another deemed "hot." Trading losses are the typical result, one study showing that on average, those following that trading policy lost nearly 4 percent in the process of discard and draw.[10]

Bubbles and Bursts

So much for ordinary market action with its alternating ups and downs. Consider now the occasional outbursts of euphoria or dysphoria that exaggerate the oscillation. The gradualness usually associated with trends and reversals is replaced by more-acute movements during booms and busts.

Part of the difference is the nature of the news. In contrast to information relevant to business performance that calls for price adjustments, irrelevant news helps sustain price derailments. This "news" can be of any nonfundamental type, but to take an obvious example, consider rumors or gossip about finance, investing, and the overall market.

Items could include that people are making big money in it, or that the stock market is poised for a bull run. Innovative financial products could be made available and marketed as news. Congress could create incentives for a tax-free retirement vehicle that attracts funding. Or a mutual fund may be launched with a neat gimmick brimming with news appeal. Most likely it is a combination of such things.

These stories can be told anywhere: the back fence, Internet chat rooms, newspapers, and financial television shows. It is amplified in trading rooms and on stock exchange floors. "News" like this catches the attention of stock-market veterans and novices alike. It quickly becomes interesting. Buy orders increase. Previous buyers see a rise in price. They repeat the stories of riches. Prices rally.

The financial sector enlarges. Brokerage houses expand. Mutual funds grow and hire more employees. New financial products are conceived. Supply creates demand, and more buyers enter the financial markets. Prices rise some more.

Hedgers and speculators who hadn't seen this blip on the horizon are now forced to get into the game. Those who had previously bet that particular stocks or the overall market was in a gloomy period and likely to head downward may hold short positions. They have borrowed shares that must be repaid, and it now seems that their bets that they'd be able to buy them later at lower prices were wrong. They have to buy them back now at higher prices.

Entrepreneurs notice that equity prices are moving higher. They decide this is a good time to raise capital. Executives notice the same thing and decide to expand with funds raised in attractively priced capital markets. Reports of initial public offerings (IPOs) and secondary offerings reinforce the view that a bull market is heating up. Underwriters disseminate promotional news about these companies and their products.

Easy access to capital lowers its cost. That means whatever level of sales a company posts, more of it flows down to the bottom line. Companies are worth more. This news feeds the process too, amplified by new investors, new IPOs, and so on, throughout the cycle.

The relatively high price of equities makes it easier for managers to buy other companies—using highly priced stock facilitates acquisitions and mergers that would be prohibitive if paid for in equivalent amounts of cash. Thus M&A volume is up. The financial sector expands again. The process repeats.

At each escalating stage of these feedback loops, strong psychological factors play a role. A dominant one throughout is overconfidence. Success breeds success, and people take credit for it. They think they can do it again, given the recent track record. Financial amateurs and pros alike are susceptible to this euphoria (pros maybe even more so, given the culture of success in which so much of the financial-services industry operates).

Biases such as mental accounting promote the feedback. For example, winners in the market may start to think of their winnings as free money, or "house money," a reference to gambling thinking that says amounts beyond one's initial stake are furnished, in effect, by the casino. Less loss aversion is placed on these funds; letting them ride is easier.

Pattern seeking is surely at work. As the market rises, people extrapolate that trend. The extrapolation continues to the point that people believe the upward trend will continue indefinitely. Stories abound.

Investors are urged to shrug off unwanted warnings: "this time it is different," and "we are in a whole new era." A New Economy.

Social proof leads people to look for opinion leaders to guide them. The media serves this role, and the opinions expressed are accepted. Beliefs take hold. The problem of social proof is magnified by errors in transmitting data. Information degrades in quality with the telling and retelling. Secondhand information, for example, is rarely conveyed verbatim. Information reported as news is often secondhand, third, fourth, or even more remote.

Distortions can arise from ongoing transmission and can be compounded by the natural desire to entertain. Broadcasters are trained to smile as much as possible throughout camera time—easy to do when reporting that the market soared, but also attempted when reporting the worst sort of financial news (smiling anchor: "The market fell sharply today on heavy volume. Over to you, Sandy!")

The media report on things that are unusual. Availability bias operates, making these things stand out in people's minds. Isolated stories of riches being made lead people to believe that riches are being made everywhere. It is the old tale of impoverished citizens in other countries, upon hearing of a few relatives making it big in the United States, believing the streets are paved with gold.

Errors arise from reporting throughout all media, especially newspapers that thrive on pulp news. Though such errors are less frequent in stories reported by elite, mainstream vehicles, such as *The New York Times* and *The Wall Street Journal*, these publications are not immune. Consider shark attacks, rarely occurring but frequently reported incidents in the summer of 2001.

The New York Times, on its front page, reported a Florida commission's decision to reduce the risk of shark attacks by banning the use of bloody bait in "interactive" shark-siting dives.[11] The story said public officials "from Virginia to Hawaii" were considering measures to reduce shark attacks, as if officials nationwide were doing so. A full read of the story carried over to page 17 mentions only 2 additional states. Page 1 also mentioned that summer's "regular reminders" of the dangers of shark attacks, as if they were common. Page 17 makes it clear that they are rare—it cites 41 for the year-to-date nationwide, and 54 the prior year.

Two weeks earlier, a *Times* op-ed piece by mathematician John Allen Paulos rightly decried the media frenzy and exaggerated public concern over shark attacks as reflecting erroneous probability calculations and the paucity of other August news.[12] He noted that shark-attack rates were as low as ever: tiny as a fraction of the millions enjoying the sea. In fact, the number of worldwide shark attacks to date in 2001 was the second lowest in a decade, according to a feature story on the cover of the Science section of the *Times*.[13] Yet during the summer, more than 1500 stories dealt with shark attacks, a sum greater than the stories from the previous 5 summers combined, as shown in Table 4-1, and *Time* magazine's July 30 cover story announced the "Summer of the Shark."

Likewise with a whole range of subjects on which media focuses disproportionate attention, generating far more stories and perspectives than substance warrants. Examples range from media exaggeration of the incidence of the West Nile virus, of wildfires raging in the western United States, and of kidnappings to the extraordinary amount of paper and ink devoted to debacles such as the Enron accounting scandal of early 2002 and the handful of anthrax letters that popped up in the postal system in late 2001.

All media outlets carry an imprimatur of authority, so the medium itself gives legitimacy to the story, even if the story is otherwise hard to believe. Beneath these exaggerations lay kernels of truth. The emergence of new industries, methods, processes, or technologies is exciting, and also often sparks hyperbole. The cotton gin, the industrial revolution, the assembly line, and plastics were all major economic milestones. Fabricated stories typically accompany the excitement, along with optimism that isn't scrutinized.

Table 4-1   Media Coverage of Shark Attacks

	2001 (50)	2000 (84)	1999 (58)	1998 (56)	1997 (60)	1996 (42)
June	95	174	41	69	43	29
July	616	193	126	50	57	76
August	818	121	89	74	78	46
TOTALS	1529	488	276	193	178	151

The table shows the number of news stories mentioning shark attacks for each month and year indicated, based on a series of searches in the LEXIS news database for each June, July, and August, from 1996 through 2001. The 1996–2000 summer total is 1286. The worldwide number of reported shark attacks for the full calendar year is indicated in parentheses after each respective year. Source of shark-attack data: Florida Museum of Natural History (http:www.flmnh.ufl.edu)

Radio, television, the Internet, and biotechnology are powerful inventions that alter and, in most cases, substantially improve lives and well being. What they can't do, however, is repeal human psychology or the principles of economics. The buoyant, spirited mood of giddy times masks this reality.

Positive moods can amplify these feedback loops, turning them into cascades. The result: inflated self-esteem, energy, and excessive demand for high-risk pleasures—including stock-market speculation. In the frenzy of a bull market, players rely on less information, process it less thoroughly, and decide more quickly. Elevated positive moods can lead to the illusion of control; manics credit themselves for good news. In the aggregate, positive moods draw people to riskier investments.

When reality begins to intercede, this can reverse. Whether or not confronting reality is the cause, the switch comes, though much quicker. Hard news makes some big financial players nervous, and they sell heavily. Others notice this, start to worry, and follow suit. News of this sell-off travels fast. Soon you have a reversal and pessimistic views circulating.

There can be much accompanying confusion. Neighborhood chat, folk wisdom, and market commentators may intone to "buy on the dips." Amateurs fall for this and continue to feed the old fire even as its embers die out. Some new volatility results, with prices gyrating against the uncertainty. That uncertainty is also news, and loss aversion heightens. Those ahead may bail out, putting downward pressure on prices. Those behind may still cling to the belief that the tide will turn.

Bull loops turn into bear loops and spin backwards through the collapse in prices. Financial-industry layoffs rise while bonuses fall, investment capital and securities offerings both dry up, and merger activity contracts. When the loops shift into bear mode, some biases also turn around. Overconfidence transforms into attribution bias or rationalization. This describes the fact that so many people attribute successes to their own handiwork and failures to factors beyond their control. When the market rises, their stock selections reflect acumen. But when it crashes, the Fed failed to follow the correct monetary policy. This blame game is well known in numerous social and cultural circles, so it is unsurprising that it plagues investment too.

As a bear market in the 2001 first quarter emerged, after a decade-long bull market and tech bubble, scores of investors looked to the Fed to bail out the sagging market. The talk was for a rate cut; the Fed cut its discount rate by half a point, but the sell-off continued. Market watchers blamed the Fed for too modest a cut, saying a 3/4-point cut was needed.

In contrast to mania, "depression" describes indecisiveness, apathy, and energy loss. This characterizes bear markets, especially early on. While many people continue to place blame elsewhere, those with more-acute feelings accept responsibility. In aggregate, negative moods lead to a willingness to accept lower rates of return.

In the mix are also speculators and manipulators. The extreme, classic example of the manipulator is the nineteenth-century British broker named Beit, poised to exploit a collapse in the price of gold-mining stocks. He sent a stock certificate to his mother in London, telling her it would rise substantially in value, but not to read the identity of the stock. Old lady Beit, natch, opened the certificate and told all her friends, who spread the price-boosting news all over town. Trader Beit, meanwhile, dumped his shares.

In modern markets, feedback loops are also fueled by technical trading strategies adopted by some investors. These include stop-loss orders that automatically prompt selling on price declines, and margin calls that result in the involuntary liquidation of all or part of a leveraged portfolio in a declining market.

Stop-loss orders, popularized by the best-selling 1960s book, *How I Made $2,000,000 in the Stock Market*, by Nicholas Darvas, by the mid-1980s evolved into "portfolio insurance" and "program trading." These played a causal role in turning the panic of 1987 into a full-blown market crash. Once the market plunged by 10 percent, these automatic loss savers kicked in, commanding the sale of more and more stocks as prices fell. Falling prices triggered the "insurance" sale, accelerating into free fall.

Lessons and Limits

Identifying and documenting psychological forces that impact the broad market does not mean these forces or their effects are predictable. Efficiency devotees correctly say that the market is impossible to predict accurately.

It is easier to describe price volatility and stock-market feedback loops than to predict their specific courses. Psychology is variable. History may repeat itself in life and in the market, but never exactly the same way. Each episode of Mr. Market's gloom-and-doom schizophrenia differs.

An immediate lesson is that an endlessly popular market technique, chartist or technical malarkey analysis, is overrated. Chartists have seized on the insights of psychology and behavioral finance to bolster claims of an ability to predict stock-market prices, as well as commodities and currencies. An entire industry is devoted to chartist techniques, with increasing attention paid to the psychology behind the charts. Nonsense. To understand the advice being peddled, consider these chart-picking techniques and how the stories of psychology are wrongly used to support them.

The *advance/decline line* takes all stocks that rise in price on a given day and subtracts those that fall. The result is offered as a barometer of investor sentiment. It probably is, for that day. It is wrong to use this barometer to extrapolate what it means for tomorrow. The record shows that this device gives premature signals and inaccurate clues.[14]

Chartists purport to gauge investor sentiment by computing the *put-to-call ratio*. Calls are rights to buy stocks in the future at today's prices, and puts are rights to sell them in the future at today's prices. So calls signify a positive outlook for stocks, while puts show pessimism. The put-call ratio captures sentiment in a single number. The historical evidence shows that players of the call and put game are wrong at key points, suggesting that paying attention to this metric is akin to practicing black magic.[15]

Wackier still is the *momentum indicator*. This compares today's price of a stock with its price 40 days or so ago. Large positive numbers indicate positive momentum; large negative numbers, negative momentum. One might have thought that the next piece of advice for a "momentum trader" is to watch for times when a stock price has fallen considerably, buy at that lower price, and conversely look out for price increases that might enable a profit. Surprise! The chartist takes the opposite approach: buy after the price has risen; sell after the price has fallen.[16]

The chartist tool kit holds a panoply of technical devices that reveal nothing more than meets the eye. Among tallied data are new highs/new lows; up volume/down volume; buying power/selling pressure; moving averages; and trend lines of every description. Don Quixote would be proud of the legions of chartists holding boundless confidence in their quest to divine from these devices the tops and bottoms in stocks and markets.

True believers in these financial voodoo dolls are now reporting that they can use psychology to predict major market events. Thus it is now possible, according to the seers, to determine when turning points will occur, what price support and resistance levels exist for particular stocks and whole markets, and when trends will emerge and how long they will last. They also name images that lines on a chart create. Favorites include the "staircase," "tea cup," "flag," and "pennant."

This is all hokum. If psychology teaches anything to investors, it is that none of this behavior is predictable. To believe otherwise is to be a poster child for cognitive biases. In believing that charts reveal profitable trends, chartists display pattern seeking. The momentum indicator in particular displays a terrible grasp of probability, ignoring basic lessons from statistics. All show a complete lack of investment skill when they ignore questions concerning fundamental business value.

Technical indicators are tempting because they can be self-fulfilling. If enough people chase trends, trends will arise. This is why some of the new models of market action describe markets in just the way the chartist tracks it. The risk is that the indicators collapse, much as a house of cards collapses. There is nothing supporting such trends but their own forces.

Attractive Prices

The only room for technical analysis is in determining whether a business is selling at an attractive price. That determination may be aided by understanding how the overall market is priced. Appreciating this requires not so much examining charts as having awareness of biases that operate in the market. It calls for detecting situations in which undue pessimism dominates, and steering clear of those where overoptimism looms large. It echoes the prudence of remaining fearful when others are greedy, and becoming greedy when others are fearful.[17]

Do you need a put-call ratio to tell you this? Clear-thinking observers of finance and industry generally discern euphoria or gloom without maps and pictures. Studying pictures promotes cognitive biases, especially the illusion of control, overconfidence, and pattern seeking. It offers no objective information useful in making clearly-thought-out investment decisions.

The lesson applies to individual-stock picking as well. Stocks priced substantially below value for psychological reasons are potentially promising investments. While predicting overreaction or underreaction is not possible, recognizing these biases and responding to them can be lucrative.

A handful of new mutual funds apply such strategies, some generating quite excellent results.[18] One private firm, Fuller & Thaler Asset Management, of which leading behavioral economist Richard H. Thaler is a principal (though not a stock-picker), reports average annual returns of 21 percent since its inception in the early 1990s (compared with about 14 percent for the S&P 500). While others sport less-exciting returns, having the behavioral approach in your investing tool kit can improve understanding and results.

In terms of reading the psychology of the overall market, "buying on the dips" is not a good strategy, because dips are unlikely to offer much opportunity to buy stocks priced below their values. The advice should be recast to buy after a panic sets in. This remains only a ground rule, not gospel to take literally or follow blindly. It defines a good time to run your critical eye over the market in search of stocks with prices depressed by unwarranted investor gloom.

Buying "after panics" is better than "on dips," because there is greater mathematical reason to believe that prices that were substantially above value now are significantly below. What constitutes a panic varies with the broader background conditions the United States is facing. If extraordinary national adversity accompanies the arrival of an economic downturn, psychological effects on market pricing exaggerate.

Drops in the Dow Jones Industrial Average range from 30 to 50 percent in the face of such national upheaval. This occurred in the depression year of 1937 and at the onset of World War II from 1940–1942. It recurred in 1966, 1969–1970, 1973–1974, and 1977, amid the Vietnam War, global gold and oil crises, the thick of the Cold War, and soaring inflation, interest, and unemployment rates.

During the 1970s, 9 intermittent panics occurred, where the Dow's closing price was down 10 percent from its highest close during the preceding 30 calendar days.[19] By comparison, there were only 9 such 10-percent panics during the 1940s, 1950s, and 1960s combined, and only 1 during the decade of the 1990s. Upon these calmer seas, setbacks to the Dow ranged from 17 to 27 percent from the market peak, as in 1948–1949, 1953, 1957, 1960, 1980, 1982, 1990, and 1998.[20]

The September 11, 2001 attack on the World Trade Center in New York City and the Pentagon in Washington, D.C. accompanied an economy teetering at the edge of recession. The immediate economic damage ran to tens of billions of dollars and threatened a domino effect on the economy reaching to multiples of that, due to declines in aviation, tourism, and industries reliant on discretionary consumer spending. The psychological effect equaled this scale, making it reasonable to estimate damage at even greater multiples. The uncertainty of the U.S. response and of subsequent replies from the perpetrators intensified the situation. The result: a 7.3 percent drop on the first day of trading following the attack, and a 14.2 percent drop for the week.

Conditions of this gravity, and market plunges of such magnitudes, scare off all but the stalwart investor, and in the case of the September 11, 2001 attack plunge, the deeply patriotic. Yet in all cases, the Dow eventually recovers, often as rapidly as three months, though sometimes stretching to many years.

This does not mean there is anything peculiar about such convulsions. The Dow has always marched upward over time, in sync with continual expansion of the U.S. and global economies. Take any point in Dow history—upon the occurrence of a tragic event or a jubilant one—and look at the Dow 6 months, 2 years, or 10 years later. You will invariably see a gain at the 10-year mark, often at the 2-year mark, and more often than not at the 6-month point.

The precise path following any national calamity or celebration cannot be predicted. To speak only of calamities, consider the many upheavals of the twentieth century, and guess what happened to the Dow on the day of the event and one week and one year after:

- While in office, President Eisenhower suffered a heart attack, President Kennedy was assassinated, President Nixon resigned, President Reagan was shot, and President Clinton was impeached.

- In a blood-strewn century, Japan bombed Pearl Harbor, bringing the United States into World War II against Japan, Germany, and Italy; and the United States later fought wars in Korea, Vietnam, and the Persian Gulf.

- The United States faced the Cuban Missile Crisis, the Arab Oil Embargo, and the Soviet Union's invasion of Afghanistan.

- The U.S. embassy was taken in Iran, with hostages held for 444 days, and U.S. embassies were bombed in Kenya and Tanzania.

- U.S. Marine barracks were bombed in Lebanon, and the USS Cole was attacked in Yemen.

- Financial crises in the United States followed the Hunt Brothers' cornering the silver market, the 1929 and 1987 market crashes, a United Kingdom currency crisis, an Asian stock-market crisis, and a Russian debt crisis.

- A bomb exploded in New York City's World Trade Center and in a Federal building in Oklahoma City; and later, commercial airplanes hijacked and piloted by suicidal fanatics demolished the Trade Center and crashed into the Pentagon in Washington, D.C.

None of these events produced like results on stock markets. In some cases, the Dow rose on the day of the event; in others it fell; in some a week later it was up, in others down; and the same was true after one year and at other intervals. All rises and falls are erratic, seeming trends running in different directions, with varying durations. So many variables operate, with conflicting responses being registered; the episodes yield no patterns.

There is one common feature of any collection of "event days" on the Dow. As the time horizon is lengthened from one day to many years, the number of gains compared to event day rises, and the number of losses falls. To illustrate, if 10 events from the list are chosen, and the Dow on event day compared with the Dow 30 days later shows 8 declines and 2 rises, when you compare it 90 days later, you will see something like 7 declines and 3 rises, a year later 4 declines and 6 rises, and so on.

That teaches a meaningful lesson, true in times of despair but also in times of jubilation: valuable businesses are underpriced, and buying them is desirable for superior financial returns. That is undoubtedly not the most important lesson for citizens to draw from the twentieth century or the opening of this one, but it is the most important finance lesson of the ages. Citizens can only hope in vain that the world itself will ever be so simple as the investment slice of it.

Behavioral theorists say people are rational in the long run but myopic in the short run. People know they ought to save, but they don't. The situation is the same comparing the short run to the past. The immediacy of the present blinds people to the lessons of the past. In trauma, people return to the past, initially for understanding, ultimately for awareness.

After every one of these tragic national events, the country looks to history for parallels, examining precedents on the list. While analogies from political, military, diplomatic, and even financial viewpoints are apparent, no pattern whatsoever emerges in investing terms. The only thing these events have in common, in the case of stock markets and business values, is that the probability of price-value differences arising is greatest in their wake.

The population of such candidates also rises at more modest drops that still resemble panics rather than dips. Consider market drops of at least seven percent in the course of a week. Table 4-2 lists these recent panics.

The key point: such circumstances create opportunities to discover issues trading at attractive prices compared to their values. The index data is only a clue, a heads up, a call to attention, not a call to action.

Table 4-2 Post-World War II Panics: Weekly Falls

Date	Dow Close	Point Decline	Percentage Decline
September 13, 1974	627.19	50.69	7.5
September 27, 1974	621.94	48.82	7.3
September 12, 1986	1,758.72	141.03	7.4
October 16, 1987	2,246.74	235.46	9.5
October 23, 1987	1,950.80	295.94	13.2
December 4, 1987	1,766.70	143.80	7.5
October 13, 1989	2,569.26	216.26	7.8
April 14, 2000	10,305.77	805.71	7.3
March 16, 2001	9,823.41	821.21	7.7
September 21, 2001	8,235.81	1,058.74	14.3

Source: www.analyzeindices.com/dowhistory

Luck and Skill

Another way to pose the question of what makes a successful investor is by asking how to tell luck from skill. Skill is at work when there is a causal link between action and result, so that success is controllable, as in selecting moves in chess or executing shots in billiards. Luck carries no such link, making success random, as in the roll of dice or the draw of cards. Simple as this sounds, most people do not distinguish these characteristics properly.

Consider Harvard University psychologist Ellen Langer's experiment involving lotteries with or without choice.[21] An office lottery is conducted using two identical collections of baseball cards. One set is put in a bin from which the winning card will be chosen at the end of the week, and the other set is distributed to players. The holder of the matching card wins. Half the players get to choose which card they will hold, and the other half are simply given a card.

Right before the drawing, players are told that no more chances are being sold, but someone wants to buy a card. The issue becomes price. Prices set by players who chose their own cards were substantially higher (nearly $9) than by those who did not (less than $2). Yet whether one was given a card or chose it makes no difference in the likelihood of winning, and does not change the fact that luck alone determines the outcome. Behavioral insights such as this led state lotteries to permit buyers to "pick their own numbers," though picking winning numbers likewise demonstrates no skill, but only luck.

Just as this illusion of control can lead investors to see trends that don't exist (and sometimes to create them), it can lead theorists to believe that they understand things they don't. The market is not as efficient as many believe, and psychological factors help explain why. In the chapters ahead, we will see how these factors influence our investment choices.

Part
II

5

Merry-Go-Rounds

We already know that in a stock market that is not efficient, a company's stock may be priced above or below its intrinsic value. That wedge offers opportunities for investors to scoop up dollar bills lying on the market floor. Finding high-quality, low-risk, underpriced businesses is how Benjamin Graham and his followers made prodigious fortunes. If Grahamites can take advantage of pricing inefficiencies, so too can corporations.

Corporations with publicly traded stock can decide when to issue new shares. These seasoned equity offerings (SEOs) are usually done when the price of outstanding shares is higher than the per-share intrinsic value of the business. Entrepreneurs and their promoters can exploit similar timing opportunities in periods of general overpricing to make initial public offerings (IPOs) at prices above values. Corporations also exploit market inefficiencies by buying back shares when the price-value difference reverses, and cash in on investor psychology by designing appealing dividend policies.

What does a corporation's exploitation of market inefficiency tell an investor? It can mean that the corporation's management is intelligent and better able than others to control sentiment. But because of the complexity of market pricing and the difficulty of exploiting it, it is possible that when a corporation exploits market inefficiency it also exploits some investors, possibly you! Management possesses a double-edged sword, forcing intelligent investors to learn how it is wielded.

Selling Hype

Intelligent investors stick with open stock-market trading, rather than buying new offerings, whether SEOs or IPOs. The main reason to prefer market trading to new issues is how prices are set. In market trading, prices are the products of interactions of lots of traders, some of whom are more accurate in their judgments than others.

Even so, this clearing price is important to investors because it determines the price at which they can buy or sell. That price will fluctuate around the intrinsic value of the business. When investors consider buying, there will be opportunities to buy quality businesses at prices below values. When price is dramatically above value, it may be prudent to prune back on a portfolio.

The price for IPOs or SEOs is set differently. It is ruled by controlling stockholders in the case of IPOs, and corporations in the case of SEOs. They ordinarily can select the timing of an offering. When the market will not accept a price at or above value, they simply pull the new issue off the market, citing "unfavorable market conditions"—unfavorable to the seller.[1] There are no bargains here. These markets always heat up when overall prices rise above values. You can expect to lose money in these deals.

IPOs historically close on the first day of trading from 5 to 10 percent above offering price, and in some boom times such as the late 1990s, at terrific multiples of that. Many take this to mean that the underwriters and issuer leave money on the table for investors. This perceived underpricing is incorrect when the long-run performance is examined. Rather, IPOs are overpriced, by about 35 percent on average, and much more in the late 1990s.

Two factors contribute. As to the overall market price level, the volume of IPOs correlates with market exuberance.[2] A reasonable estimate of historical stock-market overpricing during periods when IPOs are "hot" is 20 to 25 percent.[3] The figure is higher if you add the financial excesses of 1997–2000, when the Nasdaq quintupled as IPO volume hit record levels, before the index dropped 40 percent and the IPO market fell dormant along with it.

For particular issues, IPOs historically underperform equities that are trading at the time of the IPO, by about 12 percent compared with returns to stocks of like-sized, seasoned equities. That figure is much higher when the bacchanalian late 1990s are added, as only a handful of that era's IPOs traded above their offering prices after the party ended.[4] The high market price level coupled with the inferior comparative returns means that IPOs are historically overpriced by 32 to 37 percent,[5] a conservative estimate in light of the late 1990s.

Who is responsible for this overpricing? Underwriters, chiefly. These are agents of controlling stockholders and corporations in selling new stock. Investors sometimes believe (mistakenly) that underwriters work for them. That's wrong, even though you will also find similar impressions of judges who write opinions on the mistaken belief that underwriters are working for the public.[6] Buyers of real estate similarly believe (wrongly) that brokers work for them, probably because brokers spend more time with buyers than with sellers.

Underwriters work for the stock issuer. Their work consists of advising the company about the market environment and the process, buying the issue from the company, and then selling it to the public. They make their money selling stock, based on a percentage of the dollar amount of the offering.

The percentage of the selling commission varies but averages about six percent (for a large firm, nearly $1 billion in a good year, and three or four times that in the late 1990s). They make even more money from repeat business. This happens most often when the price at which underwriters can sell shares is high compared to the value offered.

Underwriting firms put extra marketing effort behind new issues because that's where the money is. The special salesmanship that fans demand for the offerings is fueled by hype, scarcity, and myth. Brokers talk up the issuer like it is the coolest thing since air conditioning. They persuade buyers by emphasizing that only a limited number of shares are available. And underwriters love the myth that they leave money on the table.

A popular pitch urges the novice investor that an IPO is a special opportunity to "get in on the ground floor." This is a grossly misleading form of framing. Most funds raised in IPOs are used to repay previous investors. You can't go public without an existing business, and you can't have an existing business without backers to pay. The purpose of IPOs is to repay them, so that the emphasis in the phrase "initial public offering" should be on the word "public" rather than "initial." The ground floors were built long before, and IPO buyers get on somewhere much higher, maybe the unlucky 13th floor.

Underwriters use a variety of tactics to maintain a selling price. They support the price by delivering a standing offer to buy the security in the market at the offering price. This "stabilization" means the price will not fall below the offering price because it gives the appearance of buyer interest, which, given the bias of social proof, brings buyers to the market.

Some unscrupulous underwriters are also known to support the offering price of IPOs by having analysts of their firm write favorable research reports about the stock and the company. Others have been seen to pull or withhold unfavorable reports. Lead underwriters in a syndicate restrict quick resales by imposing penalties on syndicate members if allocated shares are sold within a week or so of the offering. These are just a few of many ways to sustain overpricing.

Unsavory as it sounds, only some of this activity is illegal. Due to vague laws, only a portion of that is prosecuted. It takes extreme violations of rules—outright fraudulent manipulation of price—to land a perpetrator in jail. Headlines feature a broker at the notorious retail stock brokerage, D.H. Blair & Co., pleading guilty to stock fraud, admitting that he and other brokers manipulated stock prices after IPOs were sold at inflated prices. The Manhattan District Attorney's office said the defunct firm manipulated prices in at least 10 IPOs during a 12-year period.[7]

The rare accomplices who fall make headlines too. Shoe designer Steve Madden pled guilty to stock fraud for his role in some 20 IPOs handled by the disgraced Stratton Oakmont Inc. brokerage house,[8] and fashion executive Elliot Lavigne settled similar charges against him.[9] Stratton hid its stake in IPOs by transferring shares to these accomplices with the understanding that they would retransfer shares at preset prices once trading began. The market price would be maintained until the brokerage firm recovered the stocks and sold them at a profit, just before ceasing stabilization efforts and letting the price plummet.

These extravagant, illegal charades are unnecessary because perfectly legal psychology works masterfully in the underwriter's favor. Stories of IPO desks at all major underwriting firms at the end of the Internet-bubble market reveal how things work. The story is: These are hot IPOs. Why just look at the price gains? But not everyone can play. This selling technique pumps demand, making people want in, putting upward pressure on price. Social proof. *Q.E.D.*

Even so, underwriters can be tempted to play the demand for all it's worth, crossing legal lines. Favors go to those who do a favor in return. Some investors get more shares by agreeing to pay larger commissions in subsequent deals, by individuals agreeing to steer more future underwriting business the firm's way, or by agreeing to buy more shares once trading begins.

After the IPO fallout and Internet bust of 2001, everyone complained. Those who bought IPOs in the days following an offering said the cozy practices drove prices higher; those excluded from the IPOs thought they were excluded unfairly; bankrupted issuers disdained the whole racket. Shareholders of the underwriting firms sued, alleging that managers wasted firm assets playing these games. The U.S. Attorney's Office in New York looked into criminal wrongdoing. The Securities and Exchange Commission and National Association of Securities Dealers investigated civil violations.

Consider what happened to one IPO issuer who cried foul, Mortgage.com.[10] It went public at $8 per share on April 11, 1999, soared to about $24 within 2 weeks (up 300 percent), and later crashed to below $1 as the company went bankrupt and had its stock delisted. Whatever wrongdoing is proven, those complaining that they are shut out of IPOs ought to count themselves blessed.

Issuer complaints are rare, however, because overheated IPO markets are bonanzas for entrepreneurs. Executives taking a company public typically own stock paid for in pennies. While most are not allowed to sell shares until a few months after the IPO, sales at that time make them rich. The wealth effect is even greater if the offering price multiplies and stays aloft until they sell.

Other beneficiaries are fast money traders. These are scalpers who buy a piece of the IPO at the offering price and flip it within a few hours or weeks at ridiculously inflated prices. Sales at high prices along with accompanying profits help sustain the illusion that money is "left on the table." In truth, the profits that flippers generate show that money is put on the table by the gullible.

Whirl After Whirl

The amount of wealth that is shifted from gullible buyers to sellers, bankers, and flippers in IPOs is astonishing. Suppose average IPO proceeds per year are about $10 billion (the historical average, though the 1990s skew the figure upwards). At a 35-percent pricing premium, the intrinsic value of the stocks is about $7.4 billion (i.e., $7.4 × 1.35 = about $10 billion). That amounts to overpayment, or a wealth transfer, of $2.6 billion annually. For the period of 1997–2000, the figure is at least triple that, making the price tag of the era's IPO bazaar exceed $30 billion (conservatively estimated).

IPOs are awful for investors. Yet many investors, lots of traders, and some journalists speak longingly of the passing of an over-heated IPO market. It is as if hot IPOs signal an easy-money era for investors. This is false, except in the precisely fleeting sense that easy money comes, and easy money goes.

This is why bull markets are characterized by large numbers of private firms going public, and are followed by bear markets when large numbers of investors lick their wounds. Examples include the booms of the early and late 1960s, the early 1970s, the mid-1980s, the surge of the bull market in 1993–1994, and its peak in the late 1990s.

After each of these booms—accompanied by multitudes of IPOs—the public dumped these highflyers, and their prices plummeted. Every time, to paraphrase Ben Graham, after the usual swearing-off period of a few years, the whole tragicomedy is repeated, step-by-step, in another whirl of what Graham called the new-issue merry-go-round.[11]

It is hard for the public to learn its lesson, for reasons ranging from the myth of IPO underpricing to the social proof that sustains market bubbles. Apart from these is an additional learning hurdle that must be overcome to discourage repetition: the availability bias.

If something is easy to recall, it figures more significantly in memory, and people think it happens more often than it does. Spectacularly successful IPOs are easier to recall than the vastly greater multitude of flops. So people think (wrongly) that IPOs are money makers for investors.

People's assessments of "spectacularly successful IPOs" are misplaced. If asked to name spectacularly successful IPOs, many cite Microsoft. After adjusting for subsequent stock splits, Microsoft's public offering price in 1986 was 15 cents; it traded at under $1 three years later, before soaring 80-fold. True, the stock price nearly septupled in three years, not a shabby IPO. But the 80-fold pop is where the real money is, and an investment three years after the IPO was exposed to far less investment risk than the funds staked in the IPO.

Investors would benefit more not from remembering the "spectacular successes," but by remembering the debacles. Take three that should stand out in every investor's mind: the roaring 1920s, the go-go 1960s, and the heady 1990s.

The roaring 1920s showed IPO exuberance that culminated in the great stock-market crash of October, 1929. The dollar amount of IPOs during the first 9 months of 1929, through the month before the crash, totaled more than $5 billion, 10 times the $500 million average-IPO volume in the preceding 5 years.[12] In September, 1929 alone—the month before the crash—IPO volume tallied $1 billion. All told, nearly 100 new exchange listings appeared in 1929, bringing the total issues to 842. This IPO market was so hot it would scald its participants.

Of September, 1929's $1 billion funding, 22 percent went to what became the favor of the era, investment trusts. While valuations across the market were high, these pools of funds were entirely speculative operations, aggressively marketed to novice investors, drawing billions in capital. The pools looked solely for price appreciation in target investments, not at underlying businesses; borrowed substantially to buy securities; churned them (i.e., bought and then immediately sold) to give the appearance of action to whet the public's appetite; and used pyramid structures of multiple sponsors and affiliates to maximize leverage.

At merriment's height, $2.25 billion of IPOs for investment trusts were floated in 1929, and $790 million in 1928, dwarfing the $175 million outstanding before that time. All the venerable banking firms of the era participated. Dillon, Read & Co. created the first major investment trust in 1924, followed in the next few years by the likes of Lehman Corp., J & W. Seligman & Co., and J.P. Morgan & Co.

The most aggressive, and thus most doomed, was the trust formed by Goldman Sachs & Co., called Goldman Sachs Trading Corporation. Established in late 1928, along with affiliates Shenandoah Corp. and Blue Ridge Corp., these trusts were so leveraged—with only about 2 percent of equity at stake—they crumbled a year later in the market plunge.

Goldman Sachs Trading Corporation rose 20 percent after its IPO, recorded a high of $121 in 1929, then sank to a low the following year of below $5, and below $2 the next. Shenandoah's IPO debuted at $17.50 in July of 1929, promptly doubled in price, and reached a high of $39 before plummeting to below $4 the next year. Ditto with Blue Ridge, which went public in August of 1929, reached a high of $29, then fell below $3 during 1930. Goldman Sachs & Co. shut the trusts down and sold what was left of them, then spent months battling shareholder lawsuits alleging waste of corporate assets at Goldman Sachs Trading Corporation. (Sound familiar?)

Obviously, these trusts did not rise and fall in value in accordance with these price gyrations. Rather, as a contemporary observer put it, prices skyrocketed after IPOs were issued, because "the public was beginning to believe in magic," paying $2 or more for scrip worth $1 or less.[13] The public went wild, and could not be restrained. These giddy days ended in the greatest financial calamity of the twentieth century, and though other factors were at play, every serious investor should remember the story.

Runner-up for most-dizzying whirl of the IPO merry-go-round occurred in the early 1960s. The Dow Jones Industrial Average roared from 1959 to 1961, fell a bit, advanced bullishly again in late 1961, then declined in near panic in May of 1962, with "growth" stocks (including IBM) taking nosedives.

The period was a washout for numerous "hot" small-company IPOs made at high prices and subsequently inflated by "nearly insane" speculation.[14] The insanity, of course, is only diagnosed later, when the erstwhile hot issues lose 90-percent-plus of their prices in a few months.

Ben Graham examined a representative sample of 41 IPOs from the 1960–1962 frenzy listed in Standard & Poor's *Stock Guide*. Five lost 90 percent or more of their high price, 30 lost more than 50 percent, and the entire group 66 percent. He concluded, "The money not listed in the *Stock Guide* undoubtedly had a larger shrinkage on the whole."[15]

Which brings us to the winner: the loony toons of our era. In the 1990s boom, first-day IPO pricing (from offering to closing) doubled, tripled, and quadrupled. (One, VA Linux Systems Inc., septupled!) This made earlier periods with average first-day price rises of 5 to 10 percent seem coolheaded.

In the 6 weeks preceding Nasdaq's March 10, 2000 peak, 77 IPOs were made.[16] Nearly half doubled from offering to closing price, nearly one-third tripled, and some quadrupled. One year later, the prices on all these highflyers had plummeted, in proportion to their earlier rises: on average, the quadruples had fallen 91 percent, the triples 87 percent, the doubles 83 percent, the rest 66 percent. The higher they go the harder they fall.

The peak market cap of this class of newcomers that collectively generated nearly $2 billion in losses on less than $5 billion in revenue, was $209 billion. By comparison, on the same day IBM, with $88 billion in revenue and profits of about $8 billion, sported a market cap of $194 billion, $15 billion less.

Table 5-1 shows the top 10 best-performing IPOs as of the last day of 2000. The average arithmetic gain on these hot issues that day, compared to their respective offering prices, was nearly fivefold. The bubble soon burst, making these marquee names tombstones in the Internet graveyard.

Within six months, all but one fell at least 92 percent from their high prices in the previous period, and the sole exception lost 87 percent. All but two fell at least 66 percent from their original price, and those two didn't fare much better. All continued to slide in succeeding months. Similar results held for the next 20 hot issues of that period and no doubt, as in every earlier period, things were about as bad for all the other highly promoted stocks peddled during that frenzy.

Table 5-1 Very Hot and Very Cold—Best-Performing New IPOs in After Market as of Year End 2000 compared to Mid-2001

Company	IPO Date	IPO	y/e 00	gain	mid 01	lost v. IPO	v. high
Linux	12/9/99	30	250	733%	4	87%	98%
theglobe.com	11/12/98	9	64	606%	*	89%	99%
Foundry Networks	9/27/99	25	156	525%	21	16%	87%
FreeMarkets	12/10/99	48	280	483%	15	69%	95%
CobaltNetworks	11/5/99	22	128	432%	*	84%	97%
MarketWatch.com	1/15/99	17	98	474%	3	82%	97%
Akamai Technologies	10/29/99	26	145	458%	11	58%	92%
CacheFlow	11/19/99	24	126	427%	8	66%	94%
Sycamore Networks	10/21/99	38	185	386%	11	71%	94%
Ask Jeeves	7/1/99	14	65	364%	3	79%	95%

Source: IPO.com (prices and percentages rounded).
*Stock was delisted. Cobalt was sold to its financial backer for $3.50/share, a 79% premium to price.

These data, and the other cited studies, should put to rest the claim that IPOs are "underpriced." It may be the case, as early research emphasized, that issues often rise in price substantially above the offering prices within the first days or weeks following the offerings. But it is wrong to conclude that underwriters have "left money on the table."

Because company managers want the highest possible price for their shares, they may exaggerate a business's intrinsic value. Underwriters, in turn, may talk them down. They have to sell the shares, and those they don't sell they hold. A unit price is set and, except in broken deals, all shares are sold. The hype necessary to sell those shares doesn't naturally cease at the completion of the IPO. It lingers. People still want the stock. Upward price pressure continues. Short-term price rises do not indicate underpricing, but overhyping.

The silver lining: there may be dollar bills lying on the table in subsequently pessimistic markets. It is a smart strategy to review the IPOs of the optimistic period to hunt for bargains. Markets in disarray often provide mouthwatering opportunities. (In relatively high-insolvency periods such as the early 2000s, much of the bargain hunting is done by corporate investors shopping in bankruptcy courtrooms, not a bad place for individual investors likewise to train their attention.)

This does not mean that IPOs during post-boom periods are bargains, despite such frequently heard professional advice. While underwriters and issuers have a tougher time in bear markets selling stock at prices greater than value, an offering priced below value remains about as rare as a shark attack on a human being.

A bear period marked the aftermath of the 1990s' bull run that began to falter in early 2000. By mid-2001, the IPO market stalled. Market conditions were "unfavorable." The big offering of the period was an IPO of a portion of Kraft Foods, sold by Philip Morris, which continued to hold the controlling position.

Total proceeds ran close to $9 billion, at a per-share offering price of $31, which insiders said was at the high end of the planned range. Underwriters apparently were able to sell all the shares, but they could only boost the price to within a dollar or so below the offering price, where it languished for months afterward.

The same difficulty plagued numerous other deals offered in the same period. These are not bargains. Wait until long after the underwriter has no interest in supporting the price of an IPO before even thinking about a purchase—at least one year. From the vantage point of the 1970s, Graham summarized the situation like this:

> The heedlessness of the public and the willingness of selling organizations to sell whatever may be profitably sold can have only one result—price collapse. In many cases, the new issues lose 75 percent and more of their offering price. The situation is worsened by the fact that, at bottom, the public has a real aversion to the very kind of small issue that it bought so readily in its careless moments. Many of these issues fall, proportionately as much below their true value as they formerly sold above it.[17]

Accordingly, avoid IPOs. Their prices rise, often spectacularly, due to a speculative atmosphere evoking a sense of easy money. But except in exceedingly rare and impossible-to-predict cases, it all vanishes. Next time you are tempted, remember the losers; forget the winners. And remember Graham's admonishment that, "For every dollar you make in this way you will be lucky if you end up by losing only two."[18]

Kraft is an example of an IPO effected as a spin-off, a business carved out of a larger parent concern, in this case Phillip Morris. Generally accounting for about 20 percent or less of the overall IPO market, the dangers for investors in buying these are not as great as first-stage IPOs, though risks remain.

Famed fund manager and stock picker Peter Lynch recorded his belief that IPOs of brand-new companies are very risky—75 percent of those he chose became long-term disappointments—noting he fared better with IPOs of spin-offs, with track records that could be intelligently evaluated.[19] Beware, even so. While corporate officers choosing to spin off may not pocket the proceeds as entrepreneurs in IPOs do, they are obliged to get the best deals they can for their existing shareholders. This makes analysis of spin-offs akin to the analysis of seasoned equity offerings.

Seasoned Equity

In IPOs, controlling shareholders are sellers, and the only investors are the buyers on the other side of the deal. In seasoned equity offerings (SEOs), managers decide that the corporation should sell new shares, and shareholders don't have much voice in the matter.

But the sale of new stock dilutes shareholder percentage interests, making existing holders involuntary sellers of a piece of their company. The price at which stock is sold will determine whether that dilution is worth it or not. For a shareholder advocate, this makes SEOs trickier to analyze than IPOs because there are investors on both sides of the table, prospective buyers, and involuntary sellers.

For a company with an existing class of public stock outstanding, a good time to issue new shares to raise funds is when the market is overpricing that stock compared to value. If the stock is trading at $50, but is only worth around $40, a company can "make" $10 per share by selling new shares.

A difficult question arises that would not emerge if markets were efficient: when management offers additional stock at a price above intrinsic value, are they acting in a shareholder-friendly manner? They certainly benefit existing shareholders of the corporation by charging more than they are giving up, and that benefits the corporation as a whole.

But for new buyers of the offering, this is a bad deal. If the only owners who count in this calculus are existing ones, it becomes fine for management to sell shares to newcomers at high prices. On the other hand, this would seem defensible as a matter of integrity only if the directors disclosed their beliefs to the potential buyers before the sale was made.

So which is it? Do managers tend to overprice or underprice SEOs? A flurry of research studies gives an equivocal answer.[20] Most evidence suggests overpricing of SEOs. This is good news for existing shareholders of corporate America. It means, however, SEOs are not a profitable place to look for attractive investment opportunities. This is the case because even if you identify an underpriced SEO, managers are disserving the interests of existing shareholders in making it, and there is no reason to believe they are going to improve after the SEO, either.

Substantial price appreciation in the years following an SEO does not necessarily signify untrustworthy or incompetent management. The fundamentals may have improved. Or it could be due to the fact that the corporation needed funds at a time when the market was underpricing its shares, but an SEO remained the best way to generate required capital. Some portion of the subsequent price rise could be due to investor sentiment rather than fundamentals. And it could be that managers sometimes also suffer from the same cognitive biases everyone else faces, and simply get it wrong.

What is striking is how often managers overprice SEOs, and to what extent. A leading study indicates that SEOs do half as well as investments in seasoned companies not issuing new shares. It showed that a broad group of SEOs enjoyed average annual returns of about 7 percent compared to a group of like-sized companies without SEOs, generating 15.3 percent.[21] Another study documented an average return 31.2 percent less for SEOs than a sample of like-sized peer firms that did not issue equity.[22]

The evidence of systematic overpricing suggests management's ability to price value more accurately and with less cognitive bias than investors. Managers have informational advantages because they run the company. They also pay for advice from underwriters, whose job it is to stay abreast of values and market pricing. In effecting SEOs, managers act less like arbs and more like winning bettors at the race track who wager in the last few minutes prior to post time—once sold, the gains are firmly in the corporate coffers.

If managers deserve two cheers from existing shareholders for not giving away value for too low a price, what about buyers of SEOs? On the disclosure side, there appears to be little or no acknowledgment of the price-value relationship in SEOs. A review of a random sampling of prospectuses for SEOs reveals no indication of top management's opinion concerning the price-value relationship of an offering.

The infrequency of managers who both sell only at prices higher than values and disclose this fact is further suggested by the applause given Berkshire Hathaway managers when they offered a new class of stock in a recapitalization of the company. In doing so, they in effect said they were taking advantage of market mispricing. A conspicuous legend on page one of the prospectus for the offering included the following:

> Warren Buffett, as Berkshire's Chairman, and Charles Munger, as Berkshire's Vice Chairman, want you to know the following (and urge you to ignore anyone telling you that these statements are 'boilerplate" or unimportant):

1. Mr. Buffett and Mr. Munger believe that *Berkshire's Class A Common Stock is not undervalued at the market price stated above. Neither Mr. Buffett nor Mr. Munger would currently buy Berkshire shares at that price, nor would they recommend that their families or friends do so.*

The Berkshire managers seemed to be meeting obligations to existing shareholders (selling part of the company only for a price at least equal to value) and to prospective buyers (telling them so). Experts and practitioners of corporate law and finance alike marveled at such candor, a significant indication that the practice is not widely followed in corporate America.

Two immediate lessons can be drawn. First, stay away from direct offerings. Second, there is a range of acceptable behavior, bordered at the low end by the minimum standards of society and at the top by the extraordinary. Many in corporate America try to identify and satisfy the minimum standard only. The Berkshire disclosure is an example of the rare other extreme, showing behavior far superior to that required.[23]

Uses and Abuses of Share Buybacks

A corporation can distribute funds to equity holders either through dividends or share repurchases. Historically, cash dividends were the dominant method of giving cash to shareholders. In the closing decades of the twentieth century, however, share repurchases caught on. By the late 1990s, more dollars were returned to shareholders of industrial companies in the form of repurchases than through dividends.[24]

The timing and manner of share repurchases are influenced by market inefficiencies. In the case of share buybacks, the dynamics are the mirror image of stock offerings. Repurchases are desirable from the corporation's standpoint when the company's shares are priced in the market at levels below their values. If a company's stock is trading at $40, but it is really worth around $50, the company can improve returns to investors using surplus funds to buy back stock.

Determining the return of paying $40 to repurchase stock worth $50 is not as simple as determining the return of paying $40 to expand a warehouse that will generate a return valued at $50. The latter would generate a return of 25 percent ($50 of value is created through the outlay of $40, so $40 of outlay landed $10 of additional value, and 10/40 = 25 percent).

In the case of repurchasing one's own stock, no real investment is being made. The funds used to buy shares are transferred to selling shareholders. Even so, the purchase increases the portion of the business owned by the continuing holders. Each continuing holder has a larger share of earnings and dividends and everything else, at a cost equal to the price of the shares bought back.

When the repurchase is at a price below value, continuing shareholders gain the difference, while selling shareholders forfeit it. The benefits of share repurchases to the corporation and its continuing shareholders are greater the lower the price is compared to the value (and hurt the departing shareholders to the same extent).

At prices above value, repurchases are a poor use of corporate resources. Departing shareholders are given a bonus to leave, courtesy of the continuing holders. Thus, the only time a company should buy back its shares is when the price is below value. In addition, the basis for this conclusion should be disclosed to prospective selling shareholders, and they should be given sufficient information to enable them to assess the company's value as well.

It seems that investors take buybacks as signals of managerial belief that shares are underpriced. They believe that the number of shares outstanding will fall, thus boosting earnings and dividends per all remaining shares, and raising per-share value. Due to inefficient markets, we cannot say that they will result in an adjusted price equal to value.

One study of the effects of buybacks shows prodigious value creation among certain kinds of stocks, particularly those that were low-priced based on traditional valuation metrics when repurchase programs were implemented.[25] The overall performance differential between firms doing and not doing buybacks was a few percentage points per year. That percentage difference grew to over 10 percent among stocks with relatively low market prices compared to book values.

SEC rules on the timing and volume of share buybacks are intended to limit a company's ability to use them to prop up price. Companies can't buy back shares during the opening and closing

half-hours of each trading day, times when market-price effects res-
onate most heavily with investors. There is also a cap on how much
buying back is allowed—no more than 25 percent of the average
trading volume in the shares over the preceding month.

The SEC on rare but significant occasions relaxes these rules. It
did so informally in the wake of the 1987 crash by informing companies that it would not take legal action against those buying to
prevent panic. It did so formally after the four-day market shutdown
occasioned by the terrorist airplane bombing of the World Trade
Centers in New York City on September 11, 2001.[26]

In each case, the move reflected concern that investor fears would
lead to selling pressure that market makers would not be able to
handle. Relaxing the buyback rules permitted companies to issue
standing buy orders to offset the pressure. Effectively, the SEC gave
companies incentives to buy back stock (though it made clear it was
not trying to encourage any company to take any particular action).

When used following the attack on the World Trade Centers in
September 2001, these relaxations were effective.[27] Buyback volume
on the first day of trading was 7 to 10 times normal, with more than
100 companies announcing $12 billion in planned repurchases.
Companies included a cross-section of American industry: AllState
Insurance Co., Cardinal Health, E*Trade Group Inc., General Electric
Co., H&R Block, Intel Corp., Marriott International Inc., PepsiCo Inc.,
Pfizer Inc., Starbucks Corp., and United Parcel Service Inc. Assuming
the fundamentals were sound, these were buying opportunities that
enhanced shareholder value, and undoubtedly they played a psychological role in maintaining confidence amid a wrenching crisis.

While share repurchases are all the rage today, they were virtually
unheard of as recently as the 1970s. The spiraling growth of repurchases has been fueled by four successive mothers of necessity.

The first wave of repurchases arose in the early 1970s. Trying to
fight inflation, the Nixon administration imposed wage and price
controls throughout the economy, an intervention doomed to failure. Given the political climate, labor activists argued that if the program was going to limit members' wages, then there ought to be a
limit on the payment of things like interest and dividends.

Investors wanted cash from their equity investments. To get it to
them, corporations slyly opted to structure the distribution as a
repurchase of shares. It was a good time for this strategy, since stock

prices were extremely low compared to business values, with the return on the S&P 500 equaling –14.8 percent and –26.4 percent in 1973 and 1974 respectively.

The second wave came in response to hostile-takeover battles in the early 1980s. With the rise in tender offers waged by aggressive corporate raiders bent on throwing incumbent management out, came an arsenal of defensive responses. To repel raiders, corporations simply bought them out, in privately negotiated share repurchases. Half the amount of repurchases in 1985 were due to those of two takeover targets: Unocal ($4.2 billion) and Union Carbide ($3.3 billion).

The third repurchase wave occurred in the wake of the 1987 market crash, prodded by the SEC's relaxation of its restrictions on timing and amount of buyback. Corporate America announced $9.3 billion of buybacks in the week after the crash. There have since been episodic upticks in repurchases to suggest that corporate management takes advantage of market pessimism. Activity increased following the 1989 market break and the early 1990s' and early 2000 recessions.

The fourth engine of share buybacks is the proliferation of executive and managerial stock-option packages. As more stock is given to managers to supplement their pay, reported earnings per share (EPS) figures face substantial dilution. One way to offset dilution is to buy shares back. Growth in repurchase levels in the late 1990s correlates with the growth in stock options for managers.[25]

When the average price of equities is relatively high, yet lots of companies buy back shares, you have to wonder whether managers are overpaying departing holders at the expense of long-term investors. Both these circumstances existed in the 1997–2000 period. There are probably mixed motives for share buybacks. The rationale may be a function of managerial optimism or superior knowledge, but possibly something less fundamental, such as demonstrating confidence simply to boost the stock price or to share in the widely distributed adulation attached to buybacks. Vigilance is necessary because the selling shareholder getting $20 for stock worth $10 comes at the expense of the long-term investor.

Consider the case of Warnaco Group, an apparel maker selling its wares under license from designers such as Calvin Klein and Ralph Lauren. Before declaring bankruptcy in mid-2001, the New York-based company bought large blocks of its own shares. There were two problems with these stock repurchases. They were funded with borrowed money, and management paid a premium to underlying value, judging by the stock price falling from $45 in mid-1998 to below $1 three years later. This one-two suggests that one goal of the program was to prop up a sagging stock price.

The company's business strategy deteriorated, and while in bankruptcy it restated its previously released financial reports to show even worse results. Warnaco's place in the rag trade is being pushed out of existence.[29] Major apparel companies do little sewing these days, preferring to outsource that work in favor of concentrating on marketing and licensing. As a garment maker, Warnaco assumes the manufacturer's cost—storage, sales, discounts, returns, and liquidations. Its customers are department stores with growing power to squeeze the likes of Warnaco on price. While these stores once had a hard time getting the world's top fashion designers to let them sell their wares, those days are long gone.

Warnaco's management may not have consciously sought to use its repurchase program to support its stock price. Nor does the scenario mean that the repurchases caused its bankruptcy. But a buy-back program in circumstances suggesting repurchases at prices above value should alert intelligent investors to scrutinize underlying business conditions. That look may reveal deeper problems that can lead to bankruptcy. In the case of Warnaco, it also led to the CEO stepping down.

Management should never engage in share repurchases for the purpose of supporting a stock price, for this is the surest way to pay a premium to value that destroys value rather than builds it. Investors are seldom told that this is what management is doing, of course, so be on the lookout for cautionary flags.

One place to look for flags is the debt-to-equity ratio, which relates directly to the problem of using debt for repurchases. The debt-to-equity ratio can become excessive due to repurchases funded with debt. If a company cannot repurchase stock using retained earnings or free cash flow, it has no business doing the buyback. A simple rule of thumb applies: avoid companies that borrow to buy back stock. Heed the warning, for they are growing in number.

Large repurchases, say more than 15 percent of shares outstanding, remove too much of a company's equity cushion, causing a spike in the debt-to-equity ratio. This creates risks to shareholders, reduces creditworthiness, and increases borrowing costs. If repurchases begin to eat substantially into equity cushions, they are probably being done for reasons that do not increase shareholder value.

Beware of repurchases motivated by a desire to offset earnings dilution tied to the simultaneous issuances of shares for other reasons. Repurchases to offset earnings dilution caused by the concurrent exercise of employee stock options are particularly undesirable, even at lower prices. They are wealth transfers from shareholders to managers.

A good example of a buyback program succeeding only in offsetting dilution due to stock-option grants is Microsoft. Its average shares outstanding regularly rise incrementally, even as it spends several billion dollars annually on buybacks. This is because it releases more shares to executives than it repurchases from holders. There is an outright cost, with the buybacks being made at prices greater than the exercise price of the options. The net effect is a wealth shift from continuing owners to management insiders who take a piece of the corporate pie. To see for yourself, look at the balance-sheet line item indicating average shares outstanding from period to period, and compare this with the number of shares repurchased.[30]

A decision to repurchase shares rather than pay cash dividends is often described as an effort to address differences in shareholder needs. All shareholders receive dividends when declared and suffer requisite tax consequences. For individuals, dividends are usually treated as ordinary income. Repurchases are voluntary, so each holder gets to choose whether to take that income. For seasoned holders of shares, that usually means taxation at rates applicable to capital gains which are lower than rates applicable to ordinary income.

It is a practical impossibility for management to make decisions based on their impacts on particular shareholder groups. In capital-allocation decisions, directors cannot make decisions based on shareholder-specific factors, such as liquidity needs and tax brackets.

With repurchases, however, managers can show greater sensitivity to the positions of particular shareholders than they ordinarily do. There are two standard ways to effect corporatewide share repurchases: through formal tender offer (less common) or in the open market (most common).

The chief difference is that the tender-offer route requires a direct communication from a board to each shareholder of its offer to purchase that shareholder's shares. Each shareholder then decides whether to accept the company's offer and sell shares back to it.

In open-market repurchases, the corporation enters the market anonymously and simply instructs its brokers and dealers to purchase shares otherwise offered for sale at terms that match offers to sell. Those offers to sell are given by selling shareholders through their own brokers and dealers. The corporation and the holders do not deal directly. Holders do not know who is purchasing their shares, and the corporation likewise is in the dark about the seller's identity.

The chief regulatory difference between self-tenders and open-market purchases is that the former must comply with federal-securities laws that require certain disclosures, requirements that do not apply to open-market purchases so long as a set of fairly routine guidelines are met. Informing shareholders that management is effecting the repurchases on the grounds that it believes price is below value should be among these. Shareholders then could make more fully informed decisions about whether to discontinue all or part of their investments or, knowing management is on the other side of the trade, to buy more stock.

An even better approach would be simply to invite shareholders to contact the company whenever they want to sell shares. Make the shareholders a standing offer to buy back shares. Far-fetched? This is the standing procedure at Berkshire Hathaway.

Designer Capital

Managers have discretion over major decisions such as stock repurchases and offerings, as well as dividends, and if holders disagree they can sell their stakes. Investors choose companies as investment targets based on managerial policies, much as restaurant diners choose based on their menus.

A no-dividend policy, for example, could be justified for a company needing cash to exploit opportunities, thus appealing to investors in high tax brackets with no liquidity needs. A policy of paying out a substantial portion of earnings in cash might make sense for a company lacking growth opportunities, and would appeal more to holders who desire periodic cash returns on investments.

Communication of capital-allocation policies from managers to shareholders is vital, for they influence how share values are assessed. While efficiency theorists agree that these communications are vital, they don't think they can affect value. They say a company's value is the same no matter what portion of earnings is paid out in dividends as opposed to being reinvested (assuming investment levels and financing decisions are equal). So stock prices are unaffected by dividend designs.

Under the behavioral story, dividend policies matter to investors as components of value. Many investors value cash-flow streams differently depending on their shapes (rising, steady, declining) even when their total intrinsic values are identical. Among the biases influencing investor thinking about dividend valuation are:

- Loss aversion—The tendency of investors to value cash payments sooner rather than later at exaggerated rates suggests a preference for larger rather than smaller cash payouts.

- Framing—The manner in which capital-allocation policies are disclosed helps shape an investor's preference for cash payouts, whether as dividends or repurchases.

- Mental accounting—The process of treating income differently depending on its source may influence both these decisions as they bear on an investor's particular tax situation.

Biases such as these create preferences for a particular cash flow that attract some investors to a security while discouraging others. Such "designer dividends," along with repurchase programs, become discretionary managerial tools that can be used to market the company's securities.

The importance of dividend design explains why companies routinely maintain dividend payouts that are steady and gradually rise. Cutting is done reluctantly, even though underlying business conditions fluctuate more rapidly. Many money-losing companies maintain dividend payments at historic rates. It also explains the Berkshire Hathaway recap discussed earlier: it created a junior class of stock carrying 1/30 the rights of the senior class to enable holders of the senior class to effect do-it-yourself dividends by converting a senior share into 30 junior shares and periodically selling a junior share

The effect of capital-allocation policies on shareholder valuation assessments comes up in the related context of stock splits. Yogi Berra, when asked whether he wanted his pizza cut into four or eight slices, said, "Four, I'm not very hungry." Shareholders, when it comes to stock splits, think similarly. It is as if investors, when asked into how many shares they wish their corporate pie to be cut, say, "Eight, sixteen, thirty-two," and so on, because that makes them feel richer, due to cognitive biases.

A stock split occurs when the board of a company declares new shares for each share outstanding. They have no economic significance. Suppose you own one share of Krispy Kreme Doughnuts Inc. trading at $30, and the managers declare a two-for-one stock split. You now have two shares for every one held before. But with twice as many shares outstanding, each share now carries half the economic gain of each presplit share. You are in the same place. The price per share should drop to $15. In many cases, stock splits result in price increases, say to $17 per share in this example, due to the Yogi pizza fallacy. People (wrongly) think they are getting something for nothing.

A legitimate purpose of stock splits is reducing the market price to attractive levels, historically around $25–$50. But there are side effects. They produce upward price pressure on shares, skewing price-value gaps. They increase trading activity, causing speculation in the stock with the same result. They increase costs and turnover, and emphasize market price, not business value. Managers should design split policies in ways that will minimize these side effects while setting the stage for a price within a reasonable trading range. Above all, the best policy is to repeatedly disclose guidelines concerning when a split will be made.

Stock splits tend to rise during boom markets, and were daily facts during the gravy train of the late 1990s. In gloomier times, when average stock prices are low and falling, a tempting ploy is the reverse stock split. While stock splits slash per-share prices, reverse stock splits boost them. A 1-for-3 reverse stock split at E-Fall.com when its stock price is $1, for example, should boost it to around $3. Given cognitive biases, the attention may drive it even higher.

The popularity of reverse stock splits rose in proportion to the market's fall in 2001. Nasdaq rules generally require a minimum stock price of $1. Shares trading below that for 30 days are ordinarily delisted unless restored to above \$1 within 90 days. Many analysts won't follow unlisted shares, and top brokerage firms won't let brokers sell unanalyzed stocks. Managers are tempted to do reverse splits to keep their share prices above the radar screen, particularly when other managers are doing the same.[31] The number of reverse stock splits grows during busts, reaching hundreds per year. Don't be fooled.

Managers are keenly aware of the importance of menus to shareholders and are eager to design capital policies to influence valuation assessments. Return your attention to corporate buybacks for a moment. When a company announces a share-repurchase program, it usually sets a dollar amount and an open-ended time period (for example, "Microsoft board authorizes \$5 billion share-buyback program over next three years"). The announcement triggers no obligation to follow through; progress reports are not required. This latitude is permitted under the SEC disclosure system that gives management wide berth in deciding on the timing and content of information release, a power that enables corporate spin, the subject of our next chapter.

6

Corporate Spin

Media spin is not limited to Washington, D.C. Corporate managers are as adept as Beltway insiders at influencing how news is reported.

Most corporate announcements have predictable effects on stock price, with positive-earnings outlooks producing a rise and gloomy ones a down tick. Those that mention share repurchases, stock splits, and stock dividends boost prices; among those that depress prices are announcements of a seasoned equity offering; an abrupt, substantial change in the amount of a regular cash dividend; and the termination of a previously announced repurchase program. Knowing the usual price effects can influence the timing and extent of management's disclosure.

Intelligent investors should be alert to the reality of corporate news manipulation to manage expectations and influence share price. Particularly as the potential for information overload nears, it becomes ever more important to gauge what matters most, and to distinguish substantive information signaling relevant business data from puff, spin, hyperbole and other noise.

Effectively sorting through the avalanches of corporate information enables the wise investor to better gauge managerial intelligence and trustworthiness. Linking fundamental information to market pricing enables you to exploit gaps that informal corporate disclosure may create.

Discretion

A company about to announce a major transaction, such as a public offering or merger, must comply with a host of detailed rules concerning the timing and content of disclosure. These require financial reports and elaborate analytical discussions of operations. Likewise, public companies must file formal quarterly and annual disclosure documents reporting on a specified range of matters.

Scores of people participate in preparing these disclosure documents, from the offices of the CEO, CFO, general counsel, and others. In the case of transactional documents, there is also invariably a team of outside professional advisors, including people from Big Five accounting firms and major law and investment banking firms.

Every word in these disclosure documents is carefully weighed. Rule violations bring credible shareholder lawsuits and massive judgments against the company as well as the individuals involved. The stakes are high and the documents widely disseminated, so great care is taken to comply with the regulatory web.

Securities laws require disclosure for two policy reasons. One is to protect investors from trading on incomplete or inaccurate information, and the other is to promote efficient markets by making "material" information easily available to investors.

The effort put into these documents pays off for investors. There is no better place for an investor to get complete, accurate, and reliable information about a company than its annual report and periodic disclosure documents relating to extraordinary events such as mergers.

Between the making of these formal disclosures, the law requires very little and prescribes even less about what corporations should disclose, when, and how. The elaborate set of disclosure rules only operate on a periodic or transactional basis. Strict disclosure is required only quarterly and when a big deal is afoot, rather than continuously every day. Yet vast quantities of information gushes all around us, and we need to know what to make of it.

Management holds considerable discretion over corporate disclosures. The overall framework never explicitly requires immediate disclosure. The framework only concerns itself with things that are "material" and doesn't require information that isn't. What is considered material is hard to say in general terms.

The standard legal definition of materiality is information that an ordinary, reasonable investor would consider important in making an investment decision. There is a category of information that is almost certainly material, such as the sale of a major division. A broad range of far more mundane, but nevertheless important, business information is harder to classify. Examples include the possibility of losing a major customer, signing a new long-term lease on the company's major plant, or that the CEO is having surgery next week.

Besides items that must be disclosed is a whole range of things management might want to disclose (an engineering design award, being named company of the year). Within both categories, there is wide latitude about how to say things and through which media. Companies often make disclosure that is excessively optimistic and may amount to mere puff. Vague statements or those with obvious hyperbole do not usually cause managers any legal trouble.

One can thank efficiency theory for this. It has had a significant influence on the law concerning what is material and what management can and cannot say with legal impunity. Most courts evaluate whether statements are unlawful or not by asking whether they would lead rational investors to trade on them, affecting the stock price in a rational market. All the following statements have been approved by courts under this efficiency-inspired approach:

- The company is recession resistant.
- The company believes it can continue to grow net earnings faster than sales.
- The merger with a former arch rival is moving ahead more quickly than planned and presents compelling opportunities.
- The company should deliver income growth consistent with historical performance, and is very optimistic about the year ahead.
- The company expects 10–30-percent annual growth rates over the next several years, with growth and success continuing beyond that time
- The company is proud of its new product and believes it will be another blowout winner.

Disclosure is encouraged about things that haven't happened yet. Managers are not only free to make statements about the future, they enjoy a "safe harbor" against legal recrimination so long as they accompany these statements with appropriate caution about their prospective nature.

That is why you see and hear those scripted disclaimers in corporate press releases and at the start of corporate conference calls. The company says there will be statements about the future. Then it says what categories those statements fall into. Then it warns there can be no assurance that statements about the future will mean that the future will be as stated. It is akin to the pretakeoff safety instructions dutifully given by the attendants on every U.S. commercial flight and dutifully ignored by passengers.

With those warnings in mind, consider informal disclosure by means of a corporate press release. Stock-exchange rules are historically the key source of guidance to managers concerning press-release content, though the proliferation of press releases as a common means of disclosure has led many other private and industry groups to adopt their own standards.

The gist of the standards is to emphasize that press releases should be accurate and complete. This means that releases need numbers. They should include the quantitative information that investors must have to evaluate the relative importance of the information being disclosed. The release should also be balanced. Stock-exchange rules explain that "balanced" means:

- Gauging and reporting probabilities accurately, and especially avoiding presenting favorable probabilities as certain
- Offering only realistic projections, and accompanying these with appropriate qualifications
- Avoiding couching negative disclosures in positive terms
- Not slighting important items by burying unfavorable facts
- Avoiding promotional jargon designed to excite rather than to inform

The rules also require press releases to be clear and concise. This means they should be written in simple English so an investor doesn't need a Ph.D. to decipher them.

Take a look at Figure 6-1, a series of press releases, each announcing the same big-customer contract for a leading type of communications technology called Global System for Mobile (GSM). This GSM communications technology was among the hottest of the late-1990s tel-comm boom, spanning the globe and helping to turn

A

Press Release—February 3, 2000, Thursday—Cannes, France
Motorola and Telsim Sign **$1.5 Billion GSM Deal**—First GPRS
Trials in Turkey

Motorola, Inc (NYSE:MOT) and Turkish GSM operator Telsim have today
announced the signing of **a contract worth $1.5 billion** to provide
infrastructure handsets and associated services in order to expand the
countrywide global system for mobile (GSM) communications network.
Motorola also will implement a full trial overlay general packet radio
service (GPRS) core mobile data network.

B

Press Release—February 3, 2000, Thursday—Arlington Heights, Ill.
Motorola, Telsim Sign **GSM Deal**—First GPRS Trials in Turkey

NOTE: The following is a reissuance of an earlier press release for the
purpose of clarification.

Motorola, Inc. (NYSE:MOT) and Turkish GSM operator Telsim have
announced an agreement for Motorola to provide infrastructure, handsets
and associated services in order to expand the countrywide global system
for mobile (GSM) communications network. As part of that agreement,
Telsim has named Motorola its exclusive supplier of GSM 900 Mhz
infrastructure equipment for the next three years. **Motorola estimates that
revenues from this supplier agreement could be at least $1.5 billion
over the three years.** Motorola also will implement a full trial overlay
general packet radio service (GPRS) core mobile data network.

C

Press Release—February 3, 2000, Thursday—Schaumburg, Ill.
Motorola, Telsim Sign GSM Deal on Credit—First GPRS Trials in Turkey

NOTE: The following is a reissuance of an earlier press release for the
purpose of clarification.

Motorola, Inc. (NYSE:MOT) and Turkish GSM operator Telsim have
announced an agreement for Motorola to provide infrastructure, handsets
and associated services in order to expand the countrywide global system
for mobile (GSM) communications network. As part of that agreement,
Telsim has named Motorola its exclusive supplier of GSM 900 Mhz
infrastructure equipment for the next three years. Motorola estimates that
revenues from this supplier agreement could be at least $1.5 billion over
the three years. **All sales under this new agreement will be funded by
loans from Motorola to Telsim.** Motorola also will implement a full trial
overlay general packet radio service (GPRS) core mobile data network.

NOTE: Item C is a fictitious press release prepared for purposes of illustration in this book.

Figure 6-1 Sample press releases.

hand-held telephones into personal communications and filing systems. Worldwide interest was so great that industry players held a huge annual conference dubbed the GSM Congress, where products were launched and deals were done.

At the 2000 GSM Congress, Motorola, Inc. reached a big deal with Telsim, a major operator of GSM in Turkey. Motorola issued a press release announcing this deal—Release A quoted in Figure 6-1—on the road from the conference site in Cannes, France. The release boasts a new GSM contract "worth $1.5 billion," and includes the "$1.5 billion" value prominently in the headline to the release.

Motorola issued a second release later that day from Arlington Heights, Illinois, the location of Motorola's segment headquarters that included its GSM technology. Quoted as Release B in Figure 6-1, this "reissuance" of the earlier release qualifies the transaction's size, saying "Motorola estimates that revenues from this supplier agreement could be at least $1.5 billion over the three years." It also deletes any reference to the amount of the deal from the headline.

I created Release C in Figure 6-1 for this book to disclose an additional relevant fact (and, for the seriousness of it, used Motorola's corporate headquarters, Schaumburg, Illinois, in the dateline). It shows that the company could have gone on to disclose that it was subsidizing this new contract by providing the customer full credit: "All sales under this new agreement will be funded by loans from Motorola to Telsim."

These are quite different economic descriptions of the same contract, yet all disclosures comply with legal requirements. You can be sure that investors reading each release would reach different conclusions about the deal's significance to Motorola's business.

Even for a company of Motorola's size, with annual revenue ranging from $30 to $40 billion, $1.5 billion is a large chunk of revenue. The deal was important to Motorola's overall well-being too, as a worldwide slowdown in telecommunications spending ate away at its business, leading it to eliminate 32,000 of its 147,000 jobs over the next year and a half.[1]

A year later, the company disclosed in its annual report that Telsim was behind by $1.7 billion in payments under the contract. A few months after that the figure was up to $2 billion, Motorola was considering legal action, had retained a private investigator, and reports said even the U.S. government was offering its help.

Whether new contracts or earnings forecasts, the economic significance of events as disclosed in press releases often varies substantially from formal periodic reports. A press release can exploit the availability bias, our tendency to place undue emphasis on information that is easy to recall. It is a short document that is quickly digested. Its contents are disseminated rapidly. It is a wonderful place to spin news. Accordingly, do not treat press releases with the same reliability as periodic or transactional reports.

Treat rumors with even less respect, and be aware that corporations have little responsibility for responding to them. Rumors are longstanding problems facing every corporation, exacerbated by the expansion of information channels and ever cheaper and anonymous means to reach millions simultaneously over the Internet.

The law gives managers broad discretion in deciding what to do, with stock-exchange rules generally imposing stricter but still deferential obligations. These require listed companies to confirm or deny market rumors concerning major corporate developments that affect stock trading. Rules also require a company to investigate the causes of unusual trading volume or price gyrations.

Some corporations monitor Internet chat rooms and bulletin boards, but it is not practical to discover or address all falsehoods. On the other hand, when rumors or outright lies are big, headquarters speak up.

An example occurred in the wake of the accounting scandal at Rent Way Inc. After the company's recently hired chief financial officer (CFO) discovered accounting problems, the company began an investigation, fired its chief accounting officer, and revamped its financial accounting policies. Its stock price plummeted, and investors grew angry. They vented their anger on Yahoo! bulletin boards, with one writer alleging that the CFO concocted the shenanigans. This prompted the company's chief executive officer to go on-line to set the record straight.[2]

From responding to rumors on-line to drafting press releases, the characteristics of our disclosure system give management inordinate flexibility in the timing and content of informational reports. The discretion creates opportunities for those that manage the information flow. The motivations of managers to exercise spin control are as varied as the corporations and managers in America. But one big reason concerns their own wallets, so let's look at how disclosure discretion relates to management compensation.

Straw into Gold

Former SEC chief accountant Lynn Turner characterized many press releases as "spinning straw into gold."[3] Turner quipped that earnings press releases report not so much "EPS"—earnings per share—but "EBS"—everything but bad stuff. Disclosure of bad news and routine information that isn't easily spun can be deferred until periodic reports are due. When placed in the next quarterly or annual report, bad news does not need to be given prominence and vividness that would invoke the availability bias. It can be buried.

The opposite is also true. Bad news can be disclosed early and attention drawn to it. A press release can announce "EGS"—everything but good stuff. Good news can be deferred until the quarterly report, and even then buried if desirable. While at first glance it might be hard to see why withholding good news would be desirable, a focus on stock-option values clarifies.

Consider that the value of a stock option is greater if (a) issued when the stock price is lower and (b) exercised when the stock price is higher. Would it be a surprise to learn that managers are tempted to express (a) pessimism about company performance right before stock options are scheduled to be granted and (b) optimism ahead of exercise dates? Would it be a surprise if they chose to grant unscheduled stock options when the market expressed pessimism?

Evidence shows that managers indulge these temptations, indicating that many managers driven by stock options exploit market inefficiency.[4] Given how corporate disclosure works, managers can sharpen the market's peaks and valleys to maximize stock-option value.[5]

This market massaging is more relevant now that performance-based remuneration is a substantial part of the value of executive compensation in most major U.S. corporations. Granting executives stock options linked to company performance is firmly entrenched, resulting in multimillion-dollar payouts to top executives.

Performance-based pay is intended to deal with a fundamental concern of corporate governance: aligning the interests of managers with shareholder-owners. By linking managerial self-interest and wealth-maximizing behavior to corporate growth, performance-based pay schemes appear to put managers and shareholders on the same team.

Leading critics of performance-based remuneration, such as Graef Crystal, question the effectiveness of the structure of these remuneration packages. They prescribe fine-tuning the compensation package to achieve a more tailored fit between performance and compensation.

There is a more severe complaint. Far from creating incentives that align the interests of managers and owners, performance-based remuneration creates incentives for executives to pursue self-interest at the expense of shareholder value. For example, we all know that a CEO whose compensation consists partly of a bonus tied to an earnings increase over previous years has an incentive to manipulate earnings accruals to ensure he or she meets the target number.

Less widely recognized, a CEO whose compensation is tied to stock options has a significant incentive to manipulate the market price of his or her company's stock. The CEO reaps a greater reward if the stock price drops before issuance of the option and then rises before the exercise date.

Market manipulation takes the form of controlling the timing of corporate disclosures that are likely to affect the company's stock price, as well as controlling the content of disclosure. The flexibility of the informal disclosure system creates plenty of opportunity to do so, and even the formal rules of the periodic and transactional disclosure rules can be massaged.

Managers don't enjoy absolute discretion. Insider-trading rules prohibit corporate insiders from trading on material nonpublic information unless they first disclose the information—the famous "disclose or abstain" rule. Disclosure also must be corrected if it becomes false or misleading. And private exchanges—most notably Nasdaq and the New York Stock Exchange—impose their own disclosure rules on listed companies.

Even with these constraints, management discretion is broad. Though timing and spinning corporate disclosures to maximize executive compensation sounds like a conflict of interest, it is not illegal. Extreme forms of fraudulent disclosure or outright withholding of important information would be illegal, but such extreme behavior goes far beyond what it takes to exploit market inefficiencies enough to boost a manager's paycheck.

Let's look at two illustrations: (a) the release of negative information (for example, that earnings are likely to be less than forecast) before the grant of stock options; and (b) the withholding of material information (for example, information that merger negotiations are underway) before the exercise date.

Consider the factors that make liability difficult to prove, as in illustration (a), when the corporate manager releases negative information. The "disclose or abstain" rule applies, so executives are prohibited from trading unless they disclose all material nonpublic information they have. But the insider has done just that—disclosed; insider-trading rules impose no liability for disclosure, only nondisclosure.

Disclosing negative information would most likely not satisfy the high standard required for the statement to be found "manipulative" under the securities laws. Even if the statement about low earnings is later determined to have been inaccurate—that is, the revision of the earnings forecast was wrong—the statement is easily protected from liability by insulating it with "cautionary statements" that put it in the safe harbor. The bottom line is that a CEO who makes negative statements about his or her company shortly before the issuance of stock options has little reason to fear liability under the securities laws.

Similarly, a CEO who withholds material information as in illustration (b) may be sheltered from liability, though the situation is a little trickier. The standard for determining what a corporation has to disclose is murky because it turns on the elusive notion of materiality. It is unclear whether preliminary negotiations about uncertain future events—such as merger negotiations—would be important enough to a reasonable investor to require disclosure.

But even if the negotiations were considered material, liability for nondisclosure would still depend on showing that the CEO had the intent to deceive—or had "scienter" in the parlance of securities law. Any CEO in this situation could argue that the nondisclosure was necessary to get the best possible deal. Even if that story doesn't get him completely off the hook, it surely reduces the incentive for anyone to complain in court.

So a CEO can influence the market's assessment of his or her employer's value and remain within legal bounds, given the considerable discretion he or she has over the timing and content of disclosure. Worth emphasizing is that this discretion is not a side effect of the disclosure laws, but one of the main foundations on which the disclosure system is based. Giving managers discretion helps resolve uncertainties and conflicts that would arise in a continuous disclosure regime.

The trouble with the extensive discretion as it relates to stock options is how it turns upside down many commonsense intuitions about corporate disclosure. Consider that disclosure laws don't address wide categories of information. Managers must determine whether to disclose information in a vast gray area. Early disclosure of bad news may be resisted to avoid harming the corporation, while early disclosure of uncertain information may be encouraged to help investors make decisions. Performance-based pay alters this scheme by giving managers an incentive to disclose bad news early and to withhold uncertain news.

The loose disclosure standards are a deliberate effort to force management to make judgments about materiality. In close cases, management should disclose rather than withhold, since nondisclosure carries liability risk while disclosure does not. The incentives may be reversed for a CEO with compensation pegged to stock-price performance on a specific date.

Securities laws are narrowly construed to avoid encroaching upon the "business judgment rule"—a sacrosanct doctrine in U.S. corporate law that protects managers from liability for most business decisions. Judges defer to director decisions on a wide range of matters, from setting dividend policy and designing capital structure to closing plants and buying other companies. The general deference courts show to business judgment assumes that management is disinterested and acts in the best interests of the company and the shareholders. But this premise is undercut by the incentives created by performance-based compensation.

Finally, as seen in the earlier discussion of capital-allocation decisions, corporate governance (including securities and corporate law) assumes that responsible management exercising discretion has no reason to favor one shareholder group over another, particularly those who bought company stock on one date rather than another. Performance-based pay challenges this assumption by giving managers an interest in the stock price moving in a certain direction on a certain date.

Managerial discretion over the timing of corporate disclosures linked to performance-based pay seems to cause injury, but what is the precise nature of this injury? It is necessary to answer this question before any solutions to these issues can be considered. Unless the information disclosed is false or misleading, disclosures do not cause the type of injury that the securities laws try to protect investors against. But just because something is legal does not mean it should be done.

At stake is a bedrock principle of corporate governance: managerial trustworthiness. Shareholders rely on managers to exercise discretion in running the business for their benefit, a reliance based on trust. That trust has always been central to investors (ask duped shareholders of companies ranging from National Student Marketing to Enron). The rise of performance-based pay against the background of the loose disclosure regime puts a greater premium on trust. It forces shareholders to rely on managerial integrity to avoid conflicts between manager and shareholder interests that arise from compensation linked to a manipulatable stock price.

Apart from legal rules that are unlikely to do any good in this context of managerial trustworthiness, two sorts of pressure can help solve this governance problem. The first is to enhance monitoring of corporate managers to police possible offenders. Shareholders, their advocacy groups, and the media must play a bigger role in this enterprise. Institutional shareholders with the big clout and resources should be especially active.

The second fix, and the one on which shareholder advocates should train their sights, is the structuring of performance-based compensation. In most performance-based pay packages, options are issued infrequently and are exercisable all at once. This creates a "one big payday effect"—the CEO has a much greater interest in the stock recording a certain price on a particular day than any other time.

Take an example. Three top officers of Computer Associates, under a bonus plan approved by shareholders in 1995, would receive 6 million shares of the company's stock if the closing price exceeded $53.33 for 60 days. The target was hit on May 22, 1998, yielding the executives more than $1 billion. Eight weeks later, Computer Associates issued a press release stating that growth was slowing due to the Asian financial crisis and Y2K concerns, and also that it was taking a $675 million charge to earnings to reflect the cost of certain executive bonuses. The share price plummeted to $39.50.

While the content and timing of these disclosure decisions are controversial, the officers no doubt faced incentives to accentuate the positive news in the period ahead of the 60-day point and defer negative disclosures until afterwards.

In effect, CEOs in such positions have great incentives either to withhold or disclose information in order to take advantage of market volatility and increase their payoffs, whether or not that is in their companies' best interests. A simple solution is to restructure the compensation scheme so that the bonus is pegged to performance over an extended period; this more closely aligns the CEO's incentives with those of all shareholders. In the case of Computer Associates, for example, suppose that instead of offering 6 million shares if the price exceeded $53.33 for 60 days once, the deal offered 500,000 shares for each 6-month period during which the price exceeded that amount for at least 45 days. The payout might still strike many as exorbitant, but the suspicion that managerial manipulation played an important role would largely disappear.

Boards of directors, which ultimately approve these compensation policies, must be directed towards using spread-out pay schemes rather than one-big-payday plans. Shareholders should reward those who adopt them and penalize those who do not.

Investment Analysts

Press releases are but one source of information now at the fingertips of all investors. New channels vying for investor attention are analyst conference calls and reports, and investor road shows. While these do not offer as much value as the company's annual report, they can add some value, but only if properly used.

For many decades, the leaders in information crunching were the financial analysts. They appraise business value to help their firms or investor clients make investment decisions. Access to company information and management is obviously a valuable asset that makes the analysts more effective in doing their jobs. For many years, that access had been given almost exclusively to this cadre of Wall Street evaluators.

Access played a key role in equipping the analyst with the information necessary to spot trends and assess prospects. A good example was management providing analysts guidance in terms of earnings projections. Analysts, like others, sought to devise clear ways to measure performance and prospects. Earnings are a popular one.

Analysts would estimate a company's earnings and use this number or range of numbers as a basis for dialogue with managers at the company. The company, in turn, would offer analysts guidance as to whether the estimates were off the mark. There would be give-and-take on the variables that went into estimating the earnings figures. This would take place out of the glare of public light.

The conversations enabled analysts to report earnings estimates to the marketplace, which would use them to judge valuation. Trading decisions would be made on the basis of this information, ideally moving price closer to value.

Analysts usually have substantial experience in one or more industries they cover. Good ones can stitch together information obtained from a company's reports and managers, with other information obtained throughout the industry and marketplace, to produce a mosaic account of the companies they follow. Expert mosaic-building substantially improves information accuracy, which, when properly digested, makes markets more efficient.

Regulators from the SEC, as well as some investors, perceived a coziness between managers and analysts and began to cry foul. They suspected favoritism, speculated about accounting data being massaged and stock prices manipulated. Companies could favor analysts who saw things their way and give them greater access to information than others. Analysts generally could get information that had market value before other Wall Streeters and investors. There was also concern that some managers shared advance information selectively with large institutional shareholders at the expense of others.

The actual or perceived unfairness and abuse of this selective disclosure practice led the SEC to abolish it in favor of requiring a company that tells one investor or analyst something to tell everyone else the same thing. Since October of 2000, when a company gives earnings guidance and other information to an analyst, Regulation Fair Disclosure ("Reg FD") requires that it give that same information to all others simultaneously via press releases, conference calls, Internet announcements, and so on.[6]

Beyond these concerns exists a political/technological argument for Reg FD. The means of communication have vastly multiplied and sped up. Investors are hot-wired into the market in a way that makes shutting them off from the information flow smack of securities-industry parochialism. The securities industry has been demystified over the last three decades, opening itself up to ordinary investors, and the conference call was among the last areas off limits to individual investors.

Access to management is often by conference call. Once the preserve of the financial elite, now all interested parties have the right to listen in, including media and investors. News releases typically alert investors to scheduled calls at least several days, and sometimes up to a week, in advance. Conference calls are often archived on company Web sites that anyone can easily, unilaterally, and usually anonymously plug into. More investors are getting information this way.

Reg FD provoked controversy. One concern was that managers might simply disclose less information or disclose it later in the game, for fear that unripe information in the hands of a friendly analyst could become dangerous when viewed by the whole market.

Traditionally, many companies adhered to a self-imposed quiet period before regular earnings announcements. The concern was that this period would lengthen. While this was a credible claim, the evidence so far shows no contraction of the information flow and some indication that more information is being shared.[7]

Risks remain concerning how and when investors use disclosed information. With selective disclosure, analysts got raw information first and then turned it into a mosaic of analyzed data for the market to digest in a coherent form. Supporters of selective disclosure argued that price changes would be smoother and more accurate. Now that disclosure is made simultaneously to everyone, raw, unanalyzed data is released, and without the analyst's mosaic-building, the market is more prone to overreact or underreact to the information, promoting market inefficiencies.

Attractive as this argument supporting selective disclosure is, there is no strong evidence that analyst sifting helps market efficiency. Rather, underreaction and overreaction to information is common without regard to its form or timing. On balance, if the effect on efficiency is uncertain, at least abolishing selective disclosure achieves the goal of eliminating suspicion of analyst-manager relationships.

Another benefit of Reg FD may be to strengthen the analyst's spine. One concern of selective disclosure was that it led some analysts to fear being shunned by management. That fear may have led to the skewed distribution of recommendations toward buying and holding securities and against selling them. If all analysts receive all information simultaneously, no one can be shunned, removing this corporate hammer. Analysts should feel freer to render objective rather than biased ratings and recommendations.

Another positive side effect is that analysts are forced to broaden the scope of their research. Surveys conducted by those on both sides of the Reg FD, debate indicate increased analyst research after Reg FD using information gathered from sources in addition to the subject company.[8] Examination of such more-objective data should produce more-objective conclusions.

For investors, Reg FD offers some clear benefits. It offers direct exposure to corporate managers, providing a bird's-eye view of the players in action. That should improve an investor's ability to assess subjective managerial qualities, such as integrity and trustworthiness. Exposure to conference calls enables one to see analysts in action as well, furnishing a basis to gauge their reliability. Reg FD's other side effects will be beneficial—more-objective analyst reports and recommendations, which raises another chapter in the demystification of the securities industry.

The scrutiny that provoked Reg FD didn't stop with that rule change in October, 2000. The screws tightened on analysts from all quarters, the intensity rising during the summer of 2001, as markets fell broadly and scapegoats for the Internet bubble and burst were sought.

Congress investigated bias in analyst reports that arose due to industrywide conflicts of interest between analysts who follow companies and underwriters at the same firms who peddle their securities.[9] *The New York Times* editorialized that analysts attract clients for underwriters and then pen glowing reports on their catches, with their compensation sometimes tied to deal flow.[10] The New York attorney general, Elliot Spitzer, announced his own investigation.[11]

Against this backdrop of pressure, the securities industry adopted a statement of professional guidelines, recommending that firms prohibit tying analyst pay to deal volume, and to disallow deal-maker supervision of analysts.[12] The guidelines also call for greater disclosure of a firm's interest in analyzed securities, greater clarity in valuation and risk assessments, and more elaborate descriptions of the basis for recommendations. They also suggest barring analysts from trading against their own advice.

Industry watchers including former SEC chairman Arthur Levitt expressed skepticism, portraying the guidelines as cynical marketing gimmicks unlikely to have any substantive impact.[13] Critics note that the guidelines are not mandatory, but suggested. They point out that the securities industry always responds to pressure by emphasizing its integrity and promising to take steps to promote it.

A step up in sell recommendations made during the period of pressure was attributed to obvious but belated reality checks—stocks whose IPOs had crumbled nearly 100 percent from their offering prices were downgraded. Conflicts are part of securities-industry culture and will be difficult to remove, critics say.

The SEC echoed the skepticism, issuing an "investor alert" on analyst research reports.[14] It warned investors not to rely on these reports, advising instead to treat them as one resource among many. The SEC explained who analysts are and who they work for, cataloguing potential conflicts of interest. It also warned that disclaimers accompanying many reports—such as, "The firm and/or its employees have or may have a long or short position in the securities"—are vague in assessing conflicts that may arise.

As the critics howled, firms endorsed the trade group's guidelines and adopted their own.[15] They each adopted slightly different rules. In order from lenient to strict, here is a sampling:

- Morgan Stanley requires its analysts to disclose their holdings.[16]
- Merrill Lynch prohibits research analysts from owning stock in companies they cover.[17]
- Credit Suisse First Boston applies its similar restriction to bond analysts as well as stock analysts.[18]
- Edward D. Jones & Co. prohibits analysts from owning stocks of companies and sectors they cover.[19]
- HSBC Holdings requires analysts to issue as many negative recommendations on companies as positive ones.[20]

In the wake of the pressure and response, inevitable lawsuits followed. Buyers of stocks during the late-1990s boom alleged that they relied on misleading reports issued by top analysts at major banking firms. Some suits were settled; one was dismissed within three weeks of its filing, a well-respected Federal judge describing it as "abusive litigation" based on "media gossip," and containing "inflammatory" statements made in "grossly bad taste."[21]

One problem with all analyst reports—and much of the smoke in the debate—is the custom of boiling down the analysis to a single word.[22] While the words vary from shop to shop, the usual choices are buy, sell, or hold. These labels get all the attention, though the analyses behind them are more textured and evaluative. This may be one reason for the spectrum of terms firms use to conclude these reports, ranging from "accumulate," to "market perform," to "neutral."

Analyst's reports should be used, not reacted to. Investors should read them and add the knowledge gleaned to their information base. They should not make decisions based on analysts' conclusions and ultimate "recommendations." Their value is that they present information differently than the company, with the potential for greater objectivity. So used, analyst reports can add value to your tool kit.

Analysts often publicize a "target price" for company shares. The target is usually substantially above the prevailing price. This creates a reference-point bias, leading investors to gauge the relative attractiveness of a stock price not to its fundamental value, but to the analyst's target. The most intelligent thing any investor can do with this sort of data is ignore it; being aware of the process analysts use to reach this conclusion can help an investor resist this effect.

In the wake of the stock-market plunge, the summer of 2001 was a tough season for analysts. Yet where were all these critics—Congress, the SEC, the New York attorney general, *New York Times* editorial writers, the commentators—during the tech bubble when analysts were lavishing praise on Internet start-ups? They were mostly in the game too, spreading the word of the New Economy and joining the party. Analysts may have believed the opinions they were giving, exhibiting overconfidence, pattern-seeking, and other cognitive biases just like everybody else.

The federal judge who dismissed the lawsuits against research analysts and their firms, Milton Pollack, may as well have been describing the hyperbole in the marketplace of ideas when he described the complaint the plaintiff's lawyers drafted. Judge Pollack noted that complaints in a Federal lawsuit are supposed to contain a short and plain statement. In contrast, the complaints in these cases, over 40 pages apiece, amounted to "an unrestrained litany" of political speeches and media moralizing, full of "gross and unrestrained improprieties."[23]

The allegations. he continued, amounted to a "collection of market gossip" and that the "expectable comments of the gamblers in the world's gaming pits," arrived during "the inevitable sequel after market boom periods." The judge counseled that "Opinions turned sour by uncontrollable tidal waves of the economic cycle are substituted for considered standards of conduct." The complaint failed miserably to meet the simple standards required, instead constituting "a rhetorical exercise in length and forensic embroidery."

Investors should not count on value arising from Reg FD solely from the information spigot being opened all at once. The broader and earlier access to information does not change the fact that it must be digested with detachment and reflection. Information gleaned from conference calls is typically complex and requires time to understand; press releases remain documents crafted by experts in the spin business.

On the Road

Road shows are the other new avenue of informal disclosure available to tempt all investors. Once reserved for the elite, these forums present information about a company planning a new stock offering. They are dog-and-pony shows, with presentations by senior managers about all aspects of a business, followed by question-and-answer sessions.

Usually arranged by the underwriter of the offering, road shows were originally intended for other securities dealers who might help sell the offering, but gradually expanded to include big investors. The show would travel across the country to major cities where the underwriter sought to gauge interest in the securities.

In years past, the retail investor could not get near a road show. This was fortunate, since individual investors should avoid new securities offerings. But that's not why they weren't invited. The SEC said they could not come. Strange.

Here is a forum where managers provide reams of useful information to investors and the little guys were told they couldn't come. Issuers liked this because they'd rather huddle with the financial crowd. This crowd liked it too, because these gatherings were designed to be fun as well as informative. And the underwriters certainly liked it, because that's where the big money was.

The SEC's regulatory rationalization to exclude the retail investor was a solution to a conundrum. SEC rules say that during the period after a company formally decides to do a public offering and the day of the offering, it can make oral offers to sell securities. However, it can't make any written offers without first delivering a full-blown, formal prospectus.

Anything in writing counts as a prospectus, as do broad and wide methods of information dissemination, such as television or radio. But small, private meetings where no written information was furnished, such as road shows, didn't count. So long as not just anyone was invited.

As capabilities for broadcasting road shows by electronic means enabled them to be run without costly travel, companies sprouted up to run electronic versions of the shows that could be broadcast by closed-circuit television or over the Internet. At first, following the model, the SEC allowed these to go forward, but only following the restrictions on who could come. Retail investors remained unwelcome.

Eventually, the SEC realized the nonsense of this encrusted approach, and now allows all investors to join in these electronic road shows. Charles Schwab Co. was a leader in this pursuit, persuading the SEC to let the little guy in. Now he's in. What is he supposed to do?

Investors still should avoid buying the newly issued securities peddled at these shows, still should remain cautious in interpreting the information provided, and probably should pay only a modest amount of attention to these additional information sources. Take a lesson from the analyst community.

Important as conference calls and road shows are for conveying information, the annual report remains the most valuable source of information on any company. Star research analysts at the top investment banking firms report that this is the place they look to for most of their information on companies.[24]

Analysts highly value annual reports for content and usefulness. At the top of the value list is the "MD&A" section—"management's discussion and analysis." This provides the insider's view of the business, financial condition, and strategy of the company. The financial statements are also very useful, especially the income statement. Segment data accompanying the financials is helpful in assessing strengths and weaknesses in parts of the company's overall business.

Letters from management get high marks for clues about strategy, though analysts urge expansion of this area.

Analysts complain that they don't get enough information to enable them to gauge longer-term prospects. They get enough to figure out near-term earnings forecasts, but not enough to assess major risks to future performance. Much of this is provided in the conference call.

Analysts say that historically, they have gotten most of their information from private contacts, analyst conferences, and company annual reports, in that order. Now, conference calls and annuals are the top two sources, and both are available to investors on the Internet. Use them, along with the analyst reports, to do your homework.

For solid, stable companies with promising futures over the coming few years, press releases are far less meaningful than annual reports. Spend time with the annuals and leave the press releases alone. When press releases trumpet an issuer's hot new business acquisition, on the other hand, warning bells should ring that alert you to the risk that shareholder wealth is about to be expended to pursue managerial dreams, the concern addressed in the next chapter.

7

The Winner's Curse

If you have ever desired something so strongly that you eagerly out-did your competitors to get it, you may have experienced the win-ner's curse. This is the subsequent discovery that the object of your desire wasn't worth as much as you had hoped. You may have got-ten it, but you gave up more than you got. The experience is com-mon and fills the corporate world.

The efficiency story says the stock market is so good at properly pricing business value that managerial performance is transparent. The report card is the stock price, which is the accurate judge of value. If someone isn't running a company optimally, its stock price will show it. When that happens bidders will appear who want to buy the company and believe they can manage it better.

The implicit threat to bad managers benefits shareholders. Those owning underperforming businesses will be rescued by a superior manager; stockholders in the rescuing company enjoy the potential fruits of a bigger, well-run business.

In this "market for corporate control," when good management takes over companies from bad ones, it pays only the "right" price, never more than a modicum above the target company's real worth. If managers pay too much, they are bad managers to be run out of the market over time. After all, when someone overpays, the market reveals it. Good managers will turn around and throw out those who overpaid.

Wonderful as this story sounds, it overlooks a common fact of M&A life: bidders frequently pay too much for companies. It often appears that bad managers are those taking over, rather than being ousted. The efficiency story ducks these messy realities, but intelligent investors and shareholders face up to them.

A notable example of bidder overpayment in takeovers was Quaker Oats Co.'s purchase of Snapple Beverage Co. in 1994. Quaker paid $1.7 billion, held Snapple for 3 years, then sold it to a private equity firm, Nelson Peltz's Triarc, for S300 million. Triarc turned around and sold Snapple 3 years after that for $910 million, tripling what it paid, but still next to half of Quaker's tab.

Bidder overpayment can be measured either by comparing the bid to the actual value, or the actual value to the expected value. Either way, the winning bidder may end up losing and thus suffer the winner's curse. In the case of Snapple, Quaker made obvious estimation errors, exemplifying both forms of the winner's curse.

Hollywood is rife with high-stakes gambles illustrating the winner's curse. Movie studios often bid on new projects knowing it's likely that other studios are bidding for the same project. The tendency is to raise the bid, creating offers that are on average higher than the script's value.

Everyone has heard of big book auctions with sky-high advances. These demonstrate the winner's curse too, for most of these books do not earn the publisher's advance against future royalties. Losses are particularly staggering in the case of celebrity biographies and political memoirs.

HarperCollins paid comedian and talk show host Jay Leno a $4 million advance to write a book. Leno, who may be funny but is not known as a writer, produced a title called *Leading With My Chin*, published in 1996. By early 1997, it was available on discount tables of chain bookstores for half off, suggesting that the copies sold didn't recoup the $4 million.

Headline-grabbing advances suggesting big gambles include Simon & Schuster paying $8 million in an auction for the rights to publish Hillary Clinton's book. Other big-money books of uncertain payoff were Marcia Clark (remember her from the O.J. Simpson case?), getting an advance of $4.5 million from Viking Penguin and George Stephanopoulos (from the Clinton White House), to whom Little Brown gave $2.5 million. The books didn't sell.

Spectacular payouts for modest returns are complemented by even larger sums for major writers: HarperCollins paid $40 million to Michael Crichton, and Penguin Putnam paid $45 million to Tom

Clancy for two novels. Crichton's deal shows that the threat of a competing bidder causes others to overshoot. Crichton's incumbent publisher, Knopf, had published him for 30 years. Harper's offer dealt quite a blow and was undoubtedly formulated knowing that Knopf might try to top it.

For business-book devotees, this discussion isn't complete without noting the staggering $7.1 million paid to retiring General Electric Co. chairman John C. Welch for his autobiography, coauthored with John A. Byrne, called *Jack: Straight From the Gut*. Its publisher, Warner Books, reported that it would need to sell one million hardback copies in the United States to recoup that advance. While the release date could not have been worse (September 11, 2001), the book did make it on to many best-seller lists. Yet it was greeted with mixed critical reviews and, despite ubiquitous advertising, never really took off in a way that justifies the advance, an amount unprecedented for a business title.

Welch's book isn't the only such offering. Some justify the outlay, such as the best-in-class book *Iacocca* by legendary Chrysler man Lee Iacocca with William Novak (2.7 million copies sold in the early 1980s). However, most don't, like Sumner Redstone of Viacom, whose autobiography published in the summer of 2001 sold a fraction of the 100,000 copies printed.

Former President Bill Clinton won an advance exceeding $10 million for his memoirs from Knopf, the 25-percent edge above his wife's mark suggesting some reference-point bias, and his track record suggesting the winner's curse. Though a different genre, his earlier book—written for the 1996 campaign trail—sold fewer than 30,000 copies (out of 180,000 printed).[1] Similarly, while Simon & Schuster paid $8.5 million for Ronald Reagan's memoirs and a collection of speeches, fewer than 20,000 copies of the memoirs sold (out of a 350,000 print run), and the speech collection did no better.[2]

These books are longshots. The odds are low, but the payoff can be gigantic. Many publishers take those odds, while the more cautious prefer the sidelines Publishers often try to keep the bid prices reasonable by insisting that an in-house committee sign off on big advances. Data suggest that publisher psychology dominates over economic sense, with many publishers arguing that the cash outlays are worth their weight in bragging rights and other intangible value for publishing such books.[3]

The winner's curse also plagues major-league baseball. Salaries of baseball's free agents are often a function of owner adulation rather than their economic contribution through individual performance or team results.

Consider the 2001 salary deal made by Texas Rangers owner Thomas O. Hicks for shortstop Alex Rodriguez. Hicks is known as a shrewd businessman, having made a fortune buying companies, but something about baseball stoked even this brilliant private-equity investor's sentimental side. The deal's value over 10 years amounts to $250 million.

A-Rod, as Rodriguez is called, played spectacularly in 2001. He was among the top handful of players in all major performance categories: runs, hits, batting average, home runs, and runs batted in. He led the American League in home runs with 52; set a major-league record for home runs by a shortstop, previously held by Hall-of-Famer Ernie Banks; and set a new team record for home runs by any player. Alas, the Texas Rangers languished in last place all season, finishing with 73 wins and 89 losses.

Though this view may reflect hindsight bias, prospective indications that Hicks overpaid include that the next highest bid was just more than half his. (A bit more hindsight: the runner-up was the Seattle Mariners, the first-place team in the Rangers' division all season, and the first team in the majors to clinch a play-off berth and division title, finishing with a win-loss record of 116-46, an American League record surpassing the 1998 New York Yankees and tying a National League record set by the 1906 Chicago Cubs.)

We also see bias rather than clear thinking at work in that $250 million was the exact figure the Fox network agreed to pay for local television rights to broadcast Rangers games. This suggests Hicks succumbed to mental accounting, the tendency to treat financial resources differently depending on their sources. The astonishing sum was obviously not a calculation of the present value of the additional earnings the team would generate from having "A-Rod" help win games, set records, and attract fans.

If it can happen to Hicks, it can happen to anybody. Scores of high-priced baseball contracts are signed annually, with proof of overpayment in the statistics many of these players chalk up afterwards. Plenty of baseball-team owners recognize the winner's curse and also recognize that free-agent auctions are hotbeds for the curse.

Cures are unlikely. The baseball player's labor union won't even consider a salary cap, a way to mitigate the problem by owners' agreeing to tie their hands to the chair during the bidding process. A technique with some chance of passing is a proposal to impose a tax on high-payroll teams for reallocation to the also-ran teams.

A striking commercial example of the winner's curse occurred in offshore oil and gas lease bids. Major oil companies in oil-rich places, such as the Gulf of Mexico and Alaska, vastly overpaid for leases at auction. Despite rising oil prices, only about 20 percent of bid leases were moderately profitable, nearly 20 percent produced a loss, and the other 60 percent were dry.

Yet the ratio between the highest and lowest bids was usually on the order of 5 to 10 times and sometimes reached as high as 100 times. The total bids of winners ran to $900 million, while the total of second-place bids was only about $370 million.

Excessive enthusiasm about projected film and book sales, baseball-park attendance, and oil volume extends to the corporate world. Of greatest concern to investors and shareholders is how the winner's curse operates in takeovers. It is here that managers inflict the greatest direct economic damage on shareholders.

A Paramount Lesson

A prominent case study illustrates almost everything we need to know about overpayment in mergers, and what managers ought to know too. The case study is the early-1990s auction contest between Viacom and QVC for Paramount, the global entertainment, film, and TV-show merchandiser. Viacom, owner of such prized media assets as MTV and the Movie Channel, won the contest with a bid of $9.2 billion. QVC, whose primary business was operating a massive home-television-shopping network, bid hard and often, but lost by a hair.

Sumner Redstone, Viacom's chairman, CEO, and controlling shareholder, is a savvy media mogul with vast experience in the business, as was his counterpart at Paramount, CEO Martin Davis. They were friends. The two had been discussing a merger since early 1993. The chairman of QVC, Barry Diller was also smart and tough, but far from a friend of Davis. Instead, Diller was his long-time adversary and former underling at Gulf+Western, a Paramount corporate predecessor. Diller made a takeover overture to Davis in the summer of 1993, but was rebuffed.

The auction ensued after Paramount, under Davis's leadership, agreed to team up just with Redstone's Viacom. The two agreed to merge in fall, 1993, on terms within the range of the Diller bid. QVC jumped in with a hostile bid a week later. The battle first raged over whether Paramount could "just say no" to QVC and continue on its merry way with Redstone's Viacom. Redstone certainly thought it could, quoted in *The Wall Street Journal* and *The New York Times* saying the deal was "a marriage made in heaven that would never be torn asunder," and declaring that only a "nuclear attack" could break it.

Redstone's initial deal with Paramount called for Viacom to pay a total of $69 per Paramount share, only $9 of which was in cash and the rest in Viacom stock. His winning bid was worth $83, with $53 in cash. Paramount's stock at the time traded at around $55 per share, and its intrinsic business value ranged between $46 and $67, making Redstone's opening bid seem modest compared with the ultimate one.[4] What happened along the way?

The main event was a showdown in Delaware court where Redstone's quips to the press came back to haunt him. That court rebuked the Paramount board for neglecting to get the best deal available for shareholders.[5] It could not just say no when QVC came knocking, and cling to the embrace of Redstone's Viacom. It had to compare the two deals and pick the better one. To do that, Paramount ran an auction.[6]

When Redstone and Davis first announced their nuptials, Viacom's stock price fell while Paramount's rose, a typical pattern after acquisition announcements. When QVC destroyed the marital bliss with a hostile bid worth $80 per share, payable $30 in cash and the rest in QVC stock, the market greeted the news similarly. QVC shares declined in price as Paramount's edged up. Presumably, these price changes reflected trader fear that both bidders risked overpaying for Paramount, but hope that one of them would win.

Cross lawsuits among the parties and dueling tender offers at higher and higher bid prices, starting at $80 and rising to $90, followed. Both suitors made cash offers for half the Paramount shares and promised to squeeze the remaining shares out in a second-step merger paid for in securities. Paramount steadfastly clung to Redstone and Viacom. Davis even persuaded the Paramount board that talking to D_ler, his erstwhile nemesis, was out of the question. The skirmish ended with the Delaware court telling Paramount board members this was wrong, leading to a live, and now intensely competitive, aucion.

On December 14, Paramount announced its decision to hold an auction, saying initial bids were due December 20, and that each side would get additional chances to revise its bid, with the winner to be selected February 1. A series of bidding rounds ensued, with Paramount's bankers declaring the winner as: QVC in the first (December 21); QVC again in the second (January 12); Viacom by a nose in the third (January 21); and Viacom in the fourth and final round (February 16).

Like earlier proposals, final bids were for two-step takeovers, a front-end tender offer for half the shares paid in cash, and a second-step merger paid in securities for the rest. The value of the securities in the second step is hard to pin down, since both included bidder shares whose prices were fluctuating substantially during the period; in the case of Viacom, it included an intricate mix of stock, plus warrants, debt, cash, and other securities. The blended value of the QVC offer was between $73 and $86, and of the Viacom offer between $79 and $84.[7] Paramount's stock was then trading at $77, up about 20 percent since Redstone told *The Wall Street Journal* his deal was all sewn up, and Viacom's had declined by more than 50 percent.

Evidence is clear that both bids were substantially higher than any reasonable value of Paramount standing alone, or even after adding value for synergies that would arise after integrating the businesses. Viacom overpaid in order to "win" this auction contest by about $1.5 billion. QVC's bid was also high, though by less, about $1 billion, given its different bid composition and superior synergy values. Viacom prevailed because it was willing to overpay more.

Both parties had strong and distinctive psychological motivations for doing this, and maybe Redstone more so. Both men exuded forceful personalities famous in their organizations and the entertainment industry. Both were chairmen and CECs of their respective companies.

Redstone owned virtually all of Viacom's stock, and in the deal it proposed, he would own about 70 percent of the combined company. Diller owned shares of QVC, but not a controlling position, and nowhere near Redstone's ownership level in Viacom.

Redstone had been committed to this transaction for nearly a year; Diller badly wanted to win this jousting with his former boss, who'd rebuffed him since his early inquiries. Both knew they were facing a fierce competitor in a highly charged auction. All financial and media eyes were riveted on the contest.

Greater board oversight and disciplinary restraint may have reigned on Diller. As the principal shareholder of Viacom, Redstone could not be vetoed by his board. While his board could advise him, they could not restrain him. Diller, on the other hand, faced a board with at least the theoretical power to veto his decisions, including what to bid. True, Diller was the most powerful member of the QVC board, but not as powerful as Redstone on the Viacom board.

Consideration in the bids changed during the contest. Redstone's first bid from Viacom offered 87 percent in stock and just 13 percent in cash, whereas in his final bid the noncash piece was down to 33 percent with 67 percent in cash. A similar thing happened to QVC, with its opening bid starting out 62 percent stock and 38 percent cash, and gradually reversing. That progression from using mostly stock to increasing amounts of cash suggests escalating commitments to victory in the bidding, with the cash:stock ratio rising in proportion to the commitment bias.

In the case of both men, you had savvy and experienced financial operators making big-money decisions. Each put enormous private wealth at risk. In Redstone's case, the personal stakes were vastly greater than that of anyone else—owning virtually all of Viacom and ending up as the owner of 70 percent of the combined business, Redstone was primarily operating with his own money.[8]

Hubris[9]

Casual observers inspired by classical American economics traditions are surprised by the suggestion that business managers might overpay for businesses. How can rational, wealth-maximizing economic actors miscalculate? Those using common sense explain that it is akin to young men punching holes in their car mufflers to make the engine sound louder and therefore cooler, and middle-aged men buying cars that can clock 140 m.p.h. in a country where the highest speed limit is half that.

Acquisitions pose numerous challenges. Businesses must be integrated, cultural clashes between units smoothed, overlapping departments eliminated, data systems merged, product lines harmonized. The ordinary challenges of running any business multiply dramatically. The costs of these challenges are uncertain, but always high. In making an acquisition, it pays to be objective and conservative in evaluating these costs. It pays to use the same dispassion when estimating the gains from merger-synergies that arise from combining divisions, reducing overhead, and the like.

These qualities are often in short supply among managers interested in making acquisitions. Acquisition decisions are made by managers at the top. They did not get to the top by exuding pessimism and passivity. Top managers as a group are optimistic, overconfident, and eager for action. Acquisitions provide the thrill of action; optimism and overconfidence lead action-hungry managers to believe—often incorrectly—that they can run target businesses better than their predecessors.[10]

Dispassionate objectivity and conservatism are threatened. The first fatality of passion in mergers is value. The intrinsic worth of any business (or other productive asset) is the present value of the cash it will spin off from now until doomsday. Figuring this (in takeovers and otherwise) requires numerous judgments about operations and economic conditions over the uncertain future, guided only by historical data.

It is easy to go wrong in these calculations, even with the greatest capacity for unbiased thought. Adding overconfidence and optimism, it may be impossible not to foul up. Acquisition-hungry managers easily underestimate the business challenges a target faces. This can lead to false beliefs that a target's historical figures reflect previous management's failings, whereas once properly managed, the target business will produce as it should. The grim historical financial results are rationalized away, with superior results appearing in carefully framed projected financial results: the bottom line grows from rising operating income, profit margins widen, and inventory turnover and receivables collection speed up.

Valuation analysis also requires making risk estimates. Even small, unintentional projection errors can lead to substantially higher valuations than are justified by a realistic and objective assessment.

The other challenges acquisitions pose can be minimized as well. To take some recent examples, acquiring managers may:

- Underestimate the difficulties of melding two disparate cultures. (The lesson learned from the merger of Daimler and Chrysler, mixing Daimler's straightlaced German culture with Chrysler's more freewheeling American one.)

- Fail to anticipate how competitors will react. (Consider AT&T launching a bidding war in the long-distance market after the Worldcom-MCI deal.)

- Wrongly assume an ability to retain top talent of the acquired firm. (After buying Montgomery Securities, Bank of America watched its top bankers jump ship to join Thomas Weisel at his eponymous banking firm.)

Bidders risk overpaying even in a closed selling process, where a single bidder participates. Throw in the chance of potential competition and the risk magnifies. Other bidders induce aggressive bidding and increase the odds that the winner will overpay. In a bidding contest, bids can be driven higher by the bias of social proof: when other bidders are saying an asset you've bid $100 for is really worth $101, how easy is it to agree that it is really worth $102?

Winners of auctions with multiple bidders substantially overpay for victory.[11] This is true even if most bidders make accurate value estimates. On average, accurate bidders win only by overpaying, even when adopting a conservative tack of bidding lower than estimated value.

It is hard to escape the curse. Even bidders who know about it bid above a deep discount of their value estimate. The only way out of this trap is to bid much lower than estimated value, and run the risk of never winning. Or, better yet, staying away from auctions altogether.

Unlike books or baseball, in takeovers it can take years before overpayment manifests itself. When merger failure becomes evident, many different causes other than overpayment are often blamed. Mistakes are attributed to poor execution of the merger strategy. Managers point to failed integration efforts, a rise in the price of raw materials, or adverse changes in currency exchange rates, and so on.

If this is not enough to alarm investors whose company's CEO is regularly in the market announcing takeover deals, consider such a manager who habitually pays for these deals using stock. Acquisitions paid in stock are more common during bull markets than bear markets. This makes sense when you consider that in bull markets, the financial-services-sector expansion encourages M&A activity. Also, a buyer usually gets more using high-priced rather than low-priced stock.

But there may be an important additional psychological factor. Evidence shows that returns on mergers paid using all cash are on average greater than ones using stock or a mix.[12] The risk of the winner's curse is greater in stock acquisitions, and greater yet during bull markets.

Cash is still king. It is the ultimate business and financial measurement. Stock is secondary. Managerial extravagance with stock versus cash can be compared to Americans traveling abroad who spend more using local currency than they would paying U.S. dollars, and why all Americans spend markedly more using credit cards than cash. Using stock to fund acquisitions has the same effect as using chips in casinos: the first emotional step in parting people from their money (though in acquisitions, the money that managers wage may be yours!).

Emperors

Even a manager who is not displaying overconfidence and is unafflicted by the winner's curse still may overpay. Acquisitions are thrilling, particularly for CEOs. They give CEOs unparalleled benefits by expanding their dominions and generating more action.

In corporate America, size matters. Managers reigning over large domains get proportionally large psychological gains. Growth is a watchword on Wall Street and across corporate America. Building growth internally takes patience; buying another company adds growth instantaneously.

Prestige and fame go to those managing larger operations. Look at Sandy Weill. In the 1970s, he ran an investment firm whose business model involved acquiring others. By the late 1980s, he was running American Express, continuing the deal making. During the 1990s, he achieved widespread fame through an even more ambitious series of acquisitions: Primerica (which owned Smith Barney), Shearson (bought back from American Express), Travelers Group, Salomon Brothers, and ultimately Citicorp (renamed Citigroup).

Ego boosts arising from growth are also valuable for building a legacy. Corporate chieftains want to be remembered for something, preferably something good (such as George Eastman's philanthropy rather than Armand Hammer's treachery). Building a new conglomerate, putting together a collection of businesses, puts CEOs in the history books.

Consider Jack Welch, a very acquisitive CEO during 20 years at GE. Originally famous for his mantra of staying in businesses where GE was number one or two and getting out of others, GE spent many billions of dollars in hundreds of acquisitions, including the 1986 purchase of leading broadcasting company RCA for $6.4 billion (for a bargain price of $66.50 per share, not far from the price it traded at two decades earlier).

Weill and Welch are the success stories in a rarified league. Few are capable of making so many successful acquisitions. Other managers on the road to prestige, fame, and legacy, often fail in their efforts. Their shareholders pay the price.

Apart from the psychological benefits are employee benefits. Performance-based remuneration such as stock-option plans are routinely pegged to targets often easiest achieved by buying other businesses. Targets include rates of growth in sales and profits. Buying them, the bonuses and options grow, even if the company's return to holders is weak, dismal, or worse.

In periods when hostile takeovers are common, an additional reason to buy other businesses without sufficient regard to shareholder interests is defensive. Companies with excess cash or healthy balance sheets become targets. One way to deter the raider at the gate is to get rid of that cash, and/or load up on debt to dirty the balance sheet. Cash can be distributed to shareholders or invested in research and development, but a more temptingly thrilling use is buying other businesses. And if part of the motive to merge is to disgorge cash or leverage up, overpayment risk looms lower on the managerial checklist of concerns.

In the 1970s, among the big overpayers in corporate takeovers were the conglomerate builders, such as W.R. Grace & Co. and ITT. In the 1980s, this diversification impulse continued, and new rationales for takeovers concerning the benefits of scale were so exaggerated that the winner's curse struck Ford-Jaguar, Xerox-Scientific Data Systems, Exxon-Reliance Electric, Sohio-Kennecott, Mobil-Montgomery Ward, and the list went on.

Whatever reasons are given to rationalize a deal, the 1990s provided plenty of examples of overpriced acquisitions that suggest empire building as well as the winner's curse. These include First Union-CoreStates Financial, AT&T-NCR, Conseco-Green Tree Financial, Aetna-Prudential Healthcare, HFS-CUC (which combined to form Cendant), MCI-WorldCom, Daimler-Chrysler, and Mattel-Learning Company. As the 2000s unfold, Hewlett Packard and Compaq look poised to lead the new decade's list.

Risks are more acute for acquisitions that diversify a company's operations in remote directions (say a beverage company buying an oil-drilling business, a toy company buying a computer-chip maker, or a razor-blade company buying a battery maker). As in investing, managers who understand their core competencies and stick with them suffer less-severe cognitive biases than others. In the case of acquisitions, managers should remember their limitations and stick to their knittings.

Governance

Why can't corporate boards stonewall the overconfident, empire-building CEO about to make a dumb acquisition? Sometimes they do. A good example is the board of the Coca-Cola Co. deciding not to acquire Quaker Oats, even though CEO Douglas Daft put significant time and effort into the proposed deal.

Director interference with CEO acquisition campaigns is difficult, despite boards' having to sign off on most takeover-related decisions. Takeover proposals are usually developed by top managers, principally CEOs and their minions. The governance problem revolves around the fact that word of most acquisitions doesn't reach the board until the process is substantially underway, meaning that the CEO already has invested substantial personal capital.

Observers could interpret a board's refusal to endorse an advanced-stage acquisition proposal as a rejection of the CEO. Such refusals embarrass the CEOs when they are very much in the spotlight. Effects trickle down and out, impairing employee morale, jeopardizing customer confidence, and provoking shareholder ire. Directors face significant pressure to approve acquisitions.

Similarly, once the company goes public with its intention, backing down has serious consequences. It means being called the loser in a bidding contest. No CEO wants to be branded a loser at anything.

CEOs, from the proposal stage on, arm themselves with reassuring data showing that the company is getting a sweet deal. Projections never suggest the risk of overpaying. Boards follow along.

It would be nice if board oversight could be designed to alleviate this pressure to approve takeovers. The timing problem complicates that solution—CEOs are unlikely to announce an interest in an acquisition to a board without first doing substantial investigation. It is a mistake to think that adopting a strategic plan for measuring acquisitions would do the trick. Such plans create biases rather than promote objectivity.

One strategy to reduce the risk of bidder overpayment in takeovers is to have a regular, periodic review of past acquisitions to examine how things transpired compared to projections. This is the standard operating procedure at Johnson & Johnson Company, which made 50 acquisitions during the 1990s, including one for $4.9 billion (and is 1 of only 6 American industrial corporations sporting a "AAA" credit rating) and the Royal Dutch/Shell group of companies, an equally acquisitive and lean organization.[13]

Another governance strategy to combat the winner's curse is to have a review team, led by a rotating group of independent executives. The team studies proposed acquisitions at a preliminary level to minimize the commitment bias that can impair a CEO's objectivity. A number of financial-advisory firms run practices to help implement this control, including FleetBoston.

The winner's curse leaves an informed bidder perplexed. A sensible bidder who lowers his offer will never suffer the winner's curse because he will never win. The ideal strategy is to share knowledge and get all bids to come down. Given the characteristics required to climb the corporate ladder, that is not likely in corporate America.

Tallying the Costs

Deals afflicted by the winner's curse do not necessarily have targets that are subpar businesses or managers that are second class. All it means, as Charlie Munger puts it, is that "no business is so wonderful that it can't be ruined as an acquisition candidate by increasing the price."[14] (The same point applies to individual stocks. As Peter Lynch says, "Wonderful companies become risky when people overpay for them."[15])

You cannot usually predict who will suffer from the winner's curse. Take the case of the 1999 merger between Honeywell International Inc. and Allied Signal Corp. This $14 billion deal was intended to exploit the efficiency of Allied Signal with the innovativeness of Honeywell. The deal was reported to have been carefully researched on both sides and thoughtfully vetted by objective corporate officers.

Alas, rising oil prices, a falling euro, and management difficulties made it seem, in hindsight, like a deal plagued by the winner's curse. Subsequently when GE offered more than $40 billion for the combination, many worried that even Jack Welch may have been afflicted by the winner's curse—something we'll never know, thanks to the European Union's disapproval of the deal (Welch's successor, CEO Jeffrey R. Immelt, may be grateful).

Bidder overpayment is sometimes obscured by accounting data. Hidden accounting tricks plagued the Cendent deal in 1997, a $14-billion deal won by Henry Silverman that later exploded when accounting fraud was uncovered. While the books were not as aggressively cooked in the case of the 1998 Conseco-GreenTree deal, the major reason that the $7.6-billion deal was overpriced was huge write-offs for bad loans in GreenTree's portfolio. The worst violator was probably McKesson Corp.'s 1999 $12-billion deal for HBO (the Atlanta hospital-billing software company, not to be confused with the entertainment company Home Box Office), which blew up following accounting scandals that led to criminal charges against top executives.

Speaking of accounting tricks, all the deals just mentioned used a method that enables bidders to conceal the costs of their overpayment from investors. Called "pooling," this method of merger accounting increases the odds of committing the winner's curse. The potentially good news is that recent changes made to accounting rules governing acquisitions eliminate the pooling option.

Until recently, generally accepted accounting principles (GAAP) permitted acquisitions to be accounted for in two different ways. If only stock was used in the takeover and other restrictions were met, the acquisition could be treated as if nothing other than a business marriage had occurred. The assets and liabilities and so forth of the resulting company were pooled, basically the sum of those items beforehand.[16]

If these restrictions were not met, the acquisition had to be treated as a purchase by one company of the other. This meant that when the purchase price was greater than the fair value of the assets bought, the difference would be recorded in a new account. That account, called "goodwill," would have to be amortized over the next 40 or so years, resulting in an annual expense that lowered reported earnings.

Managers tended to prefer pooling because it liberated them from the perennial drag on earnings that goodwill entailed. Deals were structured to meet the pooling requirements and paid for in stock whenever possible, exacerbating the winner's curse. Accounting purists argued that purchases were simply being disguised.

Each side had a point. The pro-pooling party's best argument was that in most acquisitions, goodwill (the premium paid) did not decline in value in the years after the acquisition. So imposing an annual charge to earnings did not make sense. It was less like depreciating the price paid for other long-term assets that wear out with time, and more like land, which does not wear out and which GAAP does not require to be amortized. The pro-purchase party's best argument was that most acquisitions are not conceptually equivalent to a marriage, but are instead exactly like any other asset acquisition a company makes, and should be accounted for in the same way.

A hard-fought compromise to this decades-long debate was reached in 2001. The new rule requires acquisitions to be treated as purchases so that a goodwill account must be created to record the premium purchase price. But that amount will not automatically have to be amortized. As long as the goodwill value does not decline in the years after the acquisition, it does not have to be written off, so there will be no charge to earnings. Only if it is determined that the value of the goodwill is impaired will that be necessary.

After the compromise on merger accounting became effective, hundreds of billions of dollars of write-downs of goodwill accounts were taken in the middle of 2001 to reflect the high cost of acquisitions many companies made during the financial boom of 1997–2000. Goodwill write-offs were made in staggering amounts: AOL Time Warner, $50 Billion; JDS Uniphase, $45 billion; Nortel Networks, $12 billion; VeriSign, $10 billion; Corning, $5 billion; Qwest Communications, $3.5 billion; and Verizon, $3 billion.[17]

On the other side of the ledger, the bottom lines of other companies immediately benefited. Those with unimpaired but sizable amounts of goodwill on their balance sheets saw reported earnings rise, sometimes significantly. Bank of America's profits got a boost of $600 million without the burden of amortizing acquisition good- will, as did Wells Fargo's. Similar stories were told of Parker Hannifin, H&R Block, Johnson Controls, and others.[18]

The compromise approach to merger accounting may offset some problems of bidder overpayment. It will be harder to hide by struc- turing a deal as a pooling whose ultimate performance gets lost in the accounting. The premium paid will be in the goodwill account. The value of the goodwill must be examined like the value of any other asset. When that value is impaired, it must be written down. When that happens, it will be hard to deny that an overpayment occurred.

This belief may, on the other hand, be wishful thinking. It will be up to management, along with auditors, to declare goodwill impaired. That kind of admission will not come easily, except if it serves other ends. Games can be played, as the next chapter shows.

8

Corporate Ebonics

How did Kate Winslet look so lovely in the film *Titanic* even as the ship sank into the icy blue sea? Same reason some companies look good despite choppy business performance pushing them toward the abyss. Corporate accountants use accounting cosmetics for the same reason movie stars use makeup: to look better.

Among the greatest abominations of the efficiency story is its fantasy that accounting data doesn't matter. Analysts will pierce financial statements to uncover the economic substance of business activity no matter how it is reported, the tale tells us.

The efficiency story is that price is a transparent report card on managerial performance. There is no room in the story to reflect managers with incentive to grade themselves, or at least to fudge the report card. Chronicles of accounting scandals followed by price drops, with lots of money changing hands in between, suggest which account is more accurate.

In debates about accounting and markets, efficiency zealots identify a supposed paradox. It arises from two opposing arguments. Accounting purists say investors need accurate accounting data to make informed decisions. Efficiency devotees reply with this strange argument, creating the supposed paradox: when investors know enough to claim they need some data, by claiming they need it, they admit to already knowing what they need.

Thus, to argue that mergers should be accounted for as purchases rather than as poolings is to deny the significance of the requirement: if you know that this would produce more accurate accounting, then you already have as much information as you need in order to compute accurate accounting.

The paradox is false, for two reasons. Investors place greater weight on reports issued by companies than on reports issued by others. If company reports say earnings per share (EPS) are $2, then the market will believe EPS is $2—even if a financial guru applying more faithful accounting principles figured out that EPS was actually $1. Getting the accounting right is crucial.

The paradox also dissolves because the debate isn't really about whether the information is available. It is about who is responsible for the accuracy of public information. Financial statements are management's responsibility, and it falls to management to provide data that is accurate and reliable. Management is on the hook, even if researchers can discover the truth of numbers manipulation.

The incidence of accounting machinations increased in the past several decades. Formal restatements of financial data reached an annual average of about 150 by the late 1990s, 3 times greater than the decade as a whole.[1] It is true that the odds that the average stock-picking investor will hold stock in a public company that gets into an accounting mess are low. Nowadays, fewer than 1 percent of public companies engage in sufficiently bad and discovered accounting scandals that require restatements. Even so, integrity in accounting should be a top priority of smart investors.

Corporate Culture: A Lesson From Enron

Despite the statistics, many in a position to lead the way in improving corporate financial reporting are only jarred into action by drama in the scale of calamity. While dozens of major accounting frauds inflict damage on investors and others annually, most of these are relegated to the back pages of the financial press and do not prompt the SEC, Congress, or others to crack down. It takes periodic debacles of far greater magnitude to shine the spotlight on the subject of accounting, a spotlight illuminated by the Enron fiasco in 2002.

The case of Enron is instructive for investors, for it shows a corporate culture willing to tolerate and apparently even to applaud aggressive accounting that eventually crossed the line into the fraudulent. Enron was once a world leader in marketing electricity and natural gas, delivering energy and other physical commodities, and providing financial and risk management services to customers.[2]

The company melted down after it became clear in late 2001 that it had failed to disclose various "related-party transactions" and account for "off-balance-sheet" transactions that ended up costing shareholders billions. Enron made a series of deal with several partnerships it created in which both the company and Enron top executives held undisclosed interests. In fact, Enron's interests in the partnerships were so substantial that they should have been treated as consolidated entities on its books rather than as minority investments.

The immediate consequences were staggering, and only got worse. The first inkling of trouble came in an October 17, 2001 conference call, when management disclosed a reduction in equity of $1.2 billion (about 10 percent) due to losses at the partnerships. On November 8 the greater gravity of the situation emerged, with the company announcing that 20 percent of its equity was wiped out—$2.2 billion worth. On that day, the company restated its financials for the preceding four years, producing a 20 percent reduction to reported cumulative net income of nearly $600 million ($96 million in 1997, $113 million in 1998, $250 million in 1999, and $132 million in 2000). On the balance sheet, consolidation increased debt by approximately $628 million in 2000 and like amounts in earlier years.

In late 2001, the company fired its treasurer, its chief financial officer, and the general counsel of its North American division. A few months before the scandal became public, a managing director of that division quit. A few months afterward, in January 2002, a former top executive committed suicide. All reportedly had interests in the partnerships that earned them millions of dollars. Some were paid millions more by Enron to repurchase those interests.

One of the partnerships (called JEDI, reportedly after the warrior band in the *Star Wars* movies and standing for Joint Energy Development Investments Limited Partnership) should have been consolidated from the outset and was consolidated beginning the first quarter of 2001—long before the late 2001 blowup. As a result, the restatements did not materially affect earnings or debt levels for 2001. But it does suggest company awareness of trouble long before it fully began to come clean in late 2001. That suspicion is reinforced by the mind-boggling lengths that the company and its top advisors, including its outside auditor, apparently went to shred documents between the time the scandal first emerged in October 2001 and the time investigators pieced together the causes and culprits in January 2002.

The blow was so severe that Enron shopped itself around to other corporate buyers, agreeing on November 9, 2001 to be sold to an erstwhile and far more cautious arch rival in the energy business, Dynergy. Yet as the avalanche of terrible accounting news continued to flow, even that deal blew up, with Dynergy terminating the agreement on November 28. Ultimately, on December 2, Enron filed for voluntary bankruptcy protection under Chapter 11. The board appointed a special committee to investigate, as shareholders filed lawsuits against Enron, top managers, and Enron's outside auditors. The SEC also conducted an investigation, as did numerous arms of Congress and other governmental agencies.

The reason for the off-balance-sheet financing was apparently corporate concern about tarnishing the company's credit rating. It already was highly leveraged, with a substantial debt:equity ratio. Yet it desired more money to expand its energy business, as well as to venture into other fields. To attract that financing without impairing its debt rating, the company established the partnerships to do the borrowing. In some cases, other investors also contributed assets to the partnership. But even those investments were eventually repurchased by Enron affiliates. In other cases, Enron itself guaranteed the debts of the partnerships with Enron common stock.

Its would-be merger partner Dynergy exhibited a contrasting corporate culture to Enron. Enron thrived on risk, taking aggressive positions in the trading end of the energy business, while Dynergy concentrated on the old-fashioned generation and sale of energy. Trading in energy contracts was a fast money maker, whereas running power plants generated money slowly.

Enron used its fast money—from assets of $13 billion in 1995 to $64 billion in 2001—to expand its business rapidly and in many directions, ranging from the overseas retail and wholesale marketing of power to far-flung ventures in the sale of water and the laying of broadband telecommunications technology. All struck out eventually. But Enron made big promises to the financial community, creating additional pressure. Apparently to relieve that pressure, it hid problems by using sketchy financial structures and deplorable accounting.

Corporate cultures with aggressive expansion goals, diversifying in numerous directions simultaneously, and growing assets at geometric rates are ideal places for senior managers to succumb to the temptations of playing games with numbers. Wise investors eschew such cultures. As astonishing as many find the Enron debacle to be, it is merely one of numerous accounting scandals uncovered each year, all of which offer valuable lessons for investors. Let's take a further glimpse at some of the chicanery.

Snowball Accounting

The snowball effect is a self-inflicted Ponzi scheme by aggressive accountants. In the Ponzi scheme (which we'll discuss further in the next chapter), when the schemers con $1 from their first victims, they promise to pay $2, so they have to go out and find $2 plus some profit. When they get that $2-plus, they promise a payout of $4, so they need to go out and find $4-plus. And so on. The profits build, but so does the effort required. It is akin to rolling a handful of snow down a hill; the ball grows and grows.

Accounting shenanigans follow the same pattern. If Mr. Bean Counter ignores $1 in expenses this quarter, his bottom line looks that much better. But next quarter, he's got to find a way to improve on that gain or else the game isn't working. So Bean Counter must, to keep the ball rolling, pretend about $1.05 of expenses didn't arise. Next quarter, the amount grows by another dime, and so on, until soon he is near the bottom of the hill with the accounting-scandal equivalent of a massive snowball.

The snowball effect operated at Rent-Way Inc., the second-largest operator of rent-to-own stores in the country.[3] Its chief accountant ultimately admitted feeling pressure to meet analysts' earnings estimates, but said he merely pushed accounting rules in response. If by that he meant taking aggressive stances routinely and repeatedly across scores of transactions, fair enough, but when you take a penny here and take a penny there, you are no longer merely pushing the rules, but violating them.

Among the aggressive decisions, the accounting chief understated expenses such as automobile maintenance and insurance costs, and overstated assets such as inventory. Discovery came when the accountant was on vacation, and his boss started asking questions about what appeared to be high inventory levels. As he pressed, other employees came forward.

The amount of the misstatements grew as the internal probe deepened. For a company with $500 million in revenue, the amounts were significant and got more so: the misstatements were first announced at $30 million, raised to $60 million, and ultimately $110 million. Rent-Way's stock had traded in a range between $25 to $30; following the announcements it traded in the range of $5 to $10.

Where does the pressure come from? In an ordinary operating context, executives set targets and try to hit them. The pressure is on business performance. This healthy pressure in a healthy business atmosphere should not lead to cutting corners or concocted accounting. For an unhealthy business, normal pressure becomes pressure to cut corners and cook the books.

Pressure points to look for are circumstances inside a business that create temptation—a weak business model, deteriorating market share, large debt obligations—in short, all the characteristics intelligent investors shun. A little background on Rent-Way's business illustrates.

The rent-to-own business caters to low-income clientele, those who acquire the products that Rent-Way markets, such as televisions and furniture, by making weekly rental payments until they've paid enough to own and keep the merchandise outright.

Founded in 1981 by a former manager of one such store, a decade later Rent-Way owned over a dozen locations. The founder and a partner teamed up to take the company public in 1993. Over the next few years, the two set out to grow the business by buying existing stores, bringing the total to 1000 in that short time. Revenue shot up from $8 million in 1993 to nearly $600 million in 2000. Costs for acquisitions amounted to $35 million in 1999 alone. These included the costs of buying shabby stores carrying shoddy inventory.

With the CEO on the road buying stores to grow the business at this frenetic pace, the bean counters back at the home office had to contend with endless streams of new data and integration questions, along with thousands of accounting judgments. The boss was buying growth—sometimes making costly commitments—while analysts were cheering him on with excitement about the growth.

This atmosphere can lead to bad judgments. Growth is nice, but you can't go to the gym and turn yourself into Superman in a weekend. Using a common bookkeeping trick, Rent-Way recorded as an asset what should have been an expense. There is a choice to be made in making a disbursement, between treating 100 percent of it as a current expense with an immediate hit to income, or capitalizing it, allocating it as an expense over numerous future accounting periods.

Some disbursements for automobile maintenance were apparently done the latter way. This can be a close call. The basic rule is that ordinary maintenance and repairs on fixed assets are expensed when incurred; for disbursements of a more substantial kind that lengthen the asset's useful life, capitalizing them is permitted.

Rent-Way also kept on its books, as assets wore out, crummy furniture that should have been written off as an expense. This is what finally tipped superiors off: a comparison between the company's books relating to inventory and the reports of inventory held in the stores. Stores were reporting lower levels than the balance sheet indicated.

Notably, the fellow who noticed this, the company's chief financial officer, did not have an accounting background. However, it is not necessary to have an accounting background to recognize accounting shenanigans. Accounting, in the end, is a simple system, though it requires good judgment. When you see something that doesn't look quite right, you may be wrong, but it doesn't hurt to be cautious.

When accountants succumb to pressure and engage in accounting deception, psychological factors reinforce the plan. Consider the factor of overconfidence, where the cheaters really believe their employers will outperform next quarter to make up for an irregularity entered in the books this quarter. A commitment to the decision arises. It can bolster when the CEO repeatedly tells the troops and the press that success is just around the corner. Accountants want to believe.

Take the case of Critical Path, once a high-flying darling of the Internet set; this company provided corporate electronic-mail systems to its clients and promises to its investors.[4] At one exuberant time, shares reached $120 apiece. Yet it never made a dime. Its CEO repeatedly told the market that the dimes were coming, that profitability was around the next quarter.

In January of 2001, when analysts were excited by expecting profit of a penny a share, the CEO told them the company actually lost 16 cents a share. Managers denied responsibility, blaming PricewaterhouseCoopers, their auditors, for not letting them record revenue from a recently obtained licensing deal.

But the other shoe was about to drop. The 16 cents of bad news was better news than was justified because the books had been cooked. A newly hired CFO discovered later that the books reflected various "questionable transactions," making the financial reports inaccurate. In the fallout, top officials left the company, including its CEO, president and VP for sales, and several top sales staff.

With the company facing an uncertain fate, analysts reacted strongly with downgrades, including sell recommendations, and questioned whether company management could be trusted. A restructuring plan was developed, the founder was brought back from a leave of absence, and along with the CFO, tried to reassure the marketplace that the challenges were behind them.

Those preparing the books using impure accounting sometimes fool themselves and fellow insiders with their numbers. When corporate finance officers decide whether to pursue one project or another, they rely on the accounting data in much the same way outsiders conducting valuation exercises would. If those numbers are wrong, poor decisions ensue. And there is a tendency of storytellers to start to believe their stories.

Ben Graham told the parable of the oil speculator who died and went to heaven. On being told that heaven's oilman wing was full and he'd have to wait, he got St. Peter's permission to say four words to those inside. "Oil discovered in hell," he shouted. The oilmen raced out of heaven and headed for hell, creating space that St. Peter invited the oilman to occupy. He declined the invitation, announcing that he was going to follow the other guys, because "there might be some truth to that rumor after all."

This is what happened at Xerox Corp.[5] It started with business problems in its core operating unit. Copiers were being replaced by desktop printers and e-mail. Pressure to maintain growth drove financial leaders at the company to turn to the accounting department. If real growth was not possible in operations, fictional growth could be obtained by having the accountants fabricate it.

Accountants found ingenious ways to deliver. Finance staff used the misleading numbers to make business decisions about where to look for real profits. Corporate funds were allocated to money-losing ventures. Money was lost. Tough times got worse.

It is not necessary for investors to study the details of all recent accounting scandals or to know all the tricks.[6] We should recognize one unifying theme: weak underlying business conditions characterize the businesses caught in accounting scandals, along with managers willing to substitute accounting finesse for business acumen. The commonsense lesson is to search for businesses with solid economics run by trustworthy people.

Pro Forma Accounting

Linguists debate about what makes language acceptable as proper speech. Some believe it is prevailing usage by speakers, including spellings, while others insist that standards set by lexicographers are necessary.[7] The accounting profession has generally eschewed such a debate, adhering to a belief that principles of accounting should be articulated and followed so that financial reports are reliable and comparable. While it may be okay for grade-school English teachers to permit students to create words with "personal spellings" and "personal usages," allowing accountants to create "personal standards" and "personal statements" destroys the purpose of reporting.

Corporate America's equivalent of a child's personal spelling is *pro forma* presentation of accounting data. Leading Internet companies popularized the practice of offering not the hard truth of accounting reality, but an "as-if" picture of financial life—a picture not so much of performance, but of perform-ability. This may be one of the enduring legacies of the excesses of dot-com culture, for it quickly spread to mainstream businesses.

Researchers have documented the growing difference between earnings per share (EPS) determined using generally accepted accounting principles (GAAP) and *pro forma* or operating EPS.[8] In early 2000, more than 300 companies comprising the S&P 500 excluded some ordinary expenses to compute a *pro forma* number higher than real, GAAP, earnings.[9]

GAAP has a tried-and-true set of rules on what counts as an expense. Those expenses are to be subtracted from revenue to yield income. Divide by total shares outstanding to get EPS. But as the SEC's chief accountant put it, many companies now also report EBS—earnings b.s.[10] They do this by ignoring items that count as expenses in GAAP, much as a school child might choose to ignore all the "Ss" when spelling Mississippi. (Spelled "Miippi," the word looks as ridiculous as financial reports using *pro forma*.)

Examples of expenses some companies ignore are ordinary costs of doing business: sales commissions, marketing and personnel costs, and disbursements to start a new subsidiary. The typical argument for excluding these is that they are unusual, one-time events, the standard required under GAAP to exclude items. As far-fetched as that sounds for such routine items, even worse is the fact that these aggressive accountants willingly include unusual, one-time revenue events in calculating *pro forma* EPS.

This is earnings management of a quite subtle sort. We saw how snowball accounting directly alters earnings with some active manipulation of GAAP figures. *Pro forma* accounting is a more sophisticated strategy, having more to do with managing expectations than back-office manipulation. It is powerful because it appears not like shady dealing, but candid and direct. It says that this is a better way to measure performance.

In reports, the *pro forma* numbers often appear first, nominally alongside the GAAP numbers. They are accompanied by hype and an explanation of how new business models and realities require this alternative, superior presentation. These tactics exploit the availability bias, our tendency to interpret salient information as most important. The use of the phrase *pro forma* is itself an advantage, for few people even know what it means.

Traditionally, *pro forma* in the accounting profession denoted a few clear exercises. One was a hypothetical set of financial statements used for limited and special purposes, such as for testing the reasonableness and feasibility of short-term cash-flow forecasts. Another was to show how a newly merged company would have looked had the merger occurred a few years earlier.[11]

Now *pro forma* assumes a far broader meaning, usually whatever the accountant invoking it wants it to mean. The tempted accountant evokes Lewis Carroll's Humpty Dumpty: "When I use a word, it means just what I choose it to mean—neither more nor less."

Managers have been able to enlist the authority of others who endorse this new reporting, making it appear even more legitimate. Auditors have helped by providing the business of attestation. Auditing has always meant a check of a company's bookkeeping system, a testing of the numbers reported for various accounts, and an overall financial examination that led to a certification that all had been done in accordance with GAAP.

Attestation is a business that calls on the CPA firm to verify the accuracy of any of a wide variety of numerical and narrative presentations. It doesn't require much more than a review that enables an attestor to say, yes, these numbers are what they purport to be.

In the case of *pro forma* EPS, however, that attestation can be meaningless, when all it really says is yes, these *pro forma* numbers take GAAP earnings and then increase them by ignoring a specified series of expenses. The appearance of attestors carries weight of authority that exploits the psychological biases of consumers of financial data offered by corporate America.

Another source of authority are analysts, who have strongly aided the legitimizing of *pro forma* earnings by signing off on the exclusion of expanding categories of expenses. A prominent example is what happened at Staples, Inc. Its managers persuaded a cadre of analysts to prepare forecasts that excluded losses from its Internet division.[12]

The impact was severe. Staples repurchased that division's tracking stock. Following custom in such repurchase deals, management asked investment bankers to opine on whether the price of the repurchase was fair to the selling shareholders. Most banks would say yes or try to get a price increase. In this case, the bankers indicated they thought the price was "unjustifiably high" and based on "very aggressive projections."[13]

Many analysts perform an admirable role in clarifying management's complicated accounting positions. Just ask Gary Wendt, the man responsible for making GE Capital a global financial powerhouse. He was recruited to turn around an ailing finance and insurance company, Conseco, in the wake of its disastrous acquisition of the loss-riddled loan portfolio of Green Tree Financial, a business catering to high-credit-risk consumers, like those patronizing Rent-Way.

Throughout Wendt's first year at the helm, analysts raised such tough questions about the business that a major Conseco shareholder ran an ad in *The Wall Street Journal* denouncing one of them.[14] When Conseco reported its second-quarter, 2001 earnings, analysts in a conference call took Wendt and his finance colleagues to task on a range of tough accounting judgments that produced *pro forma* earnings some analysts thought were 50 percent higher than justified.[15]

In the case of analysts, there is a further psychological problem of social proof ("if everyone believes something, it must be true"). In the past decade there has been a rise of analyst tracking. Tracking involves compiling all analysts' estimates for a particular company and averaging them. Services such as First Call and others then report consensus earnings estimates. Actual earnings are then measured against that baseline. The process creates an impression that a whole group of leading financial thinkers studying a company believes the earnings will be "$X" measured in a particular way.

Anchoring is also at work. Once these estimates, calculated on a *pro forma* basis, are agreed and publicized, they become the benchmark. GAAP forecasts and earnings take a back seat.

Some rules that managers adopt in preparing *pro forma* earnings reports may be defensible and possibly should become part of GAAP. But promulgating and updating GAAP is the job of the Financial Accounting Standards Board (FASB). Corporate managers are supposed to follow GAAP and auditors to confirm whether they complied or not. That system works relatively well.

Under the *pro forma* system, managers set the accounting rules, auditors attest that they have followed those self-made rules, and analysts endorse the practice. Reposing such broad discretion in managers, with the implicit aid of analysts and auditors, is akin to giving students the power to grade themselves. Grade inflation ensues.

Pro forma accounting would not be so bad if investors continued to digest GAAP, but the evidence suggests they don't. Evidence shows that market-pricing appears to be more responsive to *pro forma* EPS figures than to GAAP figures.[16] Markets end up pricing the "*as if*" numbers rather than piercing the conventions, an unsurprising result given the widespread endorsement of the practice on Wall Street.

A good example is Computer Associates, which offered investors a menu of accounting reports. Here is the menu (see Figure 8-1). You choose:

Pro Forma	2001	2000	GAAP	2001	2000
Sales	$5.6B	$5.3B	Sales	$4.2B	$6.1B
Income	931M	787M	Income	95M	1.8M
EPS	1.61	1.30	EPS	0.16	3.11

Figure 8-1   Computer Associates earnings menu: you choose.

The *pro forma* method offers a picture of steady growth in sales, income, and earnings per share. Managers love reporting such smoothness. Techniques for doing this abound, and accounting textbooks devote entire chapters to "income smoothing."

Notice how the GAAP figures are far worse. These numbers show a company in convulsion, with a major decline in business during the period. The decline is so substantial that, on its face, it doesn't appear to be temporary.

The accounting question concerns how to treat licenses, a major source of revenue for Computer Associates and other software producers. The company grants a license, perhaps lasting several years, in exchange for a fee paid up front as well as periodically.

GAAP requires the recording of most of the revenue from such an arrangement when received, up front. So you get what you see on the right-hand panel, reflecting lots of up-front fees in 2000, meaning lots of new business, followed the next year by a mere fraction, meaning a sharp drop in new business.

Computer Associates began lengthening its license agreements around this transition year, saying that economic reality would better be reflected by recognizing revenue on these licenses gradually over their lives rather than so much up front.[17]

In the conference call reporting these approaches, company executives repeatedly congratulated themselves on this "new business model." What was new was not made exactly clear. It is possible that the new model was mainly a lengthening of the contracts, coupled with new accounting.

On the call, the managers bragged about overcoming a "challenging environment." But the most vivid information conveyed was that the purpose of the *pro forma* numbers was to give investors a "meaningful comparison" of the company's performance.[18]

Calculating the capital misallocated due to fictitious accounting is difficult. One way to gauge the costs of believing in the spurious accounting of the late 1990s examines the difference between gains reported in that period with losses revealed later. For the four quarters ending in mid-2001, 4200 Nasdaq companies reported combined losses of $148.2 billion, compared with $145.3 billion in profit over the prior five years combined.[19] Large portions of the 2001 losses came from write-downs of assets acquired at inflated prices during the frenzied financial climate of the late 1990s.

These companies attracted huge amounts of capital in the earlier period. The influx sent the market from Nasdaq 1000 in 1995 to Nasdaq 5000 in 2000, before crumbling below that during 2001. Supporting the capital call were investors succumbing to the availability bias, focusing on top-line revenue-generating power rather than bottom-line earnings results. Myopically overconfident executives were convinced that they were sailing for unstoppable success, forgetting about business cycles.

The costs are made worse by those embracing a theme from the popular television show *The X-Files*, appearing on FBI Agent Mulder's wall: "I WANT TO BELIEVE." This group continues to believe in non-GAAP measures of business performance. They argue that the reported losses were due to extraordinary items that should not count. One senior economist took the position that a write-down is "an accounting entry rather than a true loss."

Accounting is not some special place where numbers are recorded for fun without meaning. They are records of real economic activity with real effects. But plenty of people prefer to believe in the fantasy rather than reality.

If managers, analysts, and auditors are circumventing GAAP with their own *pro forma* rules, can anything be done about it? Standard setters are not so sure. The best the SEC could do was advise investors to be careful in their interpretation of *pro forma* reports,[20] and warn corporate America that when using *pro forma* presentations, management better be careful to choose only those formats that are not misleading or run afoul of the antifraud provisions of the federal securities laws.[21] The FASB also stood substantially on the sidelines, concurring implicitly in the SEC's apparent view that neither body believes it can tell companies not to include additional data along with required information. Companies hide behind the claim that they offer GAAP data, as well as more. If the regulators recognize that in this case, more is less, they could crack down, but neither the SEC nor FASB seems eager to do so.

Private organizations are playing a more proactive role, with groups such as the Financial Executives International and the National Investors Relations Institute offering guidelines to establish "best practices" on the proper scope of *pro forma* accounting presentation. The nationally recognized statistical rating agencies—such as Standard & Poor's and Moody's—have weighed in to argue against the proliferation of unbridled *pro forma* reporting. Most obviously, the press aggressively documents the scandalous state of accounting affairs in corporate America. Table 8-1 culls some excellent information on the problem of *pro forma* reporting from major financial publications.[22]

Table 8-1 Big-Name Companies Playing *Pro Forma* Games

Company	Pro Forma	GAAP	Difference
FMC	1.58	−9.62	11.20
Applied Micro Circuits	−0.05	−11.18	11.13
Great Lakes Chemical	0.35	−3.06	3.41
AMR	−0.68	−3.29	2.61
Conextant Systems	−0.45	−3.02	2.57
Eastman Chemical	0.55	−1.92	2.47
Cummins	0.06	−2.14	2.20
Qwest Communications	0.08	−1.99	2.07
Broadcom	−0.16	−1.73	1.57
Sears Roebuck	0.96	−0.60	1.56
JDS Uniphase	0.14	−1.13	1.27
Checkfree	−0.04	−1.17	1.13
Terayon	−0.43	−1.01	0.58
Amazon.com	−0.22	−0.66	0.44
PMC–Sierra	0.02	−0.38	0.40
Corning	0.29	0.14	0.15
Qualcomm	0.29	0.18	0.11
Cisco Systems	0.18	0.12	0.06
EBay	0.11	0.08	0.03
Yahoo!	0.01	−0.02	0.03

Sources: *The Wall Street Journal; Business Week*

The Surreal

Then there are the downright scoundrels. The real crooks. The psychology of the crook is, thankfully, well beyond the scope of a book on psychology and investing. But it is impossible not to consider what's out there, even at major corporations one would never have imagined. This cautionary tale is worth telling, if not for clinical understanding, then at least for raising awareness.

In March of 1999, Rite Aid announced disappointing earnings results.[23] One factor was increased interest costs associated with debt used to make a recent acquisition. That debt needed to be refinanced, or else the company faced the risk of bankruptcy.

On the news, Rite Aid's stock price fell 40 percent, slashing $4 billion off its market capitalization. The usual shareholder suits followed, naming Rite Aid, along with top management: CEO Martin L. Grass, CFO Frank Bergonzi, and COO Timothy Noonan.

Then came the bad news. On October 11, 1999, Rite Aid announced that its 1997, 1998, and 1999 financial statements would have to be restated, reducing by $500 million the company's previously reported pretax earnings. One accounting trick apparently played was that when the company sold 189 stores, it had a gain on the sale of $82.5 million. Rules say that gain is to be recorded when received, as an extraordinary item. Instead, Rite Aid's top managers apparently created a special asset of $82.5 million as a reserve that could then be drawn on in the future to offset future operating expenses. Another novel stroke was to record rebates to be received from the company's suppliers for supplies never ordered.

A few days after this announcement, the Rite Aid Board's Finance Committee met at the New York City office of Skadden, Arps, a global law firm. With most of its directors present, the issue under discussion was refinancing the acquisition debt. One director suggested that Rite Aid could improve the terms of the refinancing by pledging as collateral stock it held in a recently acquired company called PCS. At that point, Rite Aid's general counsel, Elliot Gerson, stated that the PCS stock was already pledged.

To a wide-eyed boardroom, Gerson went on to explain that on September 24, 1999, CEO Grass met with the company's bankers independently. Rite Aid needed about $800 million to pay off some commercial paper that was coming due in 3 days. The bankers offered to furnish the $800 million in short-term credit if Rite Aid would pledge assets. Grass agreed and pledged the PCS stock. So the stock was unavailable to help with the long-term refinancing.

Shocked at this explanation, Rite Aid director Leonard Stern asked incredulously, "On whose authority was this stock pledged?" According to Gerson, Grass responded by leaving the conference room "with his tail between his legs," silently resigning his position as Chairman and CEO. By this gesture, Grass admitted he lacked power to pledge the stock on his own, should have brought it to the board, and probably should have disclosed it publicly.

Grass's resignation was formally announced on October 19. This resignation was sufficiently unpleasant and unusual that Grass got no compensation or retirement benefits upon leaving, and none have been paid to him since. By contrast, when Bergonzi was earlier forced to step down as Chief Financial Officer, he made off like a bandit, receiving a lavish severance package that provided, among other benefits, annual "compensation" of $525,000 for the next 3 years.

The Audit Committee of Rite Aid's Board of Directors began an internal investigation and retained outside lawyers and forensic accountants. They uncovered facts suggesting that Grass and Bergonzi had committed serious breaches of their fiduciary duties and concealed them. There is even evidence that Grass falsified board minutes relating to his unauthorized pledge of assets. That committee worked in cooperation with the SEC's investigation of possible federal-securities-laws violations and the U.S. Attorney's Office concerning possible criminal wrongdoing.

In April 2000, the new management of Rite Aid, through Gerson, told their lawyers to attempt to settle the shareholder litigation. The plaintiffs' lawyers agreed, but only on the condition that any settlement with Rite Aid would preserve their rights against the trio of senior managers presiding during the alleged fraud, as well as Rite Aid's outside auditor.

The final settlement, approved by a federal court in August of 2001, called for paying Rite Aid shareholders $45 million cash plus $150 million in Rite Aid stock. It also granted the trio and the auditors the right to sue others—for defamation—and gave Grass the right to sue over the terms of his separation agreement.

From the time Grass skulked out of the Skadden, Arps conference room, he remained silent, refusing to cooperate with Rite Aid's board.

Forensics

The Rite Aid case shows managers engaged in grade inflation, putting themselves on their own marking curve. There is supposed to be a principal supervising grade administration. Noted accounting crusader and professor Abraham Briloff paraphrased Colonel Montgomery, a founder of the predecessor to today's PricewaterhouseCoopers, as saying that the auditor's job is "to fight the figures and find the facts."[24]

Trouble is in this school, the principal isn't always up to the detection job that the market and investors require. The result is earnings management under supine auditor supervision. Worse, when auditors partake in the *pro forma* project by attestation, the standard warning—investor beware—is more warranted than ever.

Investors should be skeptical of auditors too, for they are human beings as well. Efficiency devotees believe auditors deter fraud because they have reputations to protect and will act "rationally" to do so. But the cognitive biases that obscure "rationality" affect auditors too. They can see patterns that don't exist and exude overconfidence just as everyone else can. Traits such as these can lead auditors off the scent of financial fraud.[25] So games are played and overlooked.

A whole industry called forensic accounting has emerged to deal with this mess. It is a growth industry because financial data is a major area where managerial discretion has profound consequences. Data can be manipulated from the innocuous to the fraudulent.

The term "forensic" means "belonging to courts of justice." Branches of knowledge implicated in legal disputes have long been designated by the term. Forensic pathology, for example, is the branch of medicine dealing with diseases of the body in relation to legal principles and cases (such as whether someone who is brain-dead can have testamentary capacity), and forensic psychiatry is the branch of medicine dealing with disorders of the mind in that relation (such as fitness for trial, or insanity as a defense in a criminal prosecution).

The continental European word for this is *forensis*, which in turn derives from the Latin term *forensis homo*, indicating an advocate or a pleader of causes, one who practices in court. Specialized disciplines have practiced in this intersection with law for centuries, including forensic medicine, forensic linguistics, and forensic engineering. Relatively new to the business is forensic accounting, the branch of the public-accounting profession dealing with dysfunctional financial reporting in relation to criminal and civil law.

Investors falling for phony accounting and fraudulent disclosure may be at the mercy of management. But does it have to be that way? Two basic points can help shelter us from companies with aggressive accounting practices. Accounting shenanigans arise repeatedly in favorite spots. Revenue misstatements are the number-one reason why corporations have restated previously issued financial reports. Nearly 25 percent of all restatements from 1997 to 2000 involved revenue problems, and 66 percent of all federal class-action lawsuits alleging securities fraud included claims of fraudulent revenue reporting.[26]

Accounting games also congregate in certain industries, with computer hardware and software makers restating more often in that period (nearly 200) than all other industries. This is partly due to novel arrangements arising in technology sectors untested by accounting rules. Some of the novelty produces honest errors, but some produces gamesmanship, and these are not always easy to distinguish.

Apart from watching games played with revenue, and being particularly wary of companies operating in new business environments, what can management do to pull the wool over the eyes of investors, at least for a little while? Why are investors vulnerable? Why do people fall for financial falsehoods, generally? For insight, let's turn our attention to stings and scams designed to make even the sophisticated investor gullible.

Part
III

9

Mind Games

Most investors have heard of the notorious Ponzi scheme. Named after Charles Ponzi, a 1920s con artist from Boston, these and kindred financial schemes are rooted in mistaken beliefs in financial miracles. Smart investors should know what's behind them.

Ponzi's given name was Carlo though he called himself Charles. A forger, sign-painter, and waiter, he started his scheme with a legitimate bit of arbitrage. In 1920, he noticed price differences between "international postal reply coupons." Coupons that cost one cent in Spain sold for six cents in the United States, with similarly wide spreads between the U.S. price and that in other countries. The arbitrage play was simple: buy coupons abroad at a discount and sell them at home for a premium, pocketing a nickel profit per coupon.

Ponzi bought and sold these instruments, claiming to rack up $15,000 in arbitrage profits in his first month of operation. At 5 cents profit apiece, that would mean buying and selling some 300,000 stamps, an unlikely number given the volume of international postal activity in the 1920s. The $15,000 actually came from duped investors. They were promised a 50 percent return on their money within 45 days.

It works like this. You procure $100 from your neighbor, and promise to pay her back $150 in 45 days. You borrow that $150 from your barber promising him $225 in 45 days. You borrow that $225 from your tailor, and then continue building the pyramid in this manner. You keep borrowing amounts that increase by 50 percent to keep the promises flowing, with the amounts escalating to: $338, $506, $759, $1135, $1709, $2563, $3844. That is 40 times where you started. The amounts would even be higher depending on the commissions you charge in the process.

Word of mouth drives the scheme. As old investors make money and spread the good news, new investors emerge. A paradox of the program is that it requires ever-growing amounts of capital to circulate by attracting more investors. Eventually, the circle closes in on itself. In the meantime, however, a lot of money is lost by the last to put money in the circle. In Ponzi's case, the postal-coupon scam lasted less than a year, but unreturned principal added up to $15 million.

Con artists play the poor and rich alike. Many of our immigrant forebears were greeted at Ellis Island in the 1940s and 1950s by hustlers making false promises of nonexistent jobs and housing, while today new arrivals are hoodwinked by the hawkers of phony green cards. Amid the boom in Texas real estate and oil and gas ventures in the 1970s, opportunists wooed the wealthy with bogus offerings; during the summer of 2000, millionaires in New York's Hamptons were fleeced in a series of scams by a young artist posing as a Rockefeller. No one is immune.

Games of Boom

In the early 1990s, John G. Bennett, Jr. took the Ponzi scheme to a new level using a fake charity called the Foundation for a New Era. Bennett led the largest charity fraud ever. We will look at this contemporary example of a Ponzi scheme because it had the following characteristics: simplicity, a single promoter, hundreds of sophisticated victims, hundreds of millions of dollars changing hands, many years of life, a national appeal, an eventual implosion, and many psychology lessons for investors.

Bennett created New Era to help finance his legitimate, but failing for-profit businesses.[1] Extolled as a "new concept" in philanthropy, he told prospective contributors that one or more anonymous donors would match their contributions, and that after a six-month holding period, the contributions would at least double, and then could be transferred to their charities of choice. Hundreds of charitable organizations lined up to double their investments, giving money to Bennett, waiting six months, and telling Bennett where to send their larger holdings.

In reality, of course, there were no anonymous donors. Subsequent contributions were used to pay off earlier ones in an escalating pyramid that eventually crushed of its own "success." Bennett began his scam within the churches where he was well known. Having made his initial reputation running training programs for nonprofit managers, he was widely respected in numerous churches as a man of sterling character.

In the scheme's infancy, Bennett made his charity look real. He falsified documents filed with the Internal Revenue Service, winning New Era tax-exempt status. Later, when the IRS conducted a routine audit of New Era, Bennett produced more fake documents, generating a favorable audit letter on IRS stationery furnishing a terrific seal of New Era's legitimacy.

Bennett's persuasive personality helped exploit the authority bias, the trap of assessing merits based on characteristics of the speaker rather than his argument's substance. Bennett spent a year in medical school in his early 30s where he took a class on bedside manner. This taught him how to project authority with a slow, comforting, resonant voice, and to display superior knowledge by using technical jargon that impressed listeners.

Vital to his scheme's success was the pull of social proof, the sense that if everyone else is doing something, it must be worth doing. Early "investors" did background checks on New Era and found nothing untoward. Once they had been paid by the scheme, these people happily endorsed it. The absence of bad news combined with the ringing endorsements created positive reactions. As apparent success mounted and social proof rose, many charities didn't dare ask questions, worried that probing would cost them the opportunity to play.

Questions went unasked, and certainly unanswered. The vast religious clientele of the scheme set skepticism aside. Some church officials thought that if the fund sounded too good to be true, then it was just that—a gift from God. While there are anonymous charitable donors in the world, this belief defies common sense.

Crediting themselves as sleuths, some victims surmised that the so-called "anonymous donor" was famed mutual-fund manager Sir John Templeton. He was rich, philanthropic, a devout Christian, and he and Bennett knew each other. Apparently having met through a church, Templeton was so impressed by Bennett that the billionaire put him on the board of some of his funds. In return, Bennett listed Templeton in New Era's promotional materials as a New Era board member (a lie, since there was no board).

Bennett, a religious zealot, may have rationalized the pyramid's legitimacy. Subsequent psychological testing on Bennett suggested that he believed his scheme was morally and legally correct, however unfathomable this is to you and me. He may have convinced himself that his fantasy anonymous donors existed. Like Peter Pan, he wanted to believe.

Bennett's scam succeeded for an extraordinary six years. But as it wore into its final year, the pressure for new funds mounted and their supply dwindled. Bennett turned to borrowing, taking a major loan from Prudential Securities, on which he defaulted a year later, owing $50 million. Unable to pay, he ultimately filed for bankruptcy and revealed that there never were any anonymous donors.

During its reign, New Era collected $350 million in contributions and left losses of $135 million. Bennett was charged with 82 offenses, including a wide variety of mail and wire fraud counts. It was clear that Bennett had spent $5 million of New Era's fraudulent funds on personal items and funneled another $3 million into businesses.

In court, he pled no contest to these charges; in the press, he asserted his innocence. The sentencing judge gave him 12 years. That sentence was half the maximum, a leniency indulged to reflect Bennett's previous record of charitable works, his cooperation, and his uncertain mental state consisting of strong personality disorders, such as narcissism, hypomania, and obsessive-compulsive disorder.

Those exploited by New Era were not neophytes and rubes, but community leaders and major figures in investing circles, including the late William Simon, a former U.S. Treasury Secretary and financier, and Laurence Rockefeller, scion of one of America's wealthiest and most storied families.[2] They also included endowments of some of America's best colleges and universities, including Dartmouth College, Princeton University, and the University of Pennsylvania.

As Bennett plied his charity fraud, young stockbrokers across the country assembled in "boiler rooms," where high-pressure salespeople use banks of telephones to call as many investor targets as possible.[3] While honest stockbrokers do cold calling to find clients for the long term, dishonest brokers rely on it to find quick hits. These strangers hound their prey to buy stocks in anything from new IPOs to small, unknown companies that are high risk, or sometimes, part of a scam.

Aggressive cold callers speak from persuasive scripts that include retorts for the prey's every objection. As long as the target remains on the phone, they'll hammer away, speaking nonstop, until the victim gives in. The pitch emphasizes rarity, immediacy, and exclusivity. A gem from a cold-calling script emphasizes the "once-in-a-lifetime" opportunity. Brokers claim to have "inside" or "confidential" information and routinely promise spectacular profits and guaranteed results.

A classic boiler-room strategy is the three-call technique. The first, designed to win false trust, boasts past successes and the high quality of the firm's research staff. Solicitors sometimes offer to send free information or ask permission to call again if good deals come up. The second call is the setup, whetting the appetite with tales of a fabulous deal the prey either just missed or that the broker thinks may be available. The third call is the close, where a deal is offered and the money collected.

A variation is the two-step, bait and switch. The first step builds trust. A broker offers a new customer some stodgy, old blue-chip stock that should perform reasonably well at first. Now the bait is hooked. The second step is to get the victim to invest money in flash-in-the-pan companies without earnings, such as Internet stocks in the late 1990s and early 2000.

Another variation exploits cognitive dissonance, the tendency of people to like private associations that are hard to join. The boiler-room operator tells a client that only a small number of shares of a "hot" stock are available, even if the number strikes the listener as high. The broker reemphasizes exclusivity, so the client takes as much as possible.

Whichever *modus operandi* a broker or shop favors, the stock sold is often "house stock." These are shares of small, worthless companies whose IPO the boiler room helped arrange or in which it makes a market—that is, buys and sells for its own account. The shop can manipulate the price in ways that depart, often substantially, from value by taking advantage of substantial market inefficiencies and compounding them with psychology. They pump the price as their clients buy it, and then the house sells its shares at the top of the market, while victims lose money.

The cold call from the boiler shop is well captured in the 2000 movie *Boiler Room*, and in this excerpt from an opinion in an SEC enforcement case:

> The firm was operating a classic boiler room. The brokers sat "cheek by jowl" in a room the size of a basketball court. All their desks were lined up side by side in rows. The firm held mandatory sales meetings every morning at 8:30 at which time sales techniques were demonstrated and scripts for the firm's "house stock" were distributed. Brokers were expected to follow the scripts and only give customers the information they contained. Brokers were discouraged from doing any outside research, and told to rely on the firm's research and representations.
>
> After the morning sales meeting, brokers were expected to spend the entire day (except for a lunch break) on the telephone. The firm expected a high volume of sales, and if brokers did not stay on the phone, they were fired. One broker conceded that he falsely identified another salesman as the firm's research analyst, and gave a fictitious description of the purported analyst as "fat, bald, and badly dressed." He stated that the reason for the firm's policy of discouraging customer sales was its desire to avoid negative price pressure on house stocks, a circumstance that he did not disclose to customers.

The boiler room blossomed in the late-1980s bull market, when appetites for juicy equity returns were so voracious that people blinded themselves by the psychology that cold-calling brokers so easily exploited.

Joining the old-fashioned Ponzi scheme with the newfangled boiler room is 30-year-old Michael Gartner's contribution to financial fraud. He created a family of phony companies called InterLink Data Group in 1989, ostensibly "to develop private, fully integrated telecommunication networks and video phone systems."[4] He sold $13 million of phony securities to 600 defrauded investors.

Gartner ran his boiler-room operation for InterLink from two southern California locations, using a registered broker-dealer as a front for his operations. More than 80 salespersons, mostly unregistered, worked the phones in InterLink's boiler rooms. Gartner trained the sales force how to "pitch" the securities to investors, and prepared the scripts and other selling materials. These promotional materials contained numerous lies and distortions, as did Gartner's presentations to the sales force.

InterLink sold three offerings of securities to the public. The first raised $3 million in 1992. Investors were told funds would be used to install fiber-optic cable in downtown Los Angeles and to manufacture video telephones. Gartner instead used the funds to live the high life.

Gartner owned a Mercedes-Benz and a BMW and had given away a new Corvette to a top salesman. He leased a 16,000-square-foot mansion in the exclusive hills of San Juan Capistrano. The multimillion-dollar estate was lavishly decorated and included an eight-car garage.

Six months later, Gartner raised another $8 million in an offering investors were told would be used to fund construction of a 21-mile fiber-optic cable network in Wilshire and downtown Los Angeles. The offering documents guaranteed investors an 18-percent annual return paid monthly with full repayment of principal in 2 years. These funds were instead used to pay off previous investors and sustain Gartner's lavish life style.

The third offering began in March of 1993. Though Gartner sought to raise many millions more, this offering netted him another $1 million. These investors were told that the proceeds would be used to manufacture video telephones. They were "guaranteed" a 12-percent annual return, again payable monthly with full return of principal in 2 years. The $1 million was inadequate to pay off previous investors, marking the beginning of the end for Gartner.

To sell all these securities, Gartner and his team engaged in a nationwide solicitation of investors, predominantly through a mass telephone campaign, supported by radio and television advertising, road shows, and written and videotaped promotional materials. Investors were never given financial statements for any of these offerings.

Brokers told investors the securities were "extremely safe." Gartner gave his brokers a script suggesting that investors be told, "At all times, your investment is 100-percent secure." Investors were also told their investment was fully secured by a security interest in the (nonexistent) fiber-optic network.

Part of the allure of the InterLink securities, especially to investors living on fixed incomes, was the high rates of return. Investors were led to believe these interest payments came from revenues generated by the fiber-optic network. The only source of revenue was money raised from other investors.

Investors were told the companies held patents to optical-switch technology used in fiber-optic cable lines. In fact, these were invented and patented by ITT. Gartner falsely listed the ITT employee who invented the switch in promotional materials as InterLink's Director of Scientific Research and Technology. Gartner told his sales force the issuers held an "exclusive license" on 16 patents for video-phone technology.

Gartner lied to investors about listing InterLink securities on the American Stock Exchange or Nasdaq. He told his sales force the stocks would be listed, and urged them to tell customers the same thing. He gave them a sales script saying InterLink "has officially announced its intentions to go public on the American Stock Exchange in the next six months." The only "official" announcement was that one.

Gartner used the funds for personal extravagances. As investor money came in, he immediately diverted it to a corporate alter-ego he created for that purpose, called Photonic Technologies, Inc. The Photonic bank account would then be used to pay for his cars and house, plus indulgences such as these:

- carpet, $240,206
- chandelier, $54,250
- Steinway piano, $55,656
- bed with mirrored and illuminated headboard, $9850
- Scarab model boat made by Wellcraft, $124,436
- fish tank, $59,931

Of the 600 investors who put up $13 million in InterLink's common stock through 700 separate sales, many were retirees living on fixed incomes who could not afford the loss. Others invested their life savings. They were ruined.

The scheme unraveled in April of 1993, as unpaid investors started to complain. The SEC obtained an asset freeze and eventually won an enforcement action against Gartner. It wasn't easy. As the proceedings were underway, Gartner withdrew cash from frozen accounts, in violation of a judicial order, and started another company following the same tack. The court held Gartner in contempt for violating its asset-freeze order, and ordered him to repay withdrawn amounts.

In the enforcement proceedings, Gartner pled the Fifth Amendment privilege against self-incrimination. The judge threw the civil book at him, ordering disgorgement of the full $13 million, plus interest, and an additional penalty of another $13 million. On top of these amounts he was later ordered to pay restitution to his victims of $8 million and sentenced in a criminal action to 4 years in jail.[5]

Still, Gartner did not give up. In jail he continued to peddle securities in a video-phone company that would operate over fiber-optic cable. He even had a Web site on the Internet with a picture of himself and his video phone from the original fraudulent marketing materials.

Games of Gloom

Stockbroker con artists are on high alert for victims during times of market exuberance and technology hype, and this is also when scams such as those Bennett ran are most likely to succeed. During less exuberant times, the scam artists don't disappear. They shift their focus to where investors already are: toward the perceived safety of bonds and other more conservative investments. Scam artists perceive psychological change as naturally as a watchdog senses fear in an intruder. As the air leaked from the equity bubble of the late 1990s, con artists turned toward fixed-income securities.

The gullibility of people who should know better is showing in the latest scam, schemes known as "prime bank programs."[6] The con artist claims that investor funds will be put in "prime bank" financial instruments on clandestine overseas markets. The returns will, of course, be out of sight. Also out of sight are the securities and the markets, which simply don't exist.

Targets are the monied elite, people like those John Bennett selected. The scams are designed to appeal to financial snobs. They are offered only to a "select elite class" of rich and famous investors ("*such as yourself*"). Strict confidentiality is emphasized, and investors are often requested to sign a confidentiality agreement. These investment opportunities are typically "by invitation only," reserved for a "handful of well-heeled, special customers."

The pitch is for sophisticated financial instruments, with deceptively boring names such as "Medium Term Bank Notes," "Debentures," "Standby Letters of Credit," and "Bank Guarantees." They are part of impressive-sounding finance campaigns bearing such names as "Offshore Trading Program," "Roll Program," and "High-Yield Investment Program." All are issued under forged documents bearing the imprimaturs of fine institutions, including the World Bank, the International Monetary Fund (IMF), the Federal Reserve Board, and the International Chamber of Commerce (ICC).

The con artists take out unusually bold ads featured in such major newspapers as *USA Today* and *The Wall Street Journal*. They use elaborately forged documents that look authoritative. The rest of the package is typical of financial scams, including guaranteed outsized returns. Sponsors emphasize that these are very complicated arrangements, warning their bait not to be offended if they don't explain them in detail. They say that only financial geniuses understand them. Groucho Marx redux.

Similar appeals to confidence are the hallmarks of so-called affinity scams, those targeted to members of identifiable groups.[7] The legal version is like marketeers who sell VISA cards with university logos to alumni.

The illegal version targets senior citizens, ethnic minorities, and the religious, much like John Bennett. Promoters masquerade as members of the same group, claiming solidarity that breeds trust. They may recruit group leaders to the same purpose.

Group identity is a powerful tug of assurance for many gullible investors. The fraudsters use typical techniques. They guarantee spectacular profits, furnish limited documentation, and emphasize the warning of missing the opportunity of a lifetime. These crooks convince targets to hand over money, before fleeing with it. Their pitches are laced with tailored references, such as quotes from the Bible when the targets are Christians, or quotes from Martin Luther King, Jr. when the targets are African Americans.

Billions of dollars have been scammed this way. As one state securities regulator who investigates such scams aptly quipped, "more money is stolen in the name of God than in any other way."[8] To mention a few incidents:

- $26 million was stolen from members of the Society of Friends.[9]

- $70 million from Seventh Day Adventists.[10]
- $200 million from Christian fundamentalists in Florida, Texas, Illinois, and Wisconsin.[11]
- $450 million from Lutheran ministers, Baptists, Jews, Mormons, Hispanic Catholics, and African-American faithful.[12]
- $600 million from Baptists.[13]

The power of these scams is bolstered when the mainstream press endorses the view that different demographic groups have different investment needs. Numerous books explain how women, blacks, and gays should invest, for example. While habits may differ among demographic groups (say, a certain lack of trust of banks among new immigrants from rural Mexico), the core principles of intelligent and psychologically disciplined investing are the same for everybody.[14]

Affinity psychology affects management's ability to exploit market inefficiencies, particularly through earnings and disclosure manipulation. As a Rite Aid shareholder, for example, you are a member of a self-selected group. You may drive out of your way to buy from its pharmacy, rather than a competitor's. This *esprit de corps* is healthy to an extent, but can produce a false sense of complacency that allows managers to deceive.

Earned trust is a cornerstone of intelligent investing, making unearned trust the gullible investor's downfall. Unearned trust arises from the commitment bias, the inclination to stay the course once you've taken a position. This often leads an investor, for example, to trust a stockbroker she has chosen, just because she has chosen him. Boiler rooms thrive on this phenomenon. Trust is crucial, but must be earned and sustained.

The commitment bias is the centerpiece of "advance fee fraud," where victims are told they will receive big payoffs if they take a series of steps. Each step leads to greater participation in the scam. Greater participation raises the stakes, turning the victims into conspirators against themselves. The most prevalent and successful version begins when an investor gets an unsolicited letter from a writer claiming to be a senior civil servant in a third-world country.[15]

The writer informs the target that he is seeking a reputable U.S. citizen to help get money out of his third-world country using the target's bank account to deposit funds. The amounts range from $10 to $60 million, and are typically described as "government overpay-ments" on some procurement contract.

Criminals get the names of potential victims from sources such as trade journals, professional directories, newspapers, and libraries. They cut a broad swath, sending mass mailings. No one is safe.

The letters refer to investigations of contracts awarded by prior governments, alleging that many contracts were overpaid. Rather than return the money to the government, which certainly does not deserve it and would invariably squander it, the writer wants to move the cash out of the country. He will pay the recipient a commission of, say, 30 percent for his services and the use of his bank account.

The crook's psychological goal is to get the target thinking that he is in on something lucrative, if a bit shady. Once the target is hooked on that belief, the scammer invents a series of increasingly expen-sive stumbling blocks, such as an official needs a bribe, advance money is needed to keep someone quiet or cooperative, taxes and attorneys fees must be paid, another contractor is cut in on the action, and so on.

The target is asked to pay. Each fee is presented as the last one, but a few more come before it is over, often months later. The tar-get becomes an investor in the scam. He has made a commitment and wants it to succeed.

Victims are almost always requested to travel to the third-world country or a bordering state to complete a transaction. Individuals are often told that a visa isn't necessary to enter the country. The con artists may then bribe airport officials to pass the victims through immigration and customs. The victim is told that the completed contracts will be submitted for approval to the country's central bank. Upon approval, the funds will be remitted to the victim's bank account.

The original letter, while appearing transparent and even ridicu-lous to most, is effective. Akin to the boiler-room broker's first and second calls, it lures the victims in for the kill that occurs when they are informed the deal is off unless they pony up a few hundred thousand dollars to keep it going.

The scammer's psychological bet is also that forged documents will impress the target, appealing to the authority bias just as with John Bennett and boiler-room brokers. Documents are on official-looking paper, bear imposing seals, and include letters of credit, contract payment schedules, and bank drafts. The paperwork's bulk of detail gets so tedious and boring, it looks legitimate at a glance and doesn't bear careful study.

Here is a sample first letter, stitched together from a rhapsodic parody written by an author declaring he had received numerous letters of this genre:[16]

> It is with my profound dignity that I write you, as well as a heart full of hope. I would here crave your distinguished indulgence to a deep sense of purpose, I knowing full well how you will feel as regards to receiving a mail from somebody you have not met or seen before. There is no need to fear; I got your address from a business directory which lends credence to my humble belief. I also assure you of my honesty and trustworthiness.
>
> My late father, Sir Etienn Momoh, the former General Manager of Sierra Leone Mining Cooperative, left behind $US32,800,000. This money was the income accrued from government overpayments and personal diamond business at the mining cooperative. It was placed, by my father's good friend the late head of state, in the Luxembourg branch of German Bank Warburg, before he was ruthlessly murdered at the onset of the Civil War. Luckily for us sir, the sum of $32.8 million has eluded the eyes of the new Nigerian authorities or their agents, in safe keeping.
>
> Our family needs assistance in removing these funds from the bank without alerting the Nigerian government of the day. Rather than to launder the money through Lebanon, as our brethren have done with some risk, we wish to remove the funds to the United States, with your good aid, should we be able to interest you in our design.
>
> Rest assured that this transaction is 100% risk free as all modalities have been put in place for a smooth and successful conclusion. However, should you be interested in assisting us, I will not hesitate to furnish you with the access code of the secret account at Warburg.
>
> To my point sir, all we need is your company name to start the process of changing the certificate of the deed of deposit in your favour to enable you to come over to claim the money. We pray God touches your heart to see the urgency and importance of this pending mutually beneficial transaction.
>
> Please, note that if you cannot help I will not wish to be insulted, just save your time and do not reply. I would go to await your swift response.

> Grace and peace and love from this part of the Atlantic to
> you.
>
> Compliments of the season,
>
> Barrister Momoh Sanni Momoh, Notary Public

Despite the sweet-violet prose, violence and threats of physical
harm are employed to apply pressure in the final stages of the
scheme. It is a serious offense in destination countries to enter without a valid visa. So the victim's illegal entry may be used by the
fraudsters as leverage to coerce the victim into releasing funds.

In June, 1995, an American was murdered in Lagos, Nigeria, while
pursuing one of these scams. Numerous other Americans are
reported missing in many countries. On top of the dead and the
missing, these scams have generated hundreds of millions of dollars
for their perps.

The Song of the Sirens

The adage says that if something seems too good to be true, it usually is. The insight is incomplete. If something seems too good to be
true, assume that it is.

Promising the impossible is the theme of financial scams. Belief in
divine intervention does not belong on the investment field. Miracles
do not occur there.

These sound like trite truths. All of us know these things. But why
do so many of us fall for them? It is like the Song of the Sirens from
Homer's *The Odyssey*:[17]

> Your next land-fall will be upon the Sirens: and these craze the
> wits of every mortal who gets so far. If a man come on them
> unwittingly and lend ear to their Siren-voices, he will never
> again behold wife and little ones rising to greet him with bright
> faces when he comes home from sea. The thrilling song of the
> Sirens will steal his life away, as they sit singing in their plashet
> between high banks of mouldering skeletons which flutter with
> the rags of skin rotting upon the bones. Wherefore sail right
> past them: and to achieve this successfully you must work bees-
> wax till it is plastic and therewith stop the ears of your com-
> panions so that they do not hear a sound. For your own part,

perhaps you wish to hear their singing? Then have yourself lashed hand and foot into your ship against the housing of the mast, with other bights of rope secured to the mast itself. Ensure also that if you order or implore your men to cast you loose, their sole response shall be to bind you tighter with cord upon cord. That way you may safely enjoy the Sirens' music.

Practical ways for investors to "tighten themselves to the mast" of disciplined investing are offered in the coming chapters.

10

Living With Emotions

Benjamin Franklin is known as a paragon of rationality, and yet even he did not perceive what American economists two centuries later saw. Instead, Franklin recognized the difficulty of unbiased decision making. He promulgated "prudential algebra," an exercise to help face the tough decisions of everyday life, commonly performed by sensible decision makers.[1]

Prudential algebra is as simple as making a list of the pros and cons of any complex decision, adding to both sides of the list over a course of several days. This solves the toughest challenge of complex decision making, which is that you can't usually hold all the pros and cons in your head at the same time. The result is uncertainty.

With a full list of the pros and cons, the trade-offs can literally be made by striking out offsetting items. You don't get an algebraically precise result, but you do produce a guard against an incautious step. Franklin's prudential algebra is about recognizing one's limits. It is an example of a class of strategies that can put you a long way ahead of your peers in investing, and maybe in life.[2]

In thinking about prudential decision making, it is useful to consider what 'rational" means in the context of investment decisions. The high priests of efficiency theory co-opted the phrase to describe emotionless monomaniacs bent on maximizing wealth, and operating in a world where we are always perfect. The Austrians offered the more intuitively appealing view that rationality is making reasonable choices among alternative ways to obtain goals, where we sometimes go astray.

Franklin's prudential argument suggests an affinity with the Austrians. Where there are alternatives, there are trade-offs (pros and cons). These must be weighed against one another. In investing, trade-offs include options that are financially strong but weak in peace of mind, and vice versa. When economics and emotions conflict, there is no metric to assess which choice is "rational."

American economists devoted to efficiency theory say that happiness moves in tandem with wealth. In this view, happiness is measured as utility, and utility rises with wealth. Yet as American wealth rose dramatically in the last half century, happiness did not, and according to some survey evidence, happiness actually declined—even before the national mood was altered by the attacks on New York and Washington of September 11, 2001.[3]

The Austrians had a better explanation for this. They recognized the limits of the slogan that money cannot buy happiness. It can. But only to a point. Wealth helps to satisfy needs. But the more wealth one has, the more needs are both satisfied and created. Needs rise along with wealth, leading people to demand more from life and of their money. The gulf between wealth and happiness is self-sustaining.

Striking the balance is key, and cognitive biases help do so. As strategies hardwired into our biological makeup, they carry obviously powerful benefits. To defend the status-quo bias, for example, constancy is more common than change. In defense of overconfidence, its characteristics often spell success in life, such as high self-esteem, optimism, and perseverance. The balance cognitive biases produce is better described as "satisficing" (combining the words satisfying and sufficing) rather than "maximizing" or "optimizing."[4] Instead of "perfect decision making," there is "good enough decision making," illustrating Voltaire's point that the perfect is the enemy of the good.

So investing is both a financial and an emotional enterprise. As much attention should be given to decisions that produce desired financial results as those enabling satisfactory emotional states. Cognitive biases can help produce the right trade-off between finance and steadiness. Yet they often yield decisions that are off balance, both in terms of money and peace of mind. Alertness is required.

While experts disagree about whether people can overcome their cognitive biases, the consensus is that becoming aware of biases can improve decision making. In the context of investment decisions, this means striking the right balance between getting high returns while juggling competing goals, such as safety of principal.

A passive step is to become aware of the biases. When you know that overconfidence may mislead you, you can control for it. There are more active steps as well, and this chapter concentrates on them. These steps can be divided into two classes. The first deals with why cognitive biases come up in the first place and how various habits of mind can prevent them from interfering with clear decision making. The second addresses how to deal with persistent biases and how various investment policies can offset their effects.

Habits of Mind

The economist and investor Irving Fisher emphasized the importance of "foresight, self-control, and habits."[5] For investing, the most important habits are those of the mind; they help promote foresight and self-control.

Objectivity

The strongest way to weaken our own biases is constantly to engage in objective thought. This calls for carefully considering all new investment ideas that pop into your head. Whether you have a tendency to embrace or dismiss new ideas, try also to do the opposite each time. Be especially alert when a new idea confirms a view you hold. When new ideas seem to contradict a prior belief, immediately write that down. Those are the easiest ideas to forget, but potentially the most useful in making the best investment decisions.[6]

Objective thought can be promoted by actively seeking out conflicting points of view. These can come from research materials, such as analyst and credit-rating-agency reports, or reliable books and news articles. Getting opinions from trustworthy and intelligent people likely to hold differing viewpoints promotes objectivity. Before consulting others, conduct your own analysis, and don't tell them anything about your review to skew their conclusions. To compile a wide range of perspectives, say you want to hear from a devil's advocate against your preliminary viewpoint.

Objective thought is essential for the successful investor to combat the pitfalls of social proof. It calls for forming your own opinions, considering the evidence apart from the fact that so many others have expressed a belief. Actively seek the views of those who do not share the popular view and who are not part of the social proof around you. Do not seek out only those opinions likely to conform with your own.

Be wary of unsolicited advice from friends and acquaintances, particularly about hot stock tips. It is tempting to attribute to them authority they lack. We all wish to believe our friends have desirable characteristics—they are smart, successful, and well meaning. Maybe they are, but these traits have nothing to do with whether (a) they have the acumen and discipline required to identify good businesses at reasonable prices or (b) they understand your investment needs or behavioral biases.

The availability bias—forming beliefs skewed by recency, vividness, or other faulty-memory tricks—can only be minimized by engaging in objective thought. This calls for making decisions based on external data prepared by others rather than based upon recollection and impressions. Look at a company's financial statements reporting research and development (R&D) spending over the past three years, rather than relying on splashy ads in business magazines boasting about commitment to innovation.

When you lack data, break problems into a series of parts and assess each piece, building backup. How large a market exists for this product? How many competitors are there? What portion of revenue is allocated to fixed costs? How much is available next year to continue to invest in R&D? Will that be enough to generate the competitive advantage necessary to turn innovation into profit?

Examine your assumptions. Are you considering this investment because you think this company's new product is going to be a smash hit or because you saw an ad for it? Or because the company's stock-market-price rise reported in today's newspapers was attributed to a new product announcement? After confirming that you formed your own opinion, retrace your thought process to double-check.

The single most fundamental safeguard to promoting objective decision making is to insist that outcomes be defined in advance. We hardly ever do this in daily life, and this habit may be just as well left out of daily life. But for investing and other high-stakes settings, having predefined rules is crucial.

Investors too often lack criteria for that discipline, especially not specifying ahead of time rules for deciding when to buy or sell a stock. You have trouble deciding what to do when new information points in different directions. It is easier not to be misguided if you establish standards ahead of time. (More on particular strategies below.)

Inversion

Retracing is an example of the powerful mental habit of working problems backwards. This is sometimes called inversion. One way to do this is to take your initial assumption and try to disprove it. This is the philosophy and methodology of science. Inversion, by making yourself your own devil's advocate, neutralizes many cognitive biases. If you believe satellite television will dominate in Poland within three years, do not confine your study to its proliferation in the United States, the United Kingdom, and Germany, but consider resistance in Ukraine, Belarus, and Latvia.

Elimination is another method of inversion. This calls for rejecting certain alternatives to whittle down the problem. Suppose you are going to select the 10 stocks from the Dow Jones Industrial Average of 30 that will outperform the Dow overall. It would be superior to start by a process of eliminating those least likely to do that. You vastly improve your odds of accurate selections.[7]

Inversion counters frame dependence, the skewing influence felt due to how a decision is defined. Decisions can be described in broad or narrow terms. A choice between two alternatives often yields different selections when the choice is framed differently, despite the alternatives having identical economics. Reconsider an example given in Chapter 2.

Suppose you must buy a car and save for a child's education. Is it better to pay cash for the car and build the savings account later, or is it better to borrow for the car and start the cash deposit today? Framed broadly, the question may be which approach will maximize the dollar amount in the account in 15 years. Framed narrowly, the question might be how to get that account rising, beginning this month.

When initial framing is done more narrowly, say account-funding this month, the tendency is to select choices that produce less profitable positions. Invert. Recast the choice in broader terms. The broad frame is what the account balance will be 15 years from now.

The opposite can occur. When the initial framing is broader, say final-account balance, it may sacrifice needed discipline. Invert, by recasting the choice in narrower terms. If a separate mental account for a child's collegiate savings enables a parent to allocate more to the account and leave it untouched than would be possible if those amounts were first applied to consumption (buying a car), there may be reason to stick with the shortcut—better to have something for college than nothing.

By inverting—from narrow to broad and from broad to narrow—you see a problem from multiple viewpoints. You consciously activate economic and psychological apparatus. With both involved, the decision will more likely satisfy both. Looking at the same problem in two or more ways improves the ability to combine the best economic answer with the best emotional one.

Redefining a problem to generate different viewpoints can reveal that what looks like a dilemma is actually a matter of indifference. This is especially so in investing. Investors possess a natural proclivity to prefer securities combining much hope with little fear and to perceive identical things differently when the risk-reward matrix is framed to suggest similarity.

Compare two securities: (A) has a 95-percent chance of paying $5000 and a 5-percent chance of paying $105,000, and (B) carries a 10-percent chance of paying $118,000 and a 90-percent chance of losing $2000. The choice is shown in Figure 10-1:

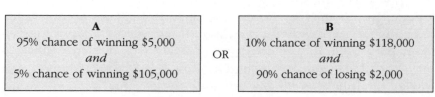

Figure 10-1   Identical alternatives framed differently.

At a glance, people prefer A. But a little inversion shows the choices have the identical expected value of $10,000. (Thus: .95 × $5000 + .05 × $105,000 = $10,000, and .10 × $118,000 −.90 × $2000 = $10,000).[8]

Inversion from narrow to broader frames helps realize the benefits of "statistical aggregation." Few single investment decisions will determine the fate of an entire fortune. Rather, a series of decisions seals one's financial future. By broadening your reference point, you become inclined to reduce amounts placed on high-risk alternatives and to increase amounts allocated to medium- and low-risk alternatives. It also helps resist ill-timed decisions by emphasizing that you will lose some and win others, and that what matters more is not each individual decision, but the aggregate over many years.

Sometimes called "global framing," another variation is to calculate aggregates rather than particulars. This applies to returns and to total states of net worth. Suppose the stocks you own, in aggregate, fell 10 percent in 2001. What happened to your bonds, real estate, collectibles such as paintings, intellectual property royalties, and so on? The year may have been better than you thought, and this knowledge may reduce emotions associated with the bad stock performance that otherwise may lead to unwise decisions.

Curiosity

Cultivate a curious mind by taking an interest in ideas. Talk and listen to people. Read widely and solve puzzles. Travel. Limit television viewing. The more mental activities one does, the more resources one has to debate new ideas, to check the continued validity of old ones, and generally to neutralize negative consequences of limited cognition.

Developing a sufficiently active mind to combat cognitive biases takes a lifetime, but it is never too late to start. A good starting point is invoking the Japanese saying that you never understand something until you ask five times, "why?"[9] To understand most problems requires getting to their cores, often requiring asking as many as five questions. For example:

Why did you buy General Electric Co. stock?
Because it is a good investment.

Why is it a good investment?
Because the value is greater than the price.
Why is the price-value relationship important?
Because it measures an investor's margin of safety.
Why is a margin of safety important?
Because it gives the greatest possible assurance of good returns.
Why are good returns important?
That is the whole point of smart investing.

A similar series of questions is usually required to reach any conclusion, from why are you reading this book, to why you did or did not go to graduate school. Asking yourself such questions when making important decisions activates the mind. (A friendly warning: overdoing it with other people can be positively annoying.)

Opportunity Cost

The concept of opportunity cost furnishes another powerful habit for investment decision making. It says that the price of choosing one course of action to the exclusion of others is the value of the highest-valued course not taken. Opportunity costs are intuitive; the mental habit of calculating them is already partly hardwired into the human brain in the form of the status-quo bias.

The opportunity-cost exercise calls for measuring prospective alternatives against opportunities, the clearest one of which is the status quo. Whether to sell a stock, for example, depends on to what use the proceeds will be put. Suppose they would buy a new stock. If the new stock is not at least as attractive as the one proposed for sale, plus an amount for transaction fees and taxes, there is no reason to sell it.

One reason for the hardwiring is that the status quo often is the best choice. The reason to be alert to the hardwiring is that when the status quo is the best choice, it is not so much because it is the status quo.

In deciding whether it is better than an alternative, ask whether you would choose the status quo if you were starting fresh. Examine the costs of switching. And do not fail to consider the possibility that the status quo, whatever it is, can improve.

Probabilities

You would be surprised at the low ability of even purportedly sophisticated investors to rank probabilities properly. Stockbrokers, for example, asked to predict future securities prices failed miserably in judging the probability that they guessed correctly, with a success rate of a mere 24 percent.[10]

Survey data repeatedly show that investors who did not live through adverse economic periods, ranging from the Great Depression to the market crash of 1987, weighed the likelihood of such economic adversities occurring far lower than either those who lived through them or than is statistically accurate.[11] One way to correct for this frightening result is to read histories of these events.

For those with an appetite for reading more than just histories of economic depression, take a tip from Statistics 101. Think of uncertain variables in terms of confidence intervals. Rather than relying solely on estimating the probability of some future event, also characterize your level of confidence in your estimate. Doing this vastly improves the quality of your judgments of probabilities.

Take an example of how this works. Estimate the level of the Dow Jones Industrial Average (the Dow) one month from today. Then pick a high level for the Dow so that you are 99-percent sure that the Dow a month from today will be lower than that. Also pick a low level for the Dow so that you are 99-percent sure that the Dow a month from today will be higher than that.[12]

Following the instructions, you state as having a 1-percent probability each that the Dow will exceed your high guess and fall short of your low guess. In statistical terms, you have set a 98-percent confidence interval of where the Dow will be. You may turn out to be correct (the actual Dow is within your confidence interval) or it may be higher (called a high surprise) or lower (called a low surprise).

People well-grounded in judgments of probability have a success rate of at least 98 percent (it is okay to be off 1 percent in each direction) but most people's success rate is more like 75 to 80 percent. This is why when someone tells you "I am 99-percent sure," you should translate that as "75 to 80 percent sure"—or less.

This is not an exercise in forecasting market levels. It is rather a study in predicting the likelihood that you correctly forecast them. This second-order prediction is about you and your ability, not about the market. You can perform this self-diagnosis using any future event. Practicing this technique can improve the accuracy of your probability judgments, limiting the effects of overconfidence and pattern seeking.[13]

As you practice, beware that people systematically overweigh low-probability events and underweigh high-probability ones. Compare the prospects of two horses: (A) believed to have a 50:1 chance of winning and a payoff of $200 if he wins, and (B) believed to have a 5:1 chance of winning and a payoff of $20 if he wins. Which do you prefer?

Most people favor (A) even though the expected value of each horse winning is identical ($4 in each case: for (B), $200/50 = $4 and for (2), $20/5 = $4). This shows that people overweigh the low probability that (A) will win and/or underweigh the high probability that (B) will win. In each case, their assessment is skewed by the much greater payoff figure on (A) compared to (B).

Take a couple of additional examples of people's tendency to put too little weight on high-probability events and too much weight on low-probability events.

- Which would you rather have, a 1-percent chance of winning $1000, or a $10 gift? Most people prefer the tiny chance of the big cash to the certainty of the small gift, even though the choices are identical (i.e., .01 × $1000 = $10). People overweight the remote possibility of getting the big payoff.

- You are given a 99-percent chance of winning $1000. How much would you pay to guarantee winning, $5, $10, $20, $30, or more? Most people are willing to pay more than $10 for the guaranteed payoff. This is the case even though it has a statistical value of $990 (i.e., .99 × $1000 = $990). Paying more than $10 to eliminate the 1-percent chance of not winning means people underweigh the near-certain outcome that odds of 99 percent give them.

The underreactions and overreactions seen in the stock market are examples of investors' ignoring the laws of probability. They may overpay for stocks with extremely low odds of paying off but have big payoffs if they actually hit (a problem running from IPOs to takeovers). They may punish a stock unduly and produce a price that is low compared to value when failing to see that the odds are very good that it will prosper. These are the characteristics of many bull and bear markets. Such phenomena are not limited to investors and markets but rather pervade human decision making. Becoming acquainted with illustrations of probability problems improves the ability to judge them. Let's take a couple more.

The Cab Accident.[14]   Suppose there are 100 cabs in town, 85 green and 15 blue; one hits a pedestrian and flees. A witness says the cab was blue. We test his ability to recall colors correctly and find he does so 80 percent of the time. Based on this, what is the probability that he was right in the case of the hit-and-run? Most people choose 80 percent, a superficially attractive benchmark, but the right answer is 40 percent, a deeper function of a "base rate."

Being right 80 percent of the time means if the witness were shown, for example, 85 green cabs, he'd say 68 were green (.80 × 85 = 68) and 17 were blue (85 − 68 = 17). If shown 15 blue cabs he'd say 12 were blue (.80 × 15 =12) and the others green. This makes a total of 29 he says were blue (17 + 12) but only 12 of those 29 were in fact blue (12 right, 17 wrong). So the probability that the witness is correct when he says a cab he saw was blue is 12/29, or about 40 percent.

Identity Games.[15]   A person is artistic by nature. Guess whether she is a sculptor or a secretary. Most people guess sculptor, though everyone knows there are more than 10 times as many secretaries as sculptors, so the more likely answer is by far secretary. A more complex variation on this example is the bank teller problem, where a story is told about a woman bank teller suggesting that she's a feminist. Then people are asked is she more likely to be (a) a bank teller or (b) a feminist bank teller. People leap to choose (b) on the strength of the feminist story imagery when this is clearly not the superior choice since (b) is a subset of (a)—and there are more bank tellers in the world than there are feminist bank tellers.

Patience

Take your time. The market doesn't act so quickly that you ought to act quickly too. Take time to absorb and assimilate information. Know what you are looking for. Wait until you've got enough information to make an intelligent, dispassionate decision. But remain decisive too—know when you must decide.

Patience helps ease negative effects of loss aversion. Investors lose money repeatedly by preferring steady returns to lumpy ones, even when lumpy ones produce greater long-term values. Everyone will agree that an average return over 5 years of 18 percent is superior to 15 percent. Yet many investors pay a premium to obtain a steady 15 percent in each of 5 years rather than 1 yielding an average of 18 percent but gyrating between 10 percent and 26 percent.

Investor Strategies

Investors spend substantial time preparing a wide variety of worksheets. They prepare statements concerning investment purposes. These range from home buying, tuition, retirement, and elder care, to bequests for heirs and philanthropic donations. They span from a few years to a lifetime. Investors prepare personal financial statements showing income and expenses along with assets and liabilities, and financial forecasts showing anticipated changes in these categories based on years until retirement, life expectancy, and so on. Investors use worksheets to define the investment universe and assess the investment outlook.

All these common steps are important to careful investment practice. Too often overlooked are a few crucial steps in the process underscored by the behavior studies we've been discussing. These call for developing an investor profile and an investment policy. Whether developed formally through written worksheets or less formally, those taking these steps hone their investment acumen. When coupled with the habits of mind just discussed, these techniques help conquer behavioral bias.

Value Function

All investors should develop a realistic sense of their degrees of loss aversion. If losses make you miserable, only conservative investments should be pursued (U.S. Treasury bills). If you can handle massive losses with unflinching emotional steadiness and are eager for like-sized gains, then a far more aggressive stance is justified (equity in Russian space-travel start-ups).

Loss aversion can be expressed in terms of your value function, the degree to which you differ in weighting gains versus losses. We have seen that, on average, investors weigh losses more heavily than gains by a factor of about 2.5. This is a good proxy for the basic value function.

A value function of 2.5 reflects someone comfortable with securities carrying profiles in between T-Bills and Russian equity. More loss-averse investors have higher value functions, feeling losses more acutely than gains by an order of 8, 9, 10, or higher. More risk-seeking investors have value functions closer to 1, with the real daredevils buying Russian equity having value functions of 1 or less.

What is your value function? How do you figure it out? It is not necessary to undergo any extensive diagnosis. A reasonable estimate based on a modest amount of reflection and objectivity will do. Review your past investment experience. Evaluate not only performance, but how performance affected your emotions.

Consider your best year or best stock pick ever. Suppose a 35-percent return one year, or a tripling of a stock well researched and bought and sold in a timely fashion. How gleeful were these successes? Then consider your worst year and worst stock pick ever. Suppose the exact opposite results. Oh, the misery. Gauge the degree to which the misery of the loss exceeded the glee from the win. Was it about 2.5 times worse? Or worse than that?

Form a judgment of your psychological profile based on this reflection, and use it to estimate your value function. Then, for the typical investor, add about 25 percent. On average, people say they are more daring than they really are, and say they are more willing to suffer losses than actual experience with losses indicates.

The value function is not consciously referred to in expressing disappointment with poor investment outcomes. But it captures the underlying feeling. It describes what people complain about when things don't turn out the way they had expected.

Likewise, the value function is not precisely what people refer to when they express concern about the risk of losing money on an investment. But it captures the degree of disappointment suffered when such a loss occurs. It is, in short, what people are usually worried about when thinking about the uncertainties of investment.

Objectives

Loss aversion should match investment objectives. The acutely loss averse should not declare their goal to be to strike it rich in investments this year. Nor should risk-seeking financial daredevils plunk all their resources into Treasury bills.

Taking this step will be familiar to anyone who has filled out a brokerage application designed to elicit these goals. When an investor opens a brokerage account, the broker is required to obtain information about the customer's financial and tax status and investment objectives, as well as other information that could be useful in making recommendations. On new-account forms, brokers fill out data such as age, income, and net worth, and check boxes to indicate various investment objectives. Forms vary by firm, but all get at the same range of alternatives, such as these:[16]

- Purchasing-power maintenance
- Principal preservation
- Income generation
- Capital growth
- Rapid capital appreciation

Also consider specific goals never listed on those forms, such as increasing the long-term intrinsic value of holdings, or to doubling the nominal value of holdings in five or six years. Or, more to the point: getting rich, staying rich, or never having to worry about money again.

Compare your value function with your stated investment objectives. Are they consistent? In many cases, the two must be reconciled through trade-offs. For example, an investor expressing "rapid appreciation" as her objective and also indicating a value function of six should reconsider at least one choice. Table 10-1 illustrates links between value functions, investment objectives, and suitable investment examples.

Note that value functions and investment objectives are affected by numerous variables that change during an investor's lifetime. These include age, years to retirement, uses of investment returns, liquidity and income needs, and tax status. Investors should periodically review their value functions and investment objectives in light of changes in these factors. Note also that most people should have portions of their assets in several asset classes, but only in classes at or above their value functions.

Table 10-1 Linking Risk Averseness, Objectives, and Suitability

	Value Function	Suitable Examples	Objectives
Conservative	9	Cash (Bank Accounts)	Eliminating all risk but inflation
	8	U.S. Treasury Bills	Preserving principal
	7	Home Ownership	Building equity + tax advantages
	6	Municipal Bonds	Safe income + nontaxable
	5	Investment-Grade Corporate Bonds	Income
	4	High-Yield Bonds	Income with risk
	3	*Blue-Chip Stocks*	*Appreciation + income*
	2	*Midcap Stocks*	*Growth + income*
	1	Commodities	Speculation/arbitrage
	0	IPOs + Venture Capital	Speculation
	−1	Emerging Markets	Total return
Aggressive	−2	Third-World Equity	Speculation/arbitrage

Steadiness

Designing an investment policy requires you to look at trading frequency. In broker-investor relations, excessive trading is unlawful. It is called churning. Brokers are not permitted to trade so as to generate trading revenue rather than to meet client objectives. Do-it-yourself investors should not permit themselves to hit turnover levels that brokers can't exceed.

A typical way to assess whether trading constitutes churning is by calculating the annual turnover rate. The simplest computation divides the total dollar amount of security purchases during the year by the average monthly balance of securities in the account. The standard benchmark is called the 2-4-6, with a rate over 2 indicating possible churning, over 4 presumed churning, and over 6 conclusively establishing churning.

This 2-4-6 rule should be correlated with your value function. The 2-4-6 rule is an average, appropriate for investors with a 2.5 value function. For more risk-tolerant investors, say those with a value function of 1, the 2-4-6 rule could be increased proportionately, say to 4-6-8. For the more risk averse, the churning points would be lower, perhaps as low as 1-2-3.

Acutely loss-averse investors—sporting say value functions of 10—yet carrying turnover rates over 2, ought to fire themselves as traders. (Take up gardening instead.) Investors turning over their own portfolios 8 times annually—and there are people in this category, at least during boom times—might consider investor rehab.

The turnover rate should be compared to investment objectives. An account intended to engage in short-term price arbitrage would ordinarily have a much higher turnover rate than one designed to preserve capital and accumulate income. The owner of that account should have a value function well below 2.5.

Selling Criteria

The value-function approach to understanding loss aversion can be extended to a broader lesson about dealing with one of the toughest investor questions: when to sell. One consequence of loss aversion is the tendency of investors to hold losers and sell winners.

To control for cognitively-induced buy/sell decisions requires setting selling criteria at the time of purchase, one of the smartest things investors can do. The mind-set in buying should be to select stocks that are least likely ever to trigger the criteria for selling. That is why the favorite holding period of top investors is forever.

Yet things can and do change for the worse. Hope is disappointed and a sale is called for. Defining what those changes are at the outset will aid analysis of when to sell, and make that analysis as free as possible of psychological bias when it is time to act.

Rules for selling should be set as part of an overall investment philosophy. Then tailor them to each investment. Sales should be made when the key criteria warranting the original purchase disappear. All factors relating significantly to the fundamental value of the business may be considered. When these deteriorate, it is time to go:[17]

- As to *operating climate*, this includes things that impair a franchise, such as—
  intensifying new competition
  disruptive technological onslaughts
  deregulation
- As to *financial performance*, this includes things that limit economic payoffs—

declining turnover rates for inventory and receivables accounts
shrunken profit margins
declining returns on equity, assets, and investment
earnings erosion

- As to *financial condition*, this includes things that erode fundamentals—
debt increased aggressively in relation to equity
debt used to pay for share repurchases
deterioration in liquidity ratios (current assets compared to current
liabilities)
impaired cash flows

- As to *management*, this includes things that produce mistrust or
incompetence—
change for the worse in behavior
change for the worse in identity
obfuscatory disclosure
exhibiting the winner's curse in acquisitions
giving dizzying executive compensation packages
reporting results using questionable accounting principles

Avoid selling when bad news arrives that is more likely to be temporary than permanent. A decline in profit margins in a single quarter should spark concern, but unless accompanied by additional red
flags, could be temporary. A management change for the worse
would justify a sale, as would actions indicating poor judgment, such
as using debt to buy back shares.

Sometimes you will be unsure whether a development justifies a
sale. Most often this will concern judgment calls as to whether a
development is permanent or temporary. Consider a major product
recall, for example. Permanent or temporary? Hard to tell. One strategy for dealing with the uncertainties is a policy to sell a portion of
one's holdings.

Notice that missing from the list of reasons to sell is price. Selling
due to price change is usually undesirable. Unless substantial and
precisely prescribed price changes occur, selling solely due to price
changes is the equivalent of an unforced error in tennis. Stock prices
jump around a lot. The observation that a stock slides down by 40
percent or gradually rises 40 percent may tell you something about
its value, but not everything.

The best thing to do with the price you paid for a stock is forget it. This will help avoid decisions to sell solely to convert a paper loss into a tax-savings event, or a paper gain into an opportunity for self-congratulations. A stock's price history will merely produce a psychological anchor inclined to trick you.

Forgetting your purchase price will help avoid "break-evenitis," the propensity to believe that losing stocks will eventually recover. Do not expect to break even on a stock that has plummeted in price. Do not even pay attention to your price. Look at its fundamentals. If they are intact, hold, whatever you paid; if they are in tatters, take your lumps, whatever they are.

In the case of a preset policy to sell when price reaches a certain high level, it is probably prudent to follow the same mixed strategy adhered to when one is unsure whether a development is permanent or temporary: sell some, but not all. This formula also should be preset. It might provide that when a company is overpriced by 50 percent to 100 percent or more, you will sell 1/4 to 1/3 or more of holdings.

Selling for nonfundamental reasons is otherwise unjustified. The sole exception is to meet extraordinary needs, such as major medical or similar contingencies. But the stock market is not the ideal place to put resources that may be needed for such events. Funds for these realities should be in strictly safe storage, such as bank accounts and T-bills.

A final price point concerns general market price levels. If the general level of stock prices in the market has swelled to levels that begin to appear to you to be unsustainable, begin to allow price to enter your equation. But again, be sure to set rules for this kind of selling at the time of purchase. The policy might echo the venerable advice of top investors to accumulate during busts and lighten up during booms or, as Lord Rothschild put it, "Buy on the cannons, sell on the trumpets."

That clarion call suggests a final no-no: avoid selling solely to give yourself something to do. This is giving into psychological-control needs. Acting on that impulse will yield little more than the illusion of control. A desire for action is the worst reason to sell a stock (or buy one). If you have not made a trade in three months, it may be because you have not been justified in doing so.

Post Mortems

Take a lesson from those managers who recognize they are susceptible to the winner's curse in acquisitions: conduct a post mortem on
all your stock acquisitions a year after you buy them. Compare all
your purchases and sales at the end of every year, and give yourself
objective feedback based on your original analysis and expectations.
Modify your behavior accordingly. At this time, also review your
requirements to buy and your rules of sale. This annual checkup is
a good time to reassess your value function and investment objectives as well, making sure they are in sync with investment selections. Resist revising any of these rules in the middle of a decision.

Before closing this discussion of disciplined investment decision
making, a word on behalf of undisciplined decision making. Don't
impose too much discipline on creative endeavors. Generating lists
of possibilities, for example, is an exercise more likely to be fruitful
when unconstrained by mental discipline. Selecting actual courses of
action from lists of possibilities, on the other hand, is where a disciplined mind is essential.

Take an interesting example of a stock picking method based on
how recognizable corporate names are to ordinary people—an
exquisite exploitation of the availability bias. Researchers asked
finance graduate students at the Universities of Chicago and Munich
as well as randomly selected nonprofessionals in those cities to indicate which companies they recognized from those listed on the New
York and several German stock exchanges.

Eight possible company lists could be made from these surveys
(for example, stocks most and least recognized by German nonprofessionals, those most and least recognized by U.S. professionals,
and so on). The researchers created hypothetical portfolios consisting of each of these groups of stocks, and tracked the respective per-
formances.

The result? German stocks most recognized by U.S. nonprofessionals outperformed the market and all other portfolios. This result
has an intuitive appeal. Companies with the greatest penetration in
the consciousness of the untutored are most likely to enjoy that penetration carried over to their product, supply, labor, and stock markets as well.[18]

Picking stocks based on surveys such as this would certainly be silly. But the results show a creative way to suggest the powerful and pervasive role psychology plays in business and investment. And psychology will always play a role, with cognitive biases influencing the way we make decisions. In many cases that is terribly useful, saving lots of time and headache. But to avoid allowing cognitive biases to lead to inferior results, the strategies and habits of mind discussed in this chapter can be harnessed to channel them to your further benefit.

11

Investor Evolution

Lives were short in hunter-gatherer societies where our ancestral brains were incubated and developed for more than 99 percent of our species' time on earth. Lives were always in danger. Planning for a child's education and retirement was simply not done.

Nowadays, the opposite is the case. Charles Darwin, a follower of Franklin's prudential algebra,[1] articulated evolutionary biology. This discipline explains how species use adaptation to meet the demands of their environment, as by evolving thumbs to grip objects. He paved the way to social Darwinism, the study of how humans adapt to changing circumstances through modifying behavior. A version of this phenomenon may characterize evolution in investor psychology.

Investing equivalents of biological thumbs are long-term value investors and, a distant second, investment clubs. In this view, *hyper-discounting*—the extreme preference for cash today rather than more cash tomorrow—is a strategy left over from times of short life spans. Long-term, value-oriented investors have left such prejudices behind.

Every man for himself—the *modus operandi* of many active traders going it alone at a computer screen—is left over from the spear-hunting hunter catching his evening meal. It is ignored by investors who, before acting, consult others.

As with many evolutionary adaptations, not everyone is wired with these perspectives. In fact, while numerous in absolute terms, there remain relatively few practicing disciples of long-term value investing, and relatively few who seriously discuss investment questions with others. But as with such evolution, it is possible to develop the ability. This chapter tells how.

First, let's look at how long-term value investing and consultation are evolved strategies. Consider an oversimplified but still useful account of what can be called the *triune brain*—a term to distinguish three sorts of brain power that humans deploy.

The three major types of brain operation reflect instinct, feeling, and reason. These brain aptitudes are layered and cumulative rather than discrete or mutually exclusive—they are more or less present in various settings. While they are also far more complex than the simple labels suggest, the three layers can be linked to types of market participants who may be particularly susceptible to some specific cognitive biases.[2]

Active traders, say at the trading desks of major investment banks or day traders at home computers, evince major use of instinct. They thrive on action and exercise reflexive, visceral decision-making capabilities. These gut actors, concerned mostly with quickness and short-term results, and usually acting alone, are probably most susceptible to the cognitive biases involving shortcuts and rules of thumb (the availability and pattern-seeking biases in particular).

Medium-term investors, say private, self-reliant individuals or fund managers, demonstrate significant use of the intermediate cranial apparatus, one revolving about judgment, feeling, and something more emotional. These folks follow their hearts, are concerned above all with avoiding cognitive dissonance (the clash between believing one is correct while perceiving evidence of error), and thus may experience greatest susceptibility to mental accounting (putting things in categories) and frame dependence (putting form over substance). They occasionally consult others on investment decisions, but not routinely.

Long-term investors, the famous fundamental investors of the world, emphasize reason, analysis, and thought. This involves regularly consulting others, whether a partner or group of advisors. Given their long-term view, these more cerebrally oriented investors avoid taking shortcuts and defeat biases of mental accounting and frame dependence. Their biggest psychological concerns relate to the need for control, and experiencing greater loss aversion than is ideal.

This typology suggests an evolutionary hierarchy of investors. Evidence shows that many cognitive biases are stronger in people who rely on instinct more than intellect.[3] It also suggests that the more one uses all cranial layers—acting from the head, the heart, and the gut in various measures—the greater the likelihood of achieving the ideal balance between financial outcomes and emotional and visceral contentment. This is common sense.

Another way to claim the superiority of long-term, value-oriented investing is to consider how many more adaptive strategies a trader must employ as compared to a long-term investor in order to beat cognitive biases. All investors must exercise prudent habits of mind and should follow the investment strategies discussed in the previous chapter.

These included admonitions to be objective, invert, cultivate a curious mind, consider opportunity cost, and improve probability calibration. These are precisely the sorts of traits that characterize successful long-term investors and that short-horizon traders would have to spend substantial time and effort to develop.

Likewise, computing value functions, defining investment objectives, examining trading frequency, and defining selling criteria are matters which, by temperament, long-term investors intuitively grasp. The shorter-term trader must think these things through from the outset.

In addition, the short-term trader must determine a range of other things, including most broadly how to measure success. For the long-term investor this is simple: maximizing the long-term value of investment—5, 10, and 15 years hence—while sleeping at night. For the trader, there is a whole range of possibilities, measured down to pennies of gains in minutes at a time and a lot of anxiety at night.

Long-term value investing, or investment with consultation, is the most evolved in the Darwinian process of investor philosophy and psychology. Since the attributes of long-term, value-oriented investing address the characteristics of cognitive biases, the commonsense case is strong to pursue this investment philosophy.

Long-Term Value

If forced to distill the principles of long-term, value-oriented investing into a top-10 list, it would look like this, drawing directly on principles articulated by Benjamin Graham and Warren Buffett:[4]

- *Don't be the patsy.* If you cannot invest with disciplined intelligence, the best way to own stocks is through an index fund that charges minimal fees. Those doing so will beat the net results (after fees and expenses) enjoyed by the great majority of investment professionals. As they say in poker, "If you've been in the game 30 minutes and you don't know who the patsy is, *you're* the patsy."

- *Operate as a business analyst.* Do not pay attention to daily excitement in the market, macroeconomic forecasts, or securities movements. Concentrate on evaluating businesses.

- *Look for a big moat.* The "moat" is a metaphor for a protective belt surrounding a business that will secure favorable long-term prospects, those whose earnings are virtually certain to be materially higher 5 and 10 years later.

- *Exploit Mr. Market.* Market prices gyrate around business value, much as a manic-depressive swings from euphoria to gloom when things are neither that good nor that bad. The market gives a price, which is what you pay, while the business gives value, and that is what you own. Take advantage of market mispricings, but don't let them take advantage of you.

- *Buy at a reasonable price.* Bargain hunting can lead to purchases that don't give long-lasting value; buying at frenzied prices results in purchases that give no value. Still it is better to buy a great business at a fair price than a fair business at a great price.

- *Insist on a margin of safety.* The difference between the price you pay and the value you get is the margin of safety. The thicker, the better.

- *Know your limits.* Avoid investment targets that are outside your circle of competence. You don't have to be an expert on every company, or even many—only those within your circle of competence. A large circle is not necessarily better; knowing its boundaries, however, is vital.

- *Invest with "sons-in-law."* Invest only with people you like, trust and admire—men you'd be happy to have your daughter marry, or women you'd be happy to have your son marry.

- *Only a few will meet these standards.* When you see one, buy a meaningful amount of its stock. Don't worry so much about diversification among stock holdings, so long as your assets are diversified in other ways, as among home equity, bank savings, and other asset classes. If you find one outstanding business, that is better than a dozen mediocre ones.

- *Avoid gin-rummy behavior.* This metaphor from the card game cautions against the short-term, quick-flipping strategy, akin to the action of picking and discarding cards each turn in the game. It is the opposite of possibly the most foolish of the Wall Street maxims: "You can't go broke taking a profit." Imagine as a stockholder that you own the business and hold the investment as you would if you owned and ran the whole thing. If you aren't willing to own a stock for 10 years, don't even think about owning it for 10 minutes.

These are the core tenets of a long-term, value-oriented investment philosophy. Notice how many of them directly combat cognitive bias. Consider these implications:

- Overconfidence is minimized by most of them, particularly by heeding the tenets to avoid being the patsy, to insist on a margin of safety and a big moat, and to know your limits.
- Excessive loss aversion is controlled by avoiding gin-rummy behavior that leads to skittishness in selling and buying.
- Frame dependence is minimized by exploiting Mr. Market's price-value differences, and the credo to buy at a reasonable price.
- Availability bias and pattern seeking are addressed by recognizing that few businesses meet the rigorous tests, and by avoiding gin-rummy behavior that requires a willingness to own stocks for 10 years.

The list goes on, though these investing principles were not developed specifically to defeat cognitive bias, but to help generate solid, long-term results with reasonable peace of mind. It is striking how the two dovetail. Let's look at each one. We'll consider them in reverse order, as they tend to build on each other in that direction.

Avoid Gin-Rummy Behavior. The goals of economic wealth maximization, emotional happiness, and psychological steadiness align over time. To sleep at night and build a fortune, look down the long road.

You can see a simple illustration of this in any random game. Take an illustration we already saw from coin flipping. If you just flip four to eight times you may end up with all heads in a row or all tails in a row. There is likely to be clumping you could not have predicted with any certainty. But if you extend that game out to hundreds and thousands of flips, there is a high degree of certainty that you will see a very nearly even (maybe exactly even) share of heads and tails.

It is the same in investing. If you make trades daily and examine your performance daily, you create a skewed picture. You see the sharp gyrations at such close resolution that you are likely to become so jittery that you make lots of decisions—draws and discards—the net of which will be bad financially, psychologically, and emotionally.

Slow things down. Trade less often. Check your performance less frequently, say monthly or annually, and you will see far less jagged spiking. You will be cooler, calmer, and you'll collect more money.

Evidence firmly supports the advice against engaging in gin-rummy behavior. Those who frequently check portfolio balances and share prices trade more, and yet have a greater aversion to loss than those who do so more leisurely. Take a look again at the charts included in Figure 2-3 (Chapter 2) to see why. Studies show that investors who check prices less frequently produce better investment results.[5] They also sleep better at night.

The lesson to cool activity down should be heeded by institutional as well as individual investors. As a couple of behavioral-finance pioneers note: "Overconfidence explains why portfolio managers trade so much, why pension funds hire active equity managers, and why even financial economists often hold actively managed portfolios—they all think they can pick winners."[6]

Only a Few Will Meet These Standards. Making fewer decisions will also result from realizing that only a few investment prospects examined will meet the standards set forth in this top-10 list. Mistakes are made at the time of decision; the regret arrives later. Regret produced by uncertainty differs depending on whether a decision resulted in an affirmative action ("commission") or a choice of not taking some action one had considered ("omission").

Most people experience greater regret due to errors of commission than of omission. To see this, suppose that on January 1 four years ago, Holder owned 1000 shares of Procter & Gamble (P&G), and Trader owned 1000 shares of Gillette. Two years ago, Trader decided to sell her Gillette and buy P&G, and Holder considered selling his P&G and buying Gillette but ultimately decided not to.

After that, Gillette started performing very well compared to P&G, so if Trader had not switched she'd be better off by $10,000, and if Holder had switched he'd be better off by $10,000. In effect, these two are in the same position, yet most people say Trader is likely to feel more regret.

There are two reasons, both variations on the availability bias. The broader one is that Trader made a more vivid form of what looks like a mistake—a commission consisting of a decision and an affirmative action Holder made the weaker sin of omission, consisting of a decision. to be sure, but not any other affirmative action. The second reason is the difference between outright losses and opportunity cost. Outright losses are more immediate, and thus felt more acutely than missed opportunities.[7]

The fewer decisions of commitment one makes, the fewer pangs of regret one feels. This correlation supports the tenet that only a few businesses will satisfy a long-term, value-oriented investor's purchase standards. And it is a good thing. If only a few investment opportunities meet the criteria, then only a few commitments will be made. Focus on the feelings that will arise from those commitments; avoid commitments unless the odds are high that you will feel no regret. The sins of omission are far less painful to face.

Invest with Sons-in-Law.   This is a top-10 investing tenet due to the importance of trust in investing. Take a lesson from the banking business, which has always been built on relationships. Bankers lend not on the strength of collateral alone, but on the trustworthiness of the borrower. Credit checks are a way to confirm trust. Collateral is a way to deal with problems when trust proves misplaced. It is ultimately all about trust, as any banker will tell you.

As an investor, you supply capital the same way bankers do. This is true even in cases where stock is acquired on the open market. The funds may be paid to another investor but the purchase benefits the issuer. And your role as a shareholder becomes that of a residual claimant on the issuer. Managers of that issuer are stewards of your capital. As such, they must earn and sustain your trust.

Adopting this view presupposes a long-term, value-oriented investment philosophy. Gin-rummy traders—people who hold stocks for a day, week, or month—put their trust in the greater fools, those people who will be stupid enough to buy their stocks at higher prices within that short time. Gin-rummy traders have no concern with managerial acumen or owner fidelity, for they barely give managers an operating cycle to do anything.

Know Your Limits. Part of the solution to cognitive biases is to improve your knowledge of your shortcomings. This is central to combating overconfidence. Legendary IBM chief Thomas J. Watson, Sr. said, "I'm smart in spots—but I stay around those spots." So stay clear of spots you know little about.

A student once asked famed investor Charles Munger what had gone wrong at the Apple Computer Co. Munger, who is not known as a techie, announced that he would copy the answer given by tech-savvy GE CEO Jack Welch to the same question: I don't know.

Underscoring this lesson to admit when you don't know something, Munger gave an example from biology. When a bee finds nectar, it is genetically wired to return to the hive and do a dance that indicates which direction to go to find the nectar and how far. A biologist performed an experiment in which he placed the nectar above the hive, where it never was. The bee found it, returned to the hive, and not being wired to give the upward direction, did some crazy dance that no bee understood. The bees went hungry. If the bee were Welch or Munger, it would have done no dance.[8]

When you don't know, don't dance. Remember this too: you will know only a tiny fraction of all there is to know. As noted financial columnist Jason Zweig put it after interviewing pioneering behavioral psychologist Daniel Kahneman, "By teaching me the paradox that the most powerful thing I can learn is how little I can ever possibly know, Danny Kahneman has set me free."[9]

One neglected piece of knowledge that smart investors have is the ability to distinguish between choices and consequences. People commonly judge the quality of a decision by how things turned out rather than by how sensible the decision was, given the probabilities when the decision was made.

You can buy shares of Starbucks based on an intelligent valuation exercise yielding a thick margin of safety the day before the Surgeon General announces a surprise decision banning coffee sales. Smart decision, bad consequence.

Or you can buy an overpriced high flyer in a hyped IPO and turn around and sell it six months later when you need the cash and the market is treating it like royalty. Stupid decision, good consequence.

Insist on a Margin of Safety.   Sticking to a margin of safety counters overconfidence. The concept of a "value-oriented" investor means an investor who understands that price is different from value, and focuses on the gap between the two. This is necessary to enable the purchase of a stock at a price sufficiently below value to give an investor a margin of safety. That margin of safety is critical because you may be wrong. Things may turn out worse than your best guess indicated.

The opposite of the cautious, value-oriented, long-term investor is the trader focused on price. Whereas intelligent investors are aware of the price-value difference and focus on value first, traders are preoccupied with price. This demonstrates a version of the availability bias called anchoring. It arises in finance and related negotiations routinely. It is why people often buy a relatively expensive model of an item when they are first shown an even pricier one, and why sales tags display the suggested retail price, and so on (as discussed in Chapter 2).

A simple experiment illustrates. Two groups of accountants are asked about the incidence of fraud at major companies, one group whether they thought more than 10 of 2000 companies had the problem, and the other whether more than 200 of 2000 had it. Not surprisingly, but certainly influenced by the suggested frequencies (10 versus 200), the latter group responded with significantly higher guesses than the former.[10]

Buy at a Reasonable Price.   Prices run along a range from outrageously high and low at the extremes, with a reasonable range somewhere in between. Recognizing this enables thinking about a deal in terms of multiple reference points, across that range. Thinking this way reduces the risk of anchoring based on prevailing price, an analyst's target price, your purchase price, and other psychological anchors. It also helps improve estimates of probabilities. Reasonable prices are far more likely to be found than bargain prices. Go for solid deals, not necessarily bargains.

Exploit Mr. Market.   If you take one thing from this book, it should be this: know that others suffer from bias that leads to substantial mispricing. Get your biases under control, and take advantage of times when the biases of others skew pricing to your advantage. There are greater fools, and lesser ones.

Big Moat.   Search for businesses with strong economic characteristics that enable them to fend off competition, meet technological challenges, raise prices without reducing market share, maintain high returns on equity with little use of debt (in short, the opposite of all the points suggested under selling criteria in the last chapter). This means that you can suffer from overconfidence and still succeed in making successful investment choices.

Business Analyst.   Regret is amplified by *hindsight bias*. It is a tendency to think that you would have known events were coming before they occurred, if you had only been on the scene or paying more attention.[11] "I should have known," is a common lament.

In financial markets, the hindsight bias regularly appears in "market-wraps." These are financial news shows discussing the market after it closes. They report why the market moved the way it did earlier in the day or the day before.

Consider such commentary as the "market moved sideways because investors were skittish about third-quarter earnings reports of technology companies." It suggests, dubiously, that the speaker could gather such information. Worse, it suggests that the market action could have been predicted—that a survey rather than market trading, for example, would have produced the same result showing investor skittishness over earnings. But if the market could have been predicted in that way, then lots of people would have acted differently, and the actual market behavior that day would have differed as a result.[12]

In contrast, consider this headline from *The New York Times*: "Investors Jolted as Stocks Tumble Sharply After 3 Days."[13] The story reports on what market participants were saying, implausibly, happened in the market:

> It was easy for analysts and strategists to explain what happened yesterday, as they once again trotted out the concerns about declining corporate earnings and worries that the end of the downturn in both the economy and profits is not in sight....

What was more difficult for analysts to explain was why the market went up so much in the previous days, given the negative background on earnings.

The reason inconsistencies like this are so hard to explain—and they happen frequently—is that storytellers impute rationality to "the market," as if everyone has the same information and responds to it accurately. Neither point is likely. Lots of information is contradictory, not everyone has it, some disbelieve it, and all interpret it differently. Markets move in weird ways that simply cannot be explained. But when a reporter at a major news organization calls a market observer or "source" seeking an explanation about today's market, the temptation is to give an opinion.

One study examined the relationship between news knowledge and investment success.[14] Researchers divided a group in half, giving to both halves sets of stock-price data and to one news reports purporting to explain why the prices moved as they did. In the ensuing stock-pricing exercise, the half with price data exclusively outperformed the group given price data plus news accounts.

Stock-price jumps accompanied by reasonable-sounding explanations lead people to perceive a trend. If the news data is not an accurate reflection of why prices moved, chance decisions are likely to be superior. Obviously, this is not to suggest putting one's head in the sand, but rather to treat explanations for market action with skepticism. Again, acting as a business analyst is far superior for clear thinking than acting as a market analyst.

Investors operating as business analysts are insulated from the contagion of hindsight bias. Market action need not concern them. Stories about market action should concern them even less. The media's daily diet of market wraps is safely left for gin-rummy players chasing, and eventually dumping, stocks they hear about. Business analysts can sit back and enjoy the entertainment.

Don't Be the Patsy. Stock picking using the long-term fundamental philosophy is the most advanced technique available to overcome sentiment. For those who recognize that the game is too high risk for them to play, attractive alternatives are available.

Index funds are mutual funds whose managers allocate capital not by selecting particular stocks, but by buying all stocks of a particular description, usually all stocks comprising a broad segment of the market as indexed by some benchmarking firm, such as Standard & Poor's (keepers of the popular S&P 500 index of America's most noted companies). The first index funds were created by Wells Fargo bank in the early 1970s and were popularized a few years later by investment legend Jack Bogle, recently retired head of The Vanguard Group of funds.

These managers choose which of the many possible indexes to invest in, ranging from the S&P 500 (larger companies), to the Russell 2000 (smaller companies), Wilshire 5000 (a mix of a majority of all companies), and others in between. Under relentless competition for capital to invest, index-fund managers often boast that their index outperforms the next guy's index. People opting for index funds know their limits and realize they can't outperform the market, whether due to lack of time, insight, money, or what have you.

Nonindex mutual funds are investment vehicles whose managers pick stocks (and sometimes bonds or other instruments). Some of these are closed-ended, meaning to buy into one you have to buy from an existing shareholder, usually in an open-market-exchange transaction. More numerous are open-ended funds, where anyone can buy in or cash out at any time directly through the fund.

Either type gives an investor professional management and the opportunity to diversify widely in a variety of investments. Neither of these features should put one off, for sometimes managers earn their fees and gain advantage from diversification by averaging out bad picks. In many cases, however, the fees are unjustified by performance.

Dividend reinvestment plans (DRIPs) are useful to impose self-discipline for those otherwise easily distracted from adding principal to their investment resources. These are accounts offered directly by stock-issuing corporations to individual investors. Dividends paid on account shares are automatically reinvested when declared, rather than sent to the holder. There are usually no or low sales commissions.

For regular dividend-paying companies, this can mean steady additions to equity securities. DRIPs also typically offer holders the chance to have funds automatically taken from bank accounts at designated times to buy additional shares. Investors can set dates to follow paydays, creating additional discipline that yields substantial sums.

Another benefit of the steadiness of DRIP funding is that dollars are invested at regular intervals, when price is below value, and when above. If maintained over a long period, these discrepancies result in owning shares purchased at an average cost lower than the average of the prices on each purchase date.[15] Hence the term, "dollar cost averaging."

DRIPs and dollar cost averaging reduce the number of decisions an investor must make. They are also attractive because few stocks meet properly defined investment criteria. Assume that only a few need to meet your requirements. Establish a DRIP with these and let things ride through roller-coaster market pricing, without the need to decide whether to buy this month. Monitor the fundamentals of the businesses, and only take action to stop buying or to sell when your preset fundamental factors have deteriorated to preset levels.

Avoid sector funds.[16] These are funds that accumulate the stock of companies in a particular industry, usually one with current sizzle. Sector funds are among the hottest things on Wall Street other than July's mercury, and are therefore the most dangerous.

A brief look at history tells the story, starting with the recent history of tech-sector funds in the late 1990s. They posted impressive returns, about 54 percent in 1998, 137 percent in 1999, and 19 percent in 2000. They grew phenomenally, boasting about $60 billion by late 1999, but also grew late, sprouting to $167 billion at the market's March 2000 peak. In the wake of the sector sell-off, losses mounted to nearly 50 percent by mid-2001.

It happens every time. Witness tech sector funds of the early 1980s that nearly doubled from 1982 to 1983, and then plummeted by a quarter in the next year. Or look at health-care and biotech-sector funds in 1991, running out of the gate at breakneck return pace of nearly 54 percent, only to collapse and lag the market average the next two years. Utility-sector funds burst onto the scene in 1993 with the same swing-set story, followed by real-estate funds, up in 1996–1997, down in 1998–1999. Of late, look at health-care and financial-service sector funds.

Sector funds constitute more than 7 percent of stock-fund assets held by small investors. Fees are about 1.7 percent, slightly above average for ordinary mutual funds. Shareholder-friendly funds try to steer all but the most daring away, imposing redemption fees on

quick-flips, establishing high minimum-investment levels, and closing funds to new investors. Take the hint.

The Pleasure of Company

If long-term, value-oriented investing is the high point of investor
evolution, second is group investment decision making. Everyone
knows the old joke that a camel is a horse designed by a committee,
and group decision has inherent problems. But evidence strongly
suggests that properly executed group decision making can help
eliminate cognitive biases that plague individual group members.

The rapid growth in the popularity of investment clubs during the
past few decades suggests that people have discovered this. For that
matter, many long-term, value-oriented investors regularly consult
others before acting, serving much the same purpose as good investment clubs. Many noted investors rely on noted right-hand people
for guidance and reality checks to keep sentiment out of investment
analysis. Warren Buffett and Charlie Munger are perhaps the most
famous.

The most well-known investment club is undoubtedly the
Beardstown Ladies. Formally known as the Beardstown Business
and Professional Women's Investment Club of Beardstown, Illinois,
this group of 16 retirees formed an investment club in 1981.[17] They
gained national attention a decade later when the club announced
10-year-average annual investment returns of a Buffett-Munger-like
23.4 percent. That whopping return not only outdid the S&P 500, but
tripled the average returns obtained by professional money managers during the same period.

The ladies were the talk of Wall Street. Their investment savvy
spread to television, then to a videotape called *Cookin' Up Profits on
Wall Street: A Guide to Common Sense Investing*. The Beardstown
Ladies' story was turned into a ghost-written book called *The
Beardstown Ladies' Common-Sense Investment Guide: How We Beat
the Stock Market, and How You Can, Too*. Four other books and
another video followed, all with folksy titles (such as *The
Beardstown Ladies' Stitch-in-Time Guide to Growing Your Nest Egg*).

Displayed prominently on the covers and other packaging of
these products were statements such as "23.4 percent Annual
Return," "59.5 percent return in 1991," "find the secret recipe for suc-

cess," and "learn how to outperform mutual funds and professional money managers 3 to 1." Peter Pans around the country scooped up these books, one of which sold nearly a million copies and spent three months atop of *The New York Times* best-seller list.

Trouble was, the investment club's actual average rate of return during the decade was 9.1 percent, a far cry from Buffett-like returns, the S&P 500, or many pros. The difference arose because when the club computed returns on investment, it counted member dues as part of the gain. That is like counting as returns on your investment additional monthly investments you make to your DRIP, 401(k), or other account. The ladies should have valued the club's investment account by deducting dues. (The phrase from the book title, "Cookin' Up Profits," gave new meaning to the phrase, "cookin' the books.")

Word of this egregious overstatement emerged gradually. On the copyright page of the first best-seller's paperback reprint, there appeared this misleading disclosure:

> NOTE: Investment clubs commonly compute their annual 'return' by calculating the increase in their total club balance over a period of time. Since this increase includes the dues that the members pay regularly, this 'return' may be different from the return that might be calculated for a mutual fund or a bank. Since the regular contributions are an important part of the club philosophy, the Ladies' returns described in this book are based on this common calculation.

This disclosure does not accurately describe how investment clubs calculate returns.[18] They calculate returns just like everyone else. The method of including dues is simply ridiculous. This is an admission that the trumpeted returns were not actually achieved. But not even this disclaimer accompanied other editions of the books or other products.

How could everyone have missed the Ladies' unorthodox computation of returns? It appears to be a case of social proof. One of the club's founding members, a retired bank trust officer, takes the blame for the calculation error. Other club members deferred to her authority, both as club treasurer and as a former banking employee. Among the public, book sales proved worth the weight in returns, and the crowds clamored for more. The herd of Beardstown devotees ran straight off the social cliff.

It would be a mistake to conclude from the Beardstown Ladies, experience that investment clubs do not help groups overcome the cognitive biases of individuals. The broader evidence suggests investment clubs outperform market averages and many pros.

The leading force in investment clubs is the National Association of Investors Corporation (NAIC). This nonprofit group was founded in Detroit in 1951 by representatives of four investment clubs, one of which is still active. Its membership includes nearly 40,000 clubs aggregating more than 500,000 members. Ten percent of the clubs are at least 25 years old.[19]

NAIC's investment philosophy is decidedly long term and value oriented. Its recommended investment objective is to double money every five years. That requires an average 14.9 percent compounded annual growth rate. To get such hefty returns, NAIC emphasizes that short-term trading doesn't work.[20] Rather, successful investment clubs adhere to the conservative philosophy that wealth building is a slow process, particularly in beginning years.[21] Conservatism pays off. The NAIC's portfolio index, called the NAIC Top 100, regularly outperforms the S&P 500.

The NAIC is primarily a volunteer organization created to help investors through a wide range of educational materials, including books, magazines, software, and stock-selection guidelines. Apart from offering fundamental guidelines designed to identify conservative investments, the NAIC champions learning that comes from group interaction, the give and take, and double–checking of analysis. Doing investment analysis as a group may help to spot occasions when investors fail to embrace lessons reviewed earlier.

The superiority of group decision making is best demonstrated in decisions used to solve abstract and complex problems, like investment prospects.[22] In contrast, group action tends to subtract value in areas requiring brainstorming or creativity, consistent with the belief that less rather than more discipline is desired here.

So within investment groups, lists of ideas are better generated by individuals, with the group choosing which of those ideas to pursue. As Linus Pauling, two-time Nobel Prize winner, said in describing the secret of success, "You need to have a lot of ideas, and then you have to throw away the bad ones."[23]

Take a look at classic group-decision-making studies performed by Marjorie Shaw in the 1930s. Called Eureka studies, teams of four solved problems that had single confirmable solutions.[24] Shaw devised word puzzles, spatial relationships, and other games to be played by individuals or groups to determine which would deliver superior results.

In her missionaries and cannibals game, players get six discs representing a group of people living on one side of a river, three missionaries and three cannibals. The goal is to design a plan to get all six to the other side using a two-person rowboat. All missionaries can row, as can one cannibal; cannibals can never outnumber missionaries, for obvious reasons. Successful solutions were more often and quickly devised by groups than by individuals.

Updated tests prove similar points.[25] One posed a question involving pure statistical probability, whether to act now or await further information (for example, whether to trade today or wait until after the next quarterly report is released). In this test, an equal number of blue and red balls were put in an urn which would at some point during the experiment shift composition to 70 percent of one color and 30 percent of the other, and the players must determine when it turns and to which color. To help, they could draw as many as 40 balls from the urn.

Two notable findings arose from repeated plays of this game, alternately using individuals and groups of the same players. Surprisingly, groups made decisions concerning directional change slightly more quickly than did individuals. Less surprisingly, groups had a better record of accuracy by a significant amount. In the context of investment decision making, this suggests that overreaction and underreaction to information are more likely to be by an individual than by a group acting after discussion.

A more rigorous set of experiments required players with some economics training to set interest-rate policy to achieve designated employment and inflation targets, alternately playing the game as individuals and as groups. The same findings resulted: no big difference in decision speed, but a significant accuracy edge in group-determined policy. Analogous results should follow in investment decision making.

Some of the observed superiority of group decision making is actually a function of the best individual decision maker in a group making the decision, rather than anything special about group power.[26] But in most studies, individual average performance indicated little about how their groups performed. And the best individual performers in each group did not predictably impact the performance of their groups.

More complex group decision making has also been studied. Complexities involve greater judgment, evaluation, and multiple solutions, the sorts of mental operations required in selecting stocks and deciding when to sell.

The classic study is the survival exercise.[27] Players are told they just survived an airplane crash in a remote place. They have to decide things like whether to stay at the crash site or walk, and also have to rank the usefulness of 15 survival aids devised by crash-disaster experts. Group rankings were better, though not always as good as the rankings made by the best members of particular groups.

Group superiority is rooted in balancing individual biases. It is easier for the group than an individual to correct errors; it is easier for me to correct your errors than to correct my own. In Shaw's studies, proposals were three times more likely to be squashed by someone other than the person who made them. Of squashed proposals, five times as many wrong ones were rejected than right ones.

Statistical studies confirm the hunch. If the only reason for group superiority was "in the numbers," then artificially created groups would also outperform individuals—that is, averaging a group of individual answers and comparing the aggregates with the individuals. The studies show that a group more critically evaluates individual judgments, and thus generates superior results.

A particularly interesting study drew on the classic film *Twelve Angry Men*, where a lone hold-out juror kept voting for acquittal and managed one-by-one to get all other jurors to come around.[28] The experiment had three steps: (1) individuals were asked to rank the order in which the other jurors would switch; (2) these results were pooled and averaged, creating artificial statistical "groups;" and (3) actual groups were formed and asked to do the ranking. The most accurate results were produced by actual groups.

Even if group decision making can neutralize individual cognitive biases, groups have their own problems that investment-club members must contend with. "Social loafing" concerns figuring out who's doing what. In groups there is some propensity of individuals to work less hard than if acting alone. Social-loafing studies showed that in rope-pulling contests, individual effort of members of teams fell as the size of their team grew, with people on two-person teams pulling at 93 percent of their solo effort level, those in trios at 85 percent, and those in octets at 49 percent.[29]

Sometimes also called the "free rider effect," investment clubs can combat this weakness in group work by specifically allocating responsibility Officers should be elected and given particular tasks, such as a president who plans and runs meetings, and a treasurer who keeps track of dues and maintains financial records (and calculates returns accurately). Each member should be required to produce one or two investment ideas per year. Each member should be required to examine at least two investment ideas brought by other members. And so on.

Social loafing can also be offset by proper group size. The NAIC recommends that clubs should be big enough so that members can divide the work, without putting too much burden on an individual, but small enough to get everyone involved. For most clubs, this number averages about 15.[30]

While the NAIC suggests groups of about 15, it is certainly possible to obtain the benefit of group exchange with smaller numbers. At the extreme, working with a single trading partner can help eliminate many cognitive biases. Checking with a partner before deciding to make a purchase or sale can reduce the risk of sentiment. Consultation can be particularly beneficial if members prepare guidelines concerning when to sell.

There is also the potential problem of group polarization. This is the risk that groups err on the side of either excess caution or aggressiveness, despite the usually moderating influence of group decisions A classic study shows that individuals who were told a story in which they were the central character and asked to choose at a decision point between a strategy of "high risk/high return," or of "moderate risk/moderate return" invariably chose the latter. But when individuals were put in a group and were asked the identical question, they generally favored the former.

For investment clubs, the implication of group-polarization risks is clear. To avoid it, members should agree on a statement of investment philosophy. This should follow the NAIC guidelines of adopting a conservative, long-term, value-oriented approach geared toward doubling money every five years. The statement's scope can vary, from a few words such as these with references to books that reflect the philosophy, to more elaborate guidelines. The chief goal is to put members on the same investment page.

This can raise another problem called "group-think." This refers to the proclivity of collegial groups to value consensus over debate, thereby negating the superiority of group decision making that arises from deliberation and give-and-take. The price of such civility and cohesion, in other words, is the self-critical and evaluative functions that overcomes biases that individuals bring to the table. To address group-think, invite members for their interest, knowledge, and ability to contribute, rather than for commonality or homogeneity.

Not all groups work. Some investment clubs fold due to divorces, deaths, or inability of members to get along. Nor are clubs immune to psychological interference. The number of investment clubs nationally fluctuates with market conditions. Amid the late 1990s boom market, 35,800 clubs were registered with the NAIC, boasting aggregate membership of 600,000; as gloom gripped the market in the early 2000s, nearly 3000 clubs dropped their registrations along with 80,000 individual members, drops too large to be explained by normal attrition.[31]

Plenty of members regard membership more as a learning experience than a profit-making one. Among the lessons members learned the hard way are those taught the painless way (in this chapter) concerning the top lessons of long-term, value-oriented investing, all of which are common sense but commonly neglected. Of the lessons, the central one is the margin-of-safety principle: insist when buying an investment that your estimate of value is significantly greater than the price you pay.[32]

12

The Opposite of Cool

Nirvana is a fallacy in markets and in life. No amount of investor education will eliminate cognitive biases or their effects, and it isn't desirable to do so anyway. You are not going to act perfectly. You are never going to be like models created by efficiency theorists, and who would want to be? We are human, we want our heads, hearts, and guts to play roles in decision making.

Armed with behavioral insights, however, you will vastly improve investment prowess and easily avoid the most egregious bias-based errors. These errors are epitomized by investing on margin and day trading, and can be exacerbated by technological advances that expose investors to more acute bias, leading to bubbles that accentuate the boom-bust cycle.

Nor is there any reason to worry that other investors will leave you in the dust, marching on their merry way to Nirvana. Two vignettes produced a century and half apart suggest that Nirvana is nowhere in sight. The first is from a letter to the editor of the *London Times* written during the railway mania of England's 1840s:

> There is not a single dabbler in scrip who does not steadfastly believe—first, that a crash sooner or later, is inevitable; and secondly, that he himself will escape it. When the luck turns, and the crack play is *sauve quipeut*, or devil take the hindmost, no one fancies that the last mail train from Panic station will leave him behind. In this, as in other respects, 'Men deem all men moral but themselves.'[1]

More recently, and likely to remain of value for the next couple of centuries, is this gem from Warren Buffett's 2000 annual report:

> The line separating investment and speculation, which is never bright and clear, becomes blurred still further when most market participants have recently enjoyed triumphs. Nothing sedates rationality like large doses of effortless money. After a heady experience of that kind, normally sensible people drift into behavior akin to that of Cinderella at the ball. They know that overstaying the festivities—that is, continuing to speculate in companies that have gigantic valuations relative to the cash they are likely to generate in the future—will eventually bring on pumpkins and mice. But they nevertheless hate to miss a single minute of what is one helluva party. Therefore, the giddy participants all plan to leave just seconds before midnight. There's a problem, though: They are dancing in a room in which the clocks have no hands.[2]

Investing on Margin

A major symptom of the short-term view that plagues many American traders is margin trading. It is borrowing funds from a brokerage firm to buy securities. It purports to exploit leverage, but can have financially dire consequences when market prices turn downward. It is akin to the error a corporation makes when it decides to borrow funds to repurchase stock.

Imagine two brokerage clients. Mr. Conservative opens a regular account depositing $5000 and buys X Company's securities with that amount, and Ms. Aggressive opens a margin account depositing $5000 cash and borrowing an additional $5000 to buy $10,000 of X Company's securities on the same day. A year later, X Company's stock has doubled in price, and both Conservative and Aggressive sell their shares. Conservative has generated a 100-percent return while Aggressive yielded a 200-percent return (less interest on the margin loan).

Suppose instead that a year later, X Company's stock has dropped in price by half, and both our clients sell then. Conservative has lost 50 percent, while Aggressive has lost 100 percent (plus interest on the margin loan). In light of the exploding volume of margin debt outstanding in the late 1990s and early 2000s, it seems doubtful that many investors who use margin accounts are aware of this abysmal downside potential.

Consider the experience of Lael Desmond, a 28-year-old medical student.[3] While the market was on the technology-driven run in 1998, he placed margin trades using money originally earmarked to supplement his income during medical school. Desmond invested through Ameritrade, an on-line brokerage. When Desmond's stock dropped during the brief slump in August of 1998, Ameritrade gave him a margin call.

Combining the losses on the stock he owned with the losses on the stock bought with the borrowed money, Desmond was down $30,000. To fund the deficit, the medical student borrowed another $12,000 on 4 credit cards. When the market rebounded, Desmond followed the well-worn path to the courthouse by suing Ameritrade, claiming it called his margin too quickly ("negligence") and that he was not properly protected by the brokerage from making novice mistakes ("suitability").

Desmond's case against Ameritrade was resolved through arbitration. Desmond won the claim and recovered $40,000. Since the proceedings are secret, the ruling for Desmond does not explain the panel's reasoning. Desmond's lawyer says that suitability was at the heart of the case, but Ameritrade insists that suitability had nothing to do with the decision.

The suitability claim was that Ameritrade shouldn't have allowed Desmond to invest on margin because he was a novice. Ameritrade had given Desmond a disclaimer warning him about potential risks, but Desmond admits that he never read it. Desmond maintains that he thought margin loans were like bank loans, requiring regular payments. He had no idea that he could lose all of his money—and more.

Concerning the negligence claim, Desmond said that the day before Ameritrade placed a margin call on his account, it demanded $13,000 within 3 business days. Because Desmond received the message after business hours, he informed Ameritrade he would make the transfer the next day. The following day, before Desmond transferred the money, Ameritrade told Desmond's brother (by mistake), that instead Desmond must now transfer $21,000 or "whatever he could send."

Desmond tried to call Ameritrade, but was put on hold for two hours, and eventually gave up, and wired the money. After he wired the money, an Ameritrade representative told him that his portfolio was intact. When Desmond contacted Ameritrade that evening to confirm that his portfolio was intact, he learned instead that it was liquidated at 9:00 a.m. by a new Ameritrade employee. Desmond contended that Ameritrade moved too quickly in liquidating his portfolio.

The arbitration decision put Desmond in the position he occupied before the margin call. Since this episode, Desmond continues to trade on-line, but forsakes investing on margin, fearing that the rules unduly favor brokers with the broad discretion they have over client stock.

Another good reason Desmond might cite for pulling out of the game is that playing it requires overconfidence. Its presence can be inferred from the high levels of debt compared to investment reached in the United States in the late 1990s and early 2000s. From 1996 to 1999, margin debt at on-line brokerage firms rose nearly fivefold, and doubled among New York Stock Exchange member firms. During the decade of the 1990s, margin debt as a percentage of total consumer debt quadrupled from 4 percent to 16 percent.[4] Margin debt peaked in March, 2000 at $280 billion.[5]

The combination of ignorance and arrogance can help foster market bubbles that not only push prices above values, but also fuel the substantial risks of uncontrollable financial fallout and devastation once the bubble bursts.

During the Internet bubble, for example, tech executives borrowed heavily against stock in their companies, using stock as collateral. As prices rose, the leverage made them feel richer, enabling an orgy of consumerism; as prices fell, the margin calls wiped them out. Companies with top executives suffering this fate spanned the entire range of businesses from the savvy to the unknown: Answerthink, NetSol, Safeguard Scientifics, Stamps.com, MP3.com, eToys, and Daleen Technologies.[6]

Borrowings were used to buy new homes and pay back-taxes. The universal view of those caught off guard was bullish optimism; the universal postmortem was never again to have a margin account they could not cover immediately. A stronger response is swearing off the habit.

The Federal Reserve first publicized concerns in the late 1990s about the effect of rising levels of margin debt on the overall supply of credit in the economy. While individuals did not seem to heed the initial warning, the private market responded with some brokerages prohibiting credit extensions for certain customers or for certain types of securities. Margin debt fell along with the Nasdaq, declining to $165 billion in summer, 2001.[7]

In the punctured bubble's aftermath, the New York Stock Exchange weighed in with rules of its own. It imposed greater margin requirements on accounts owned by a related group of overconfident market participants: day traders.

Day Trading

Those who invest on margin also often engage in day trading, and day traders were among the heaviest users of margin resources to buy stock during the late 1990s. The combination led the New York Stock Exchange to adopt rules addressing the overlap. The rules provide that whereas other market participants can open a margin account with as little as $2000, for "day traders" the minimum was increased to $25,000.[8]

Day trading describes a wide range of highly active buy-sell decisions intended to exploit market-price volatility over very short time periods. A broad definition would be the practice of buying and selling stocks during a single trading day, with the goal not to hold stocks overnight.

The swing-trading version extends the time period from a few days to a week. The swiftest version compresses it to minutes. The New York Stock Exchange margin rules define a day trader as anyone who buys and sells a stock in the same trading session at least four times in a week.

However described, the proliferation of day trading at the turn to the twenty-first century was obviously a product of overconfidence and pattern-seeking biases on a mass scale. It is an extraordinarily risky activity that became quite popular during the latter 1990s and early 2000s, with about 50,000 regular, full-time day traders. This suggests an epidemic of people suffering from an inability to calculate probabilities accurately, and other cognitive biases.

Many companies got into the day-trading business, teaching people how to trade electronically using tactics that purport to exploit minute-to-minute price changes throughout the trading day. Advertising touted fantasies of high profits and low risk, while ignoring the reality of danger from choppy markets, the ease of making mistakes, the risks that Internet service providers may shut down, and so on.

Advertising lured novices into day-trader classrooms, where newcomers were taught not to care anything about the business whose stock they trade. Lessons focused on technical trading strategies, the proven-to-be-impossible practice of predicting price movements from price history and other data. Some programs offered multiple-day seminars, others gave correspondence courses by mail, and many were supplemented by day-trading coaches available for monthly fees on Internet chat rooms to provide lessons and oft-needed reassurance.

During the 1990s heyday, one firm's CEO advertised himself as the father of day trading. All-Tech Direct Inc. opened offices across the country. At one point it even made plans for an IPO. In 1999, alas, bad press focused on the firm in the wake of the rampage shooting spree that an All-Tech customer waged at the company's Atlanta office. Still, All-Tech is one of the nation's largest day-trading firms.

In the summer of 2001, All-Tech and its CEO, Harvey Houtkin, settled charges with securities regulators relating to numerous aspects of its business, by paying fines totaling more than $600,000 and agreeing to certain restrictions.[9] Chief among All-Tech's questioned activities was advertising that made profitable day trading appear far easier than it really is. These statements, some made by Houtkin, were widely disseminated in print, radio, and on the Internet. Firm employees also allegedly failed to explain the risks of day trading and borrowing on margin to buy stocks.

A particularly questionable area of concern was how All-Tech administered margin operations. It allowed customers to skirt margin restrictions by giving them money belonging to traders associated with the firm to repay loans the firm had extended. It also used funds of some traders to make margin loans to others. During 1998, about 100 such improper loans, totaling $4 million, were allegedly made.

Regulators cracked down, but not until five percent of aggregate market trading was being done by amateur day traders trained by the likes of Houtkin.[10] The epidemic caught the attention of regulators, including the SEC. It warned against the activity. The Senate published a report about its hazards, along with statistical evidence showing how unlikely it is for a person to make money engaging in the practice. Neither Congress nor the SEC took any formal action to ban day trading.

While the New York Stock Exchange's higher margin requirements for day trading may discourage day trading on borrowed money, it is hard to ban the practice effectively. After all, it consists solely of effecting trades in an open market (on average 44 trades per day). What the regulators throughout the country did is enforce existing laws against touters of day trading who engaged in false advertising and other deceptive practices to promote the activity.

Day trading may have reached its zenith during the boom of the late 1990s. It declined during the bust that immediately followed. But after a cooling-off period, interest resumed and day-trading levels rose. Day trading was also more durable throughout the period than on-line trading as a whole.[11] It is likely to be a cyclical phenomenon, falling when the market cools and returning as it heats up.

Technology

The close connection between the epidemics of day trading and margin trading suggests a broader problem that intelligent investors must grasp. It is that purveyors of financial-services products benefit from techniques that democratize trading. Anything that makes it easier, faster, more tempting, and even cheaper will be promoted, whether or not it is valuable for the user.

Day trading became accessible to nearly everyone with the development of software tools that make it convenient to trade from home. It was made even easier by promoters around the country offering how-to seminars. Investing on margin became vastly easier with the proliferation of entrepreneurial on-line brokerages eager to attract new business and happy to extend credit with neither a handshake nor a credit check. But leverage and swiftness do not help in investing; even-minded and cool-headed decision making are what count.

Intelligent investors may welcome technological innovations, such as Webcasting, access to conference calls, and data availability through the Internet. Yet they must be cautious about related innovations, for technology is a double-sided razor.

Technology promoted price fixation, a habit that has gotten worse over the past two decades. The advent of the Quotron in the early 1980s enabled people to stop by any branch brokerage office to check stock quotes at lunchtime. The ubiquity of the Yahoo!Finance Internet site on people's desktops in the late 1990s allowed them to check prices every five minutes. A major innovation designed to transfix an investor's attention on stock price is the streaming of real-time portfolio data. This is offered by many on-line brokers and financial Web sites to funnel current price information to your screen. Don't be distracted.

Most (maybe almost all) people check and recheck their purchases and sales and rebalance portfolios over the near term. Not only does this cost substantial, direct sums of money in transaction fees and taxes, this preference for the short-term view causes other problems.

It makes people perceive greater risks than there really are. This can translate into missing opportunities within their tolerance for risk, called *myopic loss aversion*. Shockingly, this compounds the risks by active trading over that shorter and riskier period (in effect, converting risks to reality).[12]

In stocks, the near term—now through the end of the year—is riskier than the long term (five years and beyond) in numerous ways. There is greater variability of returns on individual stocks, the percentage of losing time periods compared to winning time periods in the major indexes is greater, the volatility is greater, and so on.

When you have decided to buy or sell a security in accordance with principles of intelligent investing, it is possible to exploit "direct access" technology to get a better trade. Old-fashioned and on-line broker methods of trading put a middleman between you and the trade. Your trade instruction is taken by your brokerage to the market and executed at the price found there. Exact practices vary, but they all take time and risk price changes.

Direct access eliminates that step, enabling you with a single click to execute your trade at the price you see at that instant. There is a fee, equivalent to a commission, payable to the company providing this search (routing) service. But caution should be exercised in jumping to use such direct-access trading. It tends to be comarketed by the same firms that sell day and margin trading. They are more likely to give an illusion of control in terms of good price execution.

You will hear marketers of these services make the contrary arguments, sometimes even in behavioral terms. They may point out, for example, that it is common for frugal, self-reliant investors to expend substantial effort trying to ensure that each trade they make is effected at discount brokers offering the lowest per-share trading price, say $14.95 instead of $24.95. Execution costs, however, are both unknown and usually much higher than that $10 difference.

The latest offering for individual investors is folios. These are packages of stocks selected by a customer and bundled into a broader portfolio of selections made by other customers. The firm nets its customers' matching orders each day against each other, skipping the expense of taking matching trades to the market, and clearing only unmatched trades in the market.

Cost savings are passed on to customers, yielding fees lower than those of mutual funds and discount brokerages charged on individual trades. It is nice to pay less for the privilege of seeing such action, but the action itself can be far more expensive in price gyration than the savings from lower fees.

Venture Capital

Direct access to a new asset class, venture capital, was dangled before ordinary investors just as the bull market that spawned it started to contract in the late 1990s. The sizable returns yielded by venture capital funds in that period led to the logical next step of selling a piece of the action to individual investors. The bursting of the bubble dried up the venture-capital industry, taking this temptation off the table. You can be sure that with the next roaring bull market it will be back, making a few words to the wise in order.

Funding new enterprise is a backbone of American financial history and a major key to its success. Big firms and wealthy families have funded start-ups to make national economies roar. But Americans took it to new heights in the 1980s. By then, a fully developed market existed with a full support system and infrastructure.

Specialists in this area pooled funds from investors of all types—including families, firms, funds, endowments, and foundations—and actively sought outlets for their money. Hundreds of firms eager to fund start-ups spawned an army of venture-capital law firms, accounting firms, advisory firms, consultants, and scores of books. Hundreds of billions of pooled assets poured in.

The industry began with the founding in 1946 of George Diriot's American Research and Development Corp. Credit for the name "venture capital" is given to renowned investor Benno Schmidt who, along with John Hay Whitney, turned the business into an industry during the 1950s and 1960s.[13]

A specialized vocabulary describes it. At "zero stage," there are entrepreneurs with hopes and dreams. To break out and start attracting outside capital, they have to graduate to "first-stage" financing. This stage, to rephrase Churchill's comments about Russia, amounts to an idea spun as a yarn inside a business plan.

The goal of the venture capitalist is to make a lot of money by turning ideas into profits, starting with a business plan. Often venture capitalists back ventures that offer the promise of productive contributions, in the form of improved products or services that generate profits for their owners. Backers often help develop a business, aiding with strategy, marketing, recruiting, accounting, and so on. Many successful firms began this way, including Apple Computer, Compaq, and Intel.

Risks of new ventures are great in this high-risk, high-return industry. Many ideas don't go anywhere. Six out of ten fail completely, and only one out of eight succeeds moderately well. Money is lost. Therefore, volume is key. The more deals you do, the greater the likelihood that one of them will hit it big.

So all venture capitalists worth their salt are on the hunt for a dozen or more businesses to back. Volume can matter more than risk. Social proof infects these operators in stupefying ways—if some venture capital firms are backing a sector, others hop on the bandwagon in droves.

It is the venture capital lottery, and the lines run round the block. The more tickets, the more chances. This can compromise objectivity, leading venturers to support businesses of low quality with poor chances of success.

That has always been the tradition in venture capital. American Research and Development made almost all its returns from a single big hit, Digital Equipment Corp. (DEC). With DEC, the firm boasted average annual returns over 25 years of 15.8 percent; without DEC, returns were a mere 7.4 percent.[14]

In all venture-capital programs, there are two steps. First, procure or provide the first-stage financing. Second, find more people to put up larger and larger amounts of money to pay off you and other earlier investors.

Funding continues through ever-growing rounds of financing. In some cases, the business spins off additional funds, usually a sign that the venture is worth backing. But this is not a requirement.

After the first or "angel round" of financing is secured and spent, another "round" is assembled. In it, more money is sought to pay off earlier money. A "second round" of financing pays off investors from the "first round," which, in turn, had been raised to pay off investors in the first or "angel round."

The rounds of financing raised by venture capitalists correlate with market exuberance. In early 1999, 86 VC funds raised $9 billion; by mid-2000, total VC funds rose to 167 and pooled $30 billion; a year later, after the broad market's plunge, 95 funds raised $16 billion.[15]

While most of those dollars vanished, even more vanished by means of the most distinguishing feature of the venture-capital industry: the "exit strategy." The penultimate step in the funding process is called the "bridge round," the one on the way to the ultimate payoff, the IPO. This is the end of the line, where the public buys the equity in the venture, thereby paying off the venture capitalist.[16]

The successive rounds of financing evoke the money-losing cycle of a Ponzi scheme. The VC industry is sustained by susceptibilities akin to those of targets in Ponzi schemes, ordinary investors in IPOs, and all participants in market bubbles. Venturers suspend doubt. They persuade investors to do the same.[17]

When VC activity intensifies, an overheated IPO market follows. Together, these spawn expansion of the financial industry and kick start the feedback loops that sometimes lead to market frenzies. More money chases more money to pay off prior investment. Naturally occurring Ponzi schemes recur. When the funds dry up, the bust follows.

In the next swing of this pendulum, the expansion will undoubtedly include more aggressive marketing campaigns to draw the ordinary public investor into VC funds. Just before the VC-IPO bust of the early 2000s, a few VC funds went public with New York Stock Exchange listings, promising the little guy a piece of the VC action.[18] Knowing how the business works, ordinary investors should not be eager for their slice.

Heavy Trading

The consequences of aggressive trading—whether it be highly leveraged trading, frequent trading, or frenzied trading that leads to prices soaring above values—include increased volatility of price changes, wider swings in market indexes, and ultimately, bubbles that eventually burst. Those concerned about these effects dabble with efforts to try to stop trading during the trading day. As a way to cope with aggressive trading, looking toward the consequence of crashes is a bit like closing the barn doors after the horses have gone, only worse. It is like catching their tails in the door as they flee.

Even so, since the 1987 crash, substantial attention has been paid to halting trading when stock markets start to fall significantly. Don't count on these to help control your biases or the biased behavior of others. This is the case for two reasons: as currently designed, trading curbs will not be triggered unless a crash on the order of the crashes of 1929 or 1987 recur, and even if they are triggered, they are just as likely to make things worse.

Market crashes are described quite well by the behavioral model outlined in Chapter 4. They are preceded by market bubbles, driven by psychological forces such as overconfidence, and reinforced by those seeking patterns. They are sparked by biases such as overreaction, which are reinforced by those such as hindsight bias and regret. In short, people get carried away on the way up and carried away on the way down. Should prices be regulated in either direction?

Devotees of market-price regulation eventually learn the lesson of the Vatican. In the Middle Ages, the Pope forbade charging interest on borrowed money. Later, Christians learned this was an anathema to a market economy's function of allocating scarce resources to satisfy unlimited needs, including money.[19] The Vatican itself now boasts one of the most enviable investment portfolios globally, enjoying far more than usurious rates of return on invested capital.

Usury laws persist, but limit only exorbitant interest rates on debt instruments. Their complexity and exceptions render most meaningless. California's rule against usury, for example, does not apply to sales transactions. So many loans are set up to look like sales, and high rates are lawfully charged. For example, if a house is sold using seller financing with installment payments including a usurious interest component, the payments can be described as the purchase price rather than as payments on a loan.

These laws do not extend to equity. Earning extraordinary rates of return by investing in common stock is not prohibited. Regulation of the price of money (interest) or commodities interferes with the ability of the credit and commodity markets to allocate capital or goods, and the same is true of regulatory interference in the equity markets.

Through the 1987 crash, the regulatory posture let the cards fall where they may. In October of that year, stocks steadily declined and on a single day dropped by 25 percent. No regulatory mechanisms were triggered to halt the hemorrhaging. In the crash's wake, major securities exchanges instituted trading curbs to prevent panic. Triggered when specified price-level changes are reached, these "circuit breakers" impose a trading halt for a specified period of time— a cooling-off period.

The apparent concern addressed by trading curbs is illiquidity. They are designed to bring buyers back. A behavioral problem with circuit breakers is they can heighten fears and operate as a magnet to pull the market to the trigger level. They also draw in arbs and speculators who bet whether the trigger will be hit, which can become a self-fulfilling prophecy. Moreover, many forces other than relative liquidity affect trading volume and patterns, and therefore any market or regulatory mechanism addressing market crashes must be evaluated in the larger context of such forces.

Original breakers halted trading for an hour if the Dow fell 250 points and for two hours if it fell 400 points. In 1997, with the Dow having tripled numerically, point levels were raised to 350 and 550, and in 1996 the time-outs had been halved. Breakers triggered for the first time on October 27, 1997, at 2:35 p.m. for half an hour. When lifted at 3:05 p.m., far from restoring calm and liquidity, the Dow plunged another 200 points, triggering another halt that lasted for the rest of the day and left the Dow to close down 7.19 percent or 554 points.

Breakers now are triggered if the Dow falls by various percentages compared to its average close the previous month. The length of the trading halt depends on when during the day it occurs. Any 30-percent drop shuts trading down for the rest of the day, as does a 20-percent drop after 2:00 p.m. A 20-percent drop occurring between 1:00 and 2:00 p.m. produces a half-hour halt, and one occurring before that calls for a one-hour break. Ten-percent drops before 2:00 p.m. trigger one-hour shutdowns; those occurring between 2:00 and 2:30 p.m. produce half-hour shutdowns; after that, 10-percent drops trigger no halts.

This complex scheme suggests the lesson has been learned, based on the data in Table 12-1. The Dow has never fallen on a single day by more than 30 percent; the only drop of greater than 20 percent ever was the 1987 crash; and the only other drops greater than 10 percent were during the 1929 crash.

Note two dates at the bottom of this list, not making the top 10: October, 1997 and September, 2001. Consider the latter, when stock markets closed for four consecutive trading days following the terrorist attacks on New York and Washington. The Dow Jones Industrial Average stood at 9605 at the market close on Monday, September 10, 2001. When markets reopened one week later, Monday, September 17, 2001, trading was fast-paced during the opening hour, but panic abated. The Dow fell by 484 points or 5 percent in the first half hour of trading, and another 1 percent within an hour after that, before settling down to finish the day down 685 points to close at 8920, off 7.1 percent. Trading halts were not triggered.

Table 12-1 Dow Jones Industrial Average Top Days with Greatest Percentage Drops

Date	Close	Net Change	% Drop
October 19, 1987	1738.74	−508.00	−22.61
October 28, 1929	260.64	−38.33	−12.82
October 29, 1929	230.07	−30.57	−11.73
November 6, 1929	232.13	−25.55	−9.92
December 18, 1899	58.27	−5.57	−8.72
August 12, 1932	63.11	−5.79	−8.40
March 14, 1907	76.23	−6.89	−8.29
October 26, 1987	1793.93	−156.83	−8.04
July 21, 1933	88.71	−7.55	−7.84
October 18, 1937	125.73	−10.57	−7.75
October 27, 1997	7161.15	−554.26	−7.18
October 5, 1932	66.07	−5.09	−7.15
September 17, 2001	8920.70	−684.81	−7.13

Source: http://averages.dowjones.com/dja_fact.html

Trading curbs have the virtue of subtlety. Compare them to the price-support system in place in Japan throughout the 1990s. Japan developed an asset bubble during the 1980s, with asset prices substantially above the present value of their reasonably calculated future cash flows. As investors gradually realized this, they sold assets and prices began to fall, precipitously in the case of stocks. The Nikkei Stock Average fell by half from 1990 to 1992, closing the gap between price and value, but not all the way.

Japanese market regulators embraced a host of price-support measures, such as limits on permissible price changes of individual stocks in a day and using public funds to buy stocks en masse. Despite the efforts, the Nikkei slid throughout the decade, falling by half again from 1992 to 2001, and standing at 25 percent of its 1989 peak. By the end of the 1990s, the price-value gap was far closer to reality. Traders pushed it there, despite governmental price-support efforts.

It is possible that those efforts helped ease the transition from an overpriced to a more stable economy. One cost of doing so is deferring investments by long-term investors, who would rush to buy stocks in companies whose prices plummeted to ranges below value. A more rapid adjustment by market forces acting independently produces a swifter return to stability. Either way, those steps cannot sustain prices that deviate substantially above values.

U.S.-style trading halts are modest compared to the ambitious Japanese efforts. And since artificial market controls cannot last, modesty is a virtue. As the Japanese experience shows, the investment community drives prices to comfort levels, somewhere near value.

When used to facilitate market trading rather than to dictate it, these measures help. One means of facilitating markets amid despair is to help influence the investment community's views of what proper levels are. A one-hour trading halt may not be a terrible thing. It can give market participants needed time to cool off. Broader advice to take a long-term view has the same desirable effect.

Prices are the point of markets. To interfere with them artificially is to destroy the vital function of exchange. Even when that discovery process is distorted by massive psychological infirmities, it is those infirmities that must work and pay the price. When the consequence of the error is a price level bubbling higher than the value, it is compounding the error to block the correction. And that goes not only for the abrupt arrest of the correction, but also, though more weakly, for the gradual deflation of the bubble over time.

Either way, regularly triggered circuit breakers install artificial corrections to natural problems. Hard as it may be to correct the natural errors of cognitive bias, it is simply Frankensteinian tinkering to try to correct them with artificial devices. The best strategy for the individual investor is to avoid acting in emotional ways that lead, inevitably, to regret.

A commonly attempted form of indirect tinkering is tax policy, which can help straighten out investment pricing problems that cognitive biases produce. To combat day trading, for example, different transaction taxes could be imposed on purchases and sales of securities that occur in a single hour, day, or week. It is the rare day when an investment decision in the morning followed by the opposite decision in the afternoon are both correct. Most underlying fundamentals do not change that quickly, nor do most news reports of such alteration arrive in that short time period.

One problem with such a regulation is its inability to discriminate between day traders acting noisily and under cognitive biases, from arbitrageurs who notice price/value differentials that should be corrected. Discouraging such trades in one market may also exacerbate problems of mispricing in others, for it reduces the range of opportunities an arb has to hedge risks.

A positive tax policy would reward the positive effects of such trading and express support for long-term investing. This approach would include such steps as those championed by advocates of the individual investor, such as the National Association of Investors Corporation (NAIC). It supports a capital-gains-tax program that would:

- Exempt the first $25,000 of capital (long-term) gains annually from taxation for individual investors
- Grant a lifetime exemption of $500,000 on an individual's overall equity investment
- Allow an individual investor to roll over capital gains without taxation until retirement age, and then pay on gains as they are realized, in a way similar to deferral rules for real estate investment
- Index the tax base of capital gains to offset inflation[20]

The limitations on such indirect tinkering raise another reason for letting markets do their thing, even if that results in crashes. Investors without the experience of wrenching market change estimate its likelihood to be much lower than is consistent with history. Some people have to see it to believe it. They should not be deprived of that education. They need to get smart.

"Cool" took on new meaning in the heady 1990s. Once used to characterize even-headed, deliberate, laid-back people who made difficult feats seem easy—Eric Clapton playing guitar, the James Bond character, Grace Kelly doing anything, Warren Buffett amassing a fortune—cool was now a label applied to erstwhile nerds, geeks, and dweebs who were anything but laid back. These intense technophiles focused on speeding up everything around them—computers, games, music, and communications. Wonderful as many of the resulting products and processes are, the new speed of society is swifter rather than cooler. The pace of investing is likewise faster, alas.

Dreams of fast riches have always swirled through American culture, but never have so many people been pulled into investing to make their fortunes with little more than hunches and quick mouse clicks. Yet successful investing is far more hospitable to turtles thinking clearly than to stags rushing madly, to the real cool rather than the pseudocool. The early 2000s taught this lesson to many, though it is doubtful all will have learned it. The lessons in this book are about being cool in the old-fashioned sense. Building wealth takes time, patience, and tenacity, so the temperament of top investors is not fast, faster, fastest, but cool, calm, and collected.

Conclusion

Why do people buy brand-new cars? Don't they know that upon driving a new car off the dealer's lot the car instantly loses 5 to 20 percent of its resale value? Why does a new car instantly lose so much of what someone has just paid for it? It is not the case that the intrinsic value has plummeted. It is the identical car. What has changed is the identity of the seller.

When the seller is a dealer no one wonders why he is selling the car. That is what dealers do. When the seller is a guy who just bought the car every buyer has good reason to wonder why he is selling it. After all, only a small portion of recent car buyers turn around and sell. Not all sellers suffer disappointment in their purchases, but buyers have a hard time telling them apart.

One way a seller can persuade a buyer to buy the car despite the risk that it is a lemon is to slash the price. From the new-car buyer's viewpoint, the 5-to-20-percent drop they suffer on driving off the lot is the price they pay for the comfort that they have not purchased a lemon from a rightly disappointed new-car owner.[1]

It may be a stretch to say that IPOs are akin to new-car sales in that both are sold at high prices due to a dealer's imprimatur. The analogy remains useful, however, for the price-value difference in cars carries over to the price-value difference in stocks. Circumstances and relative positions influence people in placing values on cars, leading to disagreements that produce prices that may vary from value. Investors assessing stock values and naming trading prices experience similar forces, so it is not surprising that stock prices can differ from business values. This can be the case even if the stock market is rational, as with the new-car market, in that participants behave sensibly. The result is the same: the logic in terms of value is not the same as the logic in terms of price.

That so few recognize this simple reality is a testament to the impoverished state of investment knowledge. The situation needs attention that it seems unlikely to get. In the United States, the Securities and Exchange Commission operates impressive investor-education programs, the Department of Labor leads campaigns to educate workers about the importance of retirement savings, and the Federal Reserve Board rightly proselytizes against margin trading.

These governmental arms anchor a vast industry dedicated to promoting financial intelligence, including private enterprises such as mutual funds, investment banking firms, and Internet investment sites. They offer a wide variety of publications, seminars, and other materials that seek to educate investors about investment philosophy and strategies, types and risks of various investment products, and the environment of investing, including risks associated with financial fraud. The SEC has gathered much of this material in what it bills as an integrated investor education program called the "Alliance for Investor Education."[2]

This expanding commitment to financial literacy arose in the past two decades in response to important historical and cultural forces. These include the maturation of the Baby Boom generation that will stress Social Security to meet retirement needs, as well as steadily expanding availability of private, self-directed retirement vehicles, such as IRAs and 401(k) plans. The rising concern reflects leaders' increased awareness of the financial illiteracy of most Americans.

None of these programs deal directly with behavioral finance. This may be because it is sophisticated, difficult, and new. Private providers may prefer investors who succumb to biases, for they result in substantial trading activity (and therefore commissions), margin lending (and interest income), and even greater volumes of corporate deal making (and associated fees). An extreme but instructive example of the pitfalls of leaving investor education to the private sector is the proliferation of day-trading firms in the late 1990s and early 2000s.

Congress recently directed the Department of Labor to assume a leadership role in investor education. In light of evidence of a paltry—yet declining!—national savings rate, Congress enacted the "SAVER Act," which imposed an express educational mandate on the Department of Labor.[3]

An acronym for "Savings Are Vital to Everyone's Retirement," the SAVER Act's purpose is to advance the public's knowledge of savings and investment. It requires the Labor Department to gather and disseminate this knowledge through a Web site and Presidential summits. The first was held in 1998, another required in 2001, with little fanfare and less success.[4] (Ever heard of it?)

Some of what Congress requires from the Labor Department is so mundane that it is easy to defend. For example, it requires teaching about compound interest and the virtue of early savings to take maximum advantage of it. But other topics are controversial, and when mandated by Congress or the Labor Department, parochial. For example, the legislation compels teaching the "importance" of "diversification" and "timing" in investing.[5]

While diversification is widely preached, it is too often blindly followed in stock investments. Asset allocation is the better principle, underscoring the importance of placing wealth in different vehicles, such as cash, money markets, home equity, collectibles, bonds, and stocks.[6] Within the stock class, the argument for diversification is overdrawn. Likewise, in the case of emphasizing "timing," the lesson can be downright counterproductive by encouraging high-risk practices such as day trading, and more basic errors such as focusing on price instead of value.

Even if Congress was mistaken in overspecifying the content of investor education, it was certainly correct in accepting responsibility within the federal government. However, many cylinders drive the engine of investor education. A role remains for all sources— from family, to formal schooling, to industry professionals, as well as private educators. While traditional topics need to be covered (the time value of money, risk and return, liquidity, diversification, indexing, specialized funds, tax matters, and asset allocation), they also must include investment psychology, as this book discusses.

The importance of psychology drew practical force during the wrenching 2000 market amid anxiety created by a roller-coaster stock market roaring down from its crest. A leading investment firm captured the feeling by considering for the cover of its annual report a famous painting by Edvard Munch (1863–1944) called *The Scream*.[7] (See Figure C-1).

The famous angst-riddled painting depicts the weight of modern life's daily burden. Markets of the early 2000s displayed emotions akin to the panicked, windswept form in the foreground. The painting, as with the market environment, evinces the three interrelated aspects of cognition—the emotional, cerebral, and physical. The

Figure C-1   Edvard Munch, "The Scream." The Metropolitan Museum of Art, New York, bequest of Scofield Thayer, 1982. (1984.1203.1)

complex psychology captured by the painting has nothing in common with the story of efficient markets and rational traders, and everything in common with how stock markets actually work (and life itself for that matter).

Psychology can be used to an investor's advantage. Cognition misers save time. Many tactics produce superior economic and emotional results. So long as one is aware of them, they are wonderful tools. When you and I recognize we are prone to a bias, we can deal with it. When we notice the market being infected, we can exploit it.

Let's close with a final variation of the status-quo bias called "categorization." Investors put companies in conceptual boxes and leave them there for prolonged periods. Hence the sticky categories such as hot stocks, cold stocks, value plays, growth plays, and glamour stocks.

A company can be in a particular box for reasons unrelated to the category's characteristics. The placement results from a reputation formed through a complex web of reports, opinions, and feedback. Negative repositioning occurs following a vivid event, such as a product recall (which caused the reputation of Bridgestone Tire to plunge), product-liability lawsuits (putting companies like Philip Morris near the bottom), corporate takeovers (Ben & Jerry's Ice Cream's reputation sank after being acquired by Unilever). These and similar events tend to trigger the availability bias, forging a mnemonic link between name and event that indelibly casts the company in the new light of the episode.[8]

Positive positioning is Teflon-like, with beloved companies such as Home Depot and Walt Disney regularly in the top 10. The best way to retain a positive position is to leave well enough alone. Companies least covered in the news tend to sport the best continuing positive reputations.

Category qualities can also change for the same sorts of dramatic reasons. A good example is the dot.com stock category. It was a great place for a company to be in 1999 and an awful place for the same exact company to be in 2001. What happened was a total shakeout in the industry, following a long series of news reports and changes of perception, but no real difference in fundamentals—companies in that sector as a whole continued to report no earnings, and often generated negative operating cash flows before and after the public shift in attitude.

Categorization is a variation on the lemon effect associated with the new-cars market. Price shocks to one stock can produce ripple effects on kindred stocks. When Cisco's stock price falls on disappointing earnings reports, other tech stock prices tend to fall too; likewise with bellwether stocks in the automotive, banking, consumer products, and other industries. Declines in overall industries can spell declines in the overall market.

These are lemon effects in that investors cannot always tell the winners from the losers and instead punish whole sectors or the whole market. This aggregate inability means investors overall pay too much for unattractive businesses and too little for attractive ones.

Managers respond by trying to distinguish themselves. Good ways for managers to distinguish themselves from the lemons include to avoid underpriced offerings, avoid overpriced buybacks, offer informative disclosure concerning these capital allocation policies as well as general news, refrain from expansionism for the sake of anything other than shareholder value, and be faithful to accounting reporting rules. Investors paying attention to these signals, while recognizing other cognitive tricks we play on ourselves, should be able to distinguish the lemons.

These investors discover the link between the surface perception and the underlying reality. The perception gives way to reality, but only gradually. The disciplined investor's object is not merely to think, but to think clearly.

A baseball metaphor helps. In baseball parlance, buy Dunkin' Donuts or Starbucks when they are in the on-deck circle (up-next); sell Westinghouse, Polaroid, and Xerox before their numbers are retired. To translate for the nonfan: look for the up-and-comer, bail on the down-and-out. Above all, as Aristotle advised, know thyself.

End Notes

Notes to Introduction, Pages xiii–xvii

1. Bernard Roshco, "Investor Illiteracy," *The American Prospect* (March–April, 1999).
2. With apologies to Richard Branson, owner of Virgin Atlantic Airways, who replied to the question of how to become a millionaire by saying, start as a billionaire and then buy an airline. Quoted in Warren E. Buffett and Lawrence A. Cunningham, *The Essays of Warren Buffett: Lessons for Corporate America* (1st rev. ed., The Cunningham Group, 2001), 117.

Notes to Chapter 1, Crossroads, Pages 3–22

1. John Warner and Saul Pleeter, *American Economic Review* (Spring 2001) (reported in Alan B. Krueger, "Economic Scene," *The New York Times*, May 24, 2001).
2. John Maynard Keynes, *The General Theory of Employment, Interest, and Money* (reprint ed. Prometheus Books, 1997).
3. Data relating to centennial changes are based upon materials in Theodore Caplow, Louis Hickes, and Ben J. Wattenberg, *The First Measured Century* (American Enterprise Institute Press, 2000) and for generation changes upon a study of the Congressional Budget Office as reported in Richard W. Stevenson, "Study Details Income Gap Between Rich And the Poor," *The New York Times*, May 31, 2001.
4. James M Poterba, "Stock Market Wealth and Consumption," *Journal of Economic Perspectives*, vol. 14 (2000).
5. Greg Ip, "The Outlook: Sated, Will Consumers Hurt the Economy?," *The Wall Street Journal*, June 11, 2001 (data drawn from Census Bureau, National Automobile Dealers Association, Consumer Electronics Association, and Wells Fargo)
6. William Hall, "Mass Fortunes Set For Reversal," *The Financial Times*, June 22, 2001 (*Financial Times* Survey: Private Banking).
7. The examples are drawn from Bernard Roshco, "Investor Illiteracy," *The American Prospect* (March–April 1999).

8. Glenn Ruffenach, "Fewer Americans Save for Their Retirement," *The Wall Street Journal*, May 10, 2001 (reporting study by the Employee Benefit Research Institute).

9. Letter from the U.S. Department of Labor to the House Subcommittee on Employer-Employee Relations of the House Committee on Education and the Workforce, "Opportunities to Improve DOL's SAVER Act Campaign," *Federal Document Clearing House, Inc.*, June 6, 2001.

10. Dawn Kopecki, "Law Would Require Credit Counseling," *The Wall Street Journal*, April 16, 2001.

11. Michael Jensen, "Some Anomalous Evidence Regarding Market Efficiency," *Journal of Economics*, vol. 6 (1978).

12. Eugene Fama, "The Behavior of Stock Market Prices," *Journal of Business*, vol. 38 (1965).

13. This section draws on Linda A. Schwartzstein, "Austrian Economics and the Current Debate Between Critical Legal Studies and Law and Economics," *Hofstra Law Review*, vol. 20 (1992); Gregory Scott Crespi, "Exploring the Complicationist Gambit: An Austrian Approach to Economic Analysis of Law," *Notre Dame Law Review*, vol. 73 (1998); Carl T. Bogus, "Introduction to Symposium, Rational Actors or Rational Fools?," *Roger Williams University Law Review*, vol. 6 (2000); Henry William Spiegel, *The Growth of Economic Thought* (Duke University Press, 3d ed. 1991); and Llewellyn H. Rockwell, Jr., "Why Austrian Economics Matters," *Ludwig von Mises Institute* (www.mises.org). Thanks for helpful comments to Giancarlo Ibarguen, Universidad Francisco Marroquin, Guatemala; and Todd Zywicki, George Mason University.

14. Ludwig von Mises, *Human Action* (Ludwig von Mises Institute, 1949), 56.

15. Friedrich A. Hayek, "The Pretense of Knowledge," *American Economic Review*, vol. 79 (1974).

Notes to Chapter 2, Investor Sentiment, Pages 23–40

1. Fischer Black, "Noise," *Journal of Finance*, vol. 41 (1986).

2. Oliver Wendell Holmes, Jr., "The Path of the Law," *Harvard Law Review*, vol. 10 (1897).

3. Susan T. Fiske and Shelley E. Taylor, *Social Cognition* (McGraw Hill, 1991).

4. Shlomo Benartzi and Richard H. Thaler, "Myopic Loss Aversion and the Equity Risk Premium Puzzle," *Quarterly Journal of Economics*, vol. 110 (1995).

5. Daniel Kahneman and Mark W. Riepe, "Aspects of Investor Psychology," *The Journal of Portfolio Management*, vol. 24 (1998).

6. Richard H. Thaler, *The Winner's Curse: Paradoxes and Anomalies of Economic Life* (Princeton University Press, 1992), 63–78.

7. David Hirshleifer, "Investor Psychology and Asset Pricing," *Ohio State University Working Paper* (2001) (www.ssrn.com).

8. Gary Belsky and Thomas Gilovich, *Why Smart People Make Dumb Money Mistakes* (Simon & Schuster, 1999), 70–71.

9. Terrance Odean, "Are Investors Reluctant to Realize Their Losses?," *Journal of Finance*, vol. 53 (1998).
10. Thaler, *Winner's Curse*, 64–66.
11. *Ibid.* An additional experiment showed that the "main effect of endowment is not to enhance the appeal of the good one owns, only the pain of giving it up." *Ibid.*, 68.
12. George Lowenstein and Richard H. Thaler, "Intertemporal Choice," *Journal of Economic Perspectives*, vol. 3 (1989); Richard H. Thaler, "Saving, Fungibility, and Mental Accounts," *Journal of Economic Perspectives*, vol. 4 (1990).
13. James Schembari, "A Study Dares to Question the 401(k)," *The New York Times*, May 27, 2001. The study is Jagadeesh Gokhale, Laurence J. Kotlikoff, and Todd Neumann, "Does Participating in a 401(k) Raise Your Lifetime Taxes?," *National Bureau of Economic Affairs Working Paper Number W8341* (2001) (www.ssrn.com).
14. Thaler, *Winner's Curse*, 115–116 (discussing numerous studies).
15. *Ibid.*, 117–119.
16. Kahneman and Riepe.
17. Amos Tversky and Daniel Kahneman, "The Framing of Decisions and the Psychology of Choice," *Science*, vol. 211 (1981).
18. Benartzi and Thaler; Christine Jolls, Cass R. Sunstein, and Richard H. Thaler, "A Behavioral Approach to Law and Economics," *Stanford Law Review*, vol. 50 (1998).
19. Benartzi and Thaler; Richard H. Thaler, Amos Tversky, Daniel Kahneman, and Alan Schwartz, "How Myopic Loss-Averse Investors Learn From Experience," *Quarterly Journal of Economics*, vol. 112 (1997); Uri Gneezy and Jan Potters, "An Experiment on Risk Taking and Evaluation Periods," *Quarterly Journal of Economics*, vol. 112 (1997).
20. Kahneman and Riepe.
21. The discussion of *pro forma* accounting appears in Chapter 8.
22. Theo Francis, "Company Stock Fills Many Retirement Plans Despite the Potential Risk to Employees," *The Wall Street Journal*, September 11, 2001.
23. Richard A. Oppel, Jr., "The Danger in a One-Basket Nest Egg Prompts a Call to Limit Stock," *The New York Times*, December 19, 2001 (legislation proposed by Senators Barbara Boxer, D-Cal. and Jon Corzine, D-NJ).
24. Kahneman and Riepe (drivers); Lynn A. Baker and Robert E. Emery, "Why Every Relationship Is Above Average: Perceptions and Expectations of Divorce at the Time of Marriage," *Law and Human Behavior*, vol. 17 (1993); Neil D. Weinstein, "Unrealistic Optimism About Future Life Events," *Journal of Personal and Social Psychology*, vol. 39 (1980).
25. Thomas Gilovich, Robert Vallone, and Amos Tversky, "The Hot Hand in Basketball: On the Misperceptions of Random Sequences," *Cognitive Psychology*, vol. 17 (1985).
26. Amos Tversky and Daniel Kahneman, "Judgment Under Uncertainty: Heuristics and Biases," *Science*, vol. 85 (1974).

Notes to Chapter 3, Limited Arbitrage, Pages 41–58

1. Christopher Reed, "The Damn'd South Sea," *Harvard Magazine* (May–June 1999); John D. Ayer, *Basic Finance for Lawyers* (Lexis Law Publishing, 2001), 183. Thanks to Professor Ayer, University of California (Davis).
2. Peter R. Locke and Steven C. Mann, "Do Professional Traders Exhibit Loss Realization Aversion?," *Social Science Research Network Working Paper* (2001) (www.ssrn.com).
3. Judith Chevalier and Glenn Ellison, "Career Concerns of Mutual Fund Managers," *Quarterly Journal of Economics*, vol. 114 (1999).
4. Dean LeBaron, "Reflections on Market Efficiency," *Financial Analyst's Journal* (May/June 1983).
5. Danny Hakim, "S.E.C. Censures Two Big Firms On Charges of 'Pumping'," *The New York Times*, August 11, 2001.
6. Andrei Shleifer, "Do Demand Curves for Stocks Slope Down?," *Journal of Finance*, vol. 41 (1986); Lawrence Harris and Eitan Gurel, "Price and Volume Effects Associated with Changes in the S&P 500 List: New Evidence for the Existence of Price Pressures," *Journal of Finance*, vol. 41 (1986).
7. "Market Place," *The New York Times*, May 29, 2001 (noting study by Investors.com).
8. Ken Brown, "Heard on the Street: Analysts' Top Stock Picks Get Failing Grade on Risk Meter," *The Wall Street Journal*, August 15, 2001 (noting study by Risk Metrics, an independent company spun out of J.P. Morgan in the late 1990s).
9. Gilles Hilary and Lior Menzly, "Does Past Success Lead Analysts to Become Overconfident?," *Social Science Research Network Working Paper* (2001) (www.ssrn.com).
10. Andrei Shleifer, *Inefficient Markets* (Oxford University Press, 2000), 15.
11. Roger Lowenstein, *When Genius Failed: The Rise and Fall of Long-Term Capital Management* (Random House, 2000).
12. Michael Lewis, "How the Eggheads Cracked," *The New York Times Magazine*, January 24, 1999.
13. *Ibid.*
14. Nick Leeson, *Rogue Trader* (Warner, 1997) (Barings); Martin Mayer, *Nightmare on Wall Street* (Simon & Schuster, 1993) (Salomon); Frank Portnoy, *F.I.A.S.C.O.* (W.W. Norton, 1997) (Morgan Stanley); Kathleen Sharp, *In Good Faith*, (St. Martin's Press, 1995) (Prudential).
15. Clifford Geertz, *The Interpretation of Cultures* (1st ed. 1973; rev. ed. Basic Books, 2000).
16. James M. Clash, "No Hedging Here," *Forbes*, August 6, 2001.
17. Kenneth A. Froot and Emil M. Dabora, "How Are Stock Prices Affected by the Location of Trade?," *Journal of Financial Economics*, vol. 53 (1999); Colin Young and Leonard Rosenthal, "The Seemingly Anomalous Price Behavior of Royal Dutch Shell and Unilever nv/plc," *Journal of Financial Economics,* vol. 13 (1990).
18. This portion draws on Richard H. Thaler and William T. Ziemba, "Parimutuel Betting Markets: Racetracks and Lotteries," *Journal of Economic Perspectives*, vol. 2 (1988).

19. For more of the basics, consult the Web site of the New York Racing Association, operator of Aqeduct Racetrack, Belmont Park, and Saratoga Race Course, www.nyracing.com.

Notes to Chapter 4, Diagnosing Mr. Market, Pages 59–76

1. David Hirshleifer and Tyler Shumway, "Good Day Sunshine: Stock Returns and the Weather," *Ohio State University Working Paper* (2001) (www.ssrn.com); Mark Hulbert, "Forget About Efficient Markets, Let the Sun Shine In," *The New York Times*, June 17, 2001.
2. This discussion draws on David Hirshleifer, "Investor Psychology and Asset Pricing," *Ohio State University Working Paper* (2001) (www.ssrn.com).
3. Fischer Black, "Noise," *Journal of Finance*, vol. 41 (1986).
4. Kent Daniel, David Hirshleifer, and Avanidhar Subrahmanyam, "Investor Psychology and Security Market Under- and Over-Reactions," *Journal of Finance*, vol. 53 (1998).
5. Andrei Shleifer, *Inefficient Markets* (Oxford University Press, 2000), 129–30.
6. Thomas Gilovich, *How We Know What Isn't So: The Fallibility of Human Reason in Everyday Life* (Free Press, 1991), 23–24.
7. Nicholas Barberis, Andrei Shleifer, and Robert Vishny, "A Model of Investor Sentiment," *Journal of Financial Economics*, vol. 49 (1998).
8. Robert Bloomfield and Jeffrey Hales, "Predicting the Next Step of a Random Walk: Experimental Evidence of Regime-Shifting Biases," *Cornell University Working Paper Series* (2001) (www.ssrn.com).
9. Harrison Hong and Jeremy C. Stein, "A Unified Theory of Underreaction, Momentum Trading and Overreaction in Asset Markets," *Journal of Finance*, vol. 54 (1999); David M. Cutler, James M. Poterba, and Lawrence H. Summers, "Speculative Dynamics and the Role of Feedback Traders," *American Economic Review*, vol. 80 (1990).
10. Terrance Odean, "Are Investors Reluctant to Realize Their Losses?," *Journal of Finance*, vol. 53 (1998).
11. Dana Canedy, "Florida Curbs the Operators Of Popular Shark Excursions," *The New York Times*, September 7, 2001.
12. John Allen Paulos, "How to Find a Trend When None Exists," *The New York Times*, August 25, 2001.
13. William J. Broad, "Protect Sharks? Attacks Fuel Old Argument," *The New York Times*, September 11, 2001.
14. William J. O'Neil, 24 *Essential Lessons for Investment Success* (McGraw-Hill, 2000), 82–83.
15. Ibid.
16. Lars Tvede, *The Psychology of Finance* (John Wiley & Sons, 1999), 198–206.
17. Warren E. Buffett and Lawrence A. Cunningham, *The Essays of Warren Buffett: Lessons for Corporate America* (1st ed. 1997; rev. ed. The Cunningham Group, 2001).
18. Elizabeth Harris, "Some Funds Try to Read Your Mind," *The New York Times*, August 19, 2001.

19. Victor Niederhoffer, *The Education of a Speculator* (John Wiley & Sons, 1997), 36–45.
20. O'Neil, 67.
21. Ellen J. Langer, "The Illusion of Control," *Journal of Personality and Social Psychology*, vol. 32 (1975).

Notes to Chapter 5, Merry-Go-Rounds, Pages 79–102

1. Benjamin Graham, *The Intelligent Investor* (1st ed. 1949, 4th rev. ed. Harper & Row, 1973), 68.
2. Tim Loughran and Jay R. Ritter, "The New Issues Puzzle," *Journal of Finance*, vol. 50 (1995); Jonathan A. Shayne and Larry D. Soderquist, "Inefficiency in the Market for Initial Public Offerings," *Vanderbilt Law Review*, vol. 48 (1995). Shayne and Soderquist computed the correlation of IPO volume to market exuberance for the period from 1970 to 1993 by comparing (a) IPO volume determined by dividing the total dollar amount of IPOs by the size of the national economy measured by gross domestic product (to accommodate for inflation and real growth in the national economy) to (b) market valuation measured by the multiple it accorded to dividends paid on the average stock, as compiled by the *Value Line Investment Survey*.
3. Shayne and Soderquist estimated stock-market overpricing by comparing returns yielded by a steady investment policy of buying equivalent amounts of a basket of seasoned securities annually, versus making purchases in proportion to the number of IPOs each year. Returns on the IPO-concentrated strategy lagged by 82%, suggesting that buyers of that portfolio would have paid about 22% too much (i.e., $1.00 − $0.82 / $0.82 = about 22%).
4. Kate Kelly, "Investors Discover Gravity As IPOs Return to Earth," *The Wall Street Journal*, March 7, 2001.
5. Shayne and Soderquist, *Inefficiency*.
6. *Morgan Stanley & Co., Inc. v. Archer Daniels Midland Co.*, 570 Federal Supplement 1529 (U.S. Southern District of New York, 1983); *Broad v. Rockwell International Corp.*, 642 Federal Reporter 2d 929 (U.S. Fifth Circuit Court of Appeals, 1981).
7. "D.H. Blair Ex-Broker Pleads Guilty to Charges of Stock Fraud in IPOs," *The Wall Street Journal*, June 6, 2001.
8. Kenneth N. Gilpin, "Shoe Designer Pleads Guilty To Charges of Stock Fraud," *The New York Times*, May 24, 2001.
9. John Labate, "Ex-Donna Karan Executive Fined," *The Financial Times*, August 3, 2001.
10. Randall Smith, "Client Brought Public in IPO Sues CSFB," *The Wall Street Journal*, June 5, 2001.
11. Graham, *Intelligent Investor*, 69, 39.
12. Barrie A. Wigmore, *The Crash and Its Aftermath* (Greenwood Press, 1985), 4–5, 26, 42–46, 248–250, 535.
13. Laurence Sloan, *Everyman and His Common Stocks* (McGraw-Hill, 1931), 241.

14. Graham, *Intelligent Investor*, 34.
15. *Ibid.*, 71.
16. Floyd Norris, "What Were Once Ladders Are Now Chutes," *The New York Times*, March 8, 2001.
17. Graham, *Intelligent Investor*, 70–71.
18. *Ibid.*, 71.
19. Peter Lynch and John Rothschild, *One Up On Wall Street* (1st ed. 1989; rev. ed. Fireside, 2000), 159.
20. A sampling of the research, in addition to those discussed below: Alon Brav, Christopher Geczy, and Paul Gompers, "Is the Abnormal Return Following Equity Issuances Anomalous?," *Duke University Working Paper* (1999); Kenneth Kim and Hyun-Han Shin, "The Underpricing of Seasoned Equity Offerings: 1983–1998," *Social Science Research Network Working Paper Series* (1999) (www.ssrn.com); Mark Bayless and Susan Chaplinsky, "Is There a Window of Opportunity for Seasoned Equity Issuance?," *Journal of Finance*, vol. 51 (1996); Michael Alderson and Brian Betker, "The Long-Run Performance of Companies that Withdraw Seasoned Equity Offerings," *Journal of Financial Research* (1999); Victor Soucik and David Allen, "Long Run Under-performance of Seasoned Equity Offerings: Fact or an Illusion?," *Social Science Research Network Working Paper Series* (1999) (www.ssrn.com).
21. Tim Loughran and Jay R. Ritter, "The Operating Performance of Firms Conducting Seasoned Equity Offerings," *Journal of Finance*, vol. 52 (1997).
22. Debra Katherine Spiess and John Felix Affleck-Graves, "Long-Run Stock Returns Following Seasoned Equity Offerings," *University of Notre Dame Working Paper Series* (1999).
23. Lawrence A. Cunningham, "Conversations from the Warren Buffett Symposium," *Cardozo Law Review*, vol. 19 (1997).
24. Gustavo Grullon, "The Information Content of Share Repurchase Programs" *Social Science Research Network Working Paper* (2000) (www.ssrn.com).
25. Daivd Ikenberry, Josef Lakonishok, and Theo Vermaelen, "Market Under-reaction to Open Market Share Repurchases," *Journal of Financial Economics*, vol. 39 (1995).
26. Securities and Exchange Commission Release No. 34-44791, "Emergency Order Pursuant to Section 12(k)(2) of the Securities Exchange Act of 1934 Taking Temporary Action to Respond to Market Developments" (September 14, 2001); Stephen Labaton, "S.E.C. Waives Some Rules to Try to Ease Market Volatility," *The New York Times*, September 15, 2001.
27. Michael Rapoport, "Numerous Companies Move to Buy Back Shares," *The Wall Street Journal*, September 18, 2001; Cassell Bryan-Low, "Firms Step Up By the Dozens With Buybacks," *The Wall Street Journal*, September 19, 2001.
28. Scott J. Weisbenner, "Corporate Share Repurchases in the 1990s: What Role Do Stock Options Play?," *Social Science Research Network Working Paper* (2000) (www.ssrn.com).
29. Robert Lohrer, "The CEO Was Only One of Warnaco's Troubles," *The Wall Street Journal*, June 18, 2001.

30. Anne Tergesen, "When Buybacks Are Signals to Buy," *Business Week*, October 1, 2001.
31. Aaron Elstein, "Battered Companies Do the Reverse Split," *The Wall Street Journal*, June 21, 2001.

Notes to Chapter 6, Corporate Spin, Pages 103–124

1. Andrea Petersen, "Motorola Cuts Forecasts and Jobs Again," *The Wall Street Journal*, September 7, 2001.
2. Peter Panepento, "CEO of Erie, Pa.-Based Rental Firm Responds to Message Board Comments," *Erie Times-News* (March 31, 2001).
3. Lynn E. Turner, "Accounting Irregularities II: What's an Audit Committee To Do?" (Speech, Atlanta, Georgia February 21, 2001) (available at www.sec.gov).
4. David Aboody and Ron Kasznick, "CEO Stock Option Awards and Corporate Voluntary Disclosures," *Social Science Research Network Working Paper Series* (www.ssrn.com) (November 1998); David Yermack, "Good Timing: CEO Stock Option Awards and Company News Announcements," *Journal of Finance*, vol. 52 (1997); Del Jones, "CEOs Might Time News Releases: Announcements Can Have Impact on Stock Options," *USA Today*, November 8, 1999.
5. This section is adapted with permission from my friends and colleagues Charles M. Yablon and Jennifer Hill, "Timing Corporate Disclosures to Maximize Performance-Based Remuneration: A Case of Misaligned Incentives?," *Wake Forest Law Review*, vol. 35 (2000).
6. The rule does not prohibit a company from making selective disclosure to the media, to rating agencies, in the ordinary course of business, or to professional advisors, such as lawyers and accountants, or others who expressly promise to keep the disclosure confidential.
7. Phyllis Plitch, "Dire Effects of Disclosure Rule Doubted," *The Wall Street Journal*, July 24, 2001; Frank Heflin, K.R. Subramanyam, and Yuan Zhang, "Regulation FD and the Financial Information Environment," *Social Science Research Network Working Paper Series* (2001) (www.ssrn.com).
8. PricewaterhouseCoopers, "Technology Barometer" (April 23, 2001); Association for Investment Management and Research, "Regulation FD e-Survey Summary" (January 31, 2001); Securities Industry Association, "Costs and Benefits of Regulation Fair Disclosure" (May 2001).
9. Michael Schroeder, "Lawmakers Urge Broad Inquiry Of Analysts, Securities Business," *The Wall Street Journal*, June 15, 2001.
10. Editorial, "Wall Street's Conflicted Research," *The New York Times*, June 15, 2001.
11. Karen Talley, "Probe Focuses on Legitimacy of Stock Advice From Analysts," *The Wall Street Journal*, June 7, 2001.
12. Securities Industry Association, *Best Practices for Research* (June 2001).
13. Karen Talley, "Levitt Expects Wall Street to Fall Short," *The Wall Street Journal*, July 24, 2001; Brian Lund, "Why Should We Trust Analysts Now?," *The Motley Fool* (June 13, 2001) (www.fool.com).
14. Securities and Exchange Commission Press Release, "SEC Cautions Investors About Analyst Recommendations," Release No. 2001-66 (June 28, 2001);

Securities and Exchange Commission, "Investor Alert: Analyzing Analyst Recommendations" (July 13, 2001); Jeff D. Opdyke, "SEC Issues 'Investor Alert' on Analysts' Reports," *The Wall Street Journal*, June 29, 2001.

15. Gretchen Morgenson, "Wall Street Firms Endorse Ethics Standards for Analysts." *The New York Times*, June 13, 2001.

16. Bloomberg News, "Morgan Requires Analysts' Disclosure," *The Wall Street Journal*, August 25, 2001.

17. Charles Gasparino and Jeff D. Opdyke, "Merrill Alters a Policy on Analysts," *The Wall Street Journal*, July 11, 2001.

18. Susanne Craig, "Credit Suisse Limits Holdings of Its Analysts," *The Wall Street Journal*, July 25. 2001.

19. Staff Reporter, "Edward D. Jones Puts Limits on Stock Owned by Analysts," *The Wall Street Journal*, July 12, 2001.

20. Avital Louria Hahn, "Bring on the Sells' Newest Twist: Some Street Firms Order Analysts to Go Negative," *Investment Dealers Digest*, September 10, 2001.

21. Colleen DeBaise "Judge Dismisses Lawsuits Against Analyst Meeker," *The Wall Street Journal*, August 22, 2001.

22. Jeff D. Opdyke, "Analysts' Reports: Don't Believe the Hype," *The Wall Street Journal*, July 10, 2001.

23. *Pludo v. Morgan Stanley Dean Witter & Co.*, 2001 U.S. Dist. LEXIS 12666 (SDNY August 21, 2001) (Milton Pollack, Senior United States District Judge).

24. Marc J. Epstein and Krishna G. Palepu, "What Financial Analysts Want," *Strategic Finance* (April 1999).

Notes to Chapter 7, The Winner's Curse, Pages 125–142

1. John H Fund "Bill's Book Deal: The Triumph of Hope Over History," *The Wall Street Journal* August 8, 2001.

2. David D. Kirkpatrick, "Publisher Will Pay Clinton Over $10 Million for Book," *The New York Times*, August 7, 2001; John H. Fund, "Bill's Book Deal: The Triumph of Hope Over History," *The Wall Street Journal*, August 8, 2001 (quoting Simon & Schuster head Michael Korda's comments on C-Span's "Booknotes" program).

3. Jeffrey Krames, "The Big Gamble on a Hillary Book," *The New York Times*, December 20, 2000.

4. Pekka Hietala, Steven N. Kaplan and David T. Robinson, "What is the Price of Hubris? Using Takeover Battles to Infer Overpayments and Synergies," *Social Science Research Network Working Paper* (July 18, 2000) (www.ssrn.com). This paper cites a University of Chicago Business School case note on Paramount by Mr. Kaplan indicating this valuation.

5. Geraldine Fabrikant, "Delaware Court Ruling Aids QVC in Struggle to Acquire Paramount," *The New York Times*, December 10, 1993 (front-page story quoting the author as saying "This is a stinging rebuke to the Paramount management and board for not taking shareholder rights seriously.").

6. For more on the duties boards in the situation of Paramount owe to their shareholders, consult Lawrence A. Cunningham and Charles M. Yablon, "Delaware

Fiduciary Duty Law after *QVC* and *Technicolor*: A Unified Standard (and the End of *Revlon* Duties?)," *The Business Lawyer*, vol. 49 (1994).

7. Hiatala, Kaplan and Robinson.

8. Redstone's 2001 biography emphasizes repeatedly his interest in winning, indicated by the book's title, *A Passion to Win*, and reflected in various reviews of the book by content and title, including Roger Lowenstein, "A Sore Winner's Play-By-Play," *The Wall Street Journal*, June 8, 2001.

9. This portion draws on Richard H. Thaler, "The Winner's Curse," *Journal of Economic Perspectives*, vol. 2 (1988) and Bernard S. Black, "Bidder Overpayment in Takeovers," *Stanford Law Review*, vol. 41 (1989).

10. Nikhil P. Varaiya, "The 'Winner's Curse' Hypothesis and Corporate Takeovers," *Managerial and Decision Economics*, vol. 9 (1988).

11. James F. Nielsen and Ronald W. Melicher, "A Financial Analysis of Acquisition and Merger Premiums," *Journal of Financial and Quantitative Analysis*, vol. 8 (1973).

12. Black.

13. *Outstanding Investor Digest* (December 29, 1998) (quoting remarks of Charles T. Munger, Chairman, Wesco Financial, annual meeting).

14. Charles T. Munger, *Wesco Financial Annual Report* (1989) (also giving the list of deals from the 1980s noted).

15. Peter Lynch and John Rothschild, *One Up On Wall* Street (1st ed. 1989; rev. ed. Fireside, 2000), 14.

16. Standard accounting textbooks provide more specifics, including one I wrote for nonaccountants: Lawrence A. Cunningham, *Introductory Accounting and Finance for Lawyers* (2d ed. West Group, 1999), Chapter 12.

17. Thor Valdmanis, "Big Names Feel Pain of Goodwill: Rules Change Means Many Forced Into Huge Write-Downs," *USA Today*, August 1, 2001.

18. Aaron Elstein, "Heard on the Street: Firms Fatten Up Profit Outlooks on FASB Rule," *The Wall Street Journal*, August 21, 2001.

Notes to Chapter 8, Corporate Ebonics, Pages 143–162

1. Financial Executives International, "Financial Reporting Quality" (June 2001), reported in Jonathan Weil, "Restatement of Earnings Have Multiplied," *The Wall Street Journal*, June 7, 2001.

2. The discussion of Enron draws substantially on the company's press release and public filings made with the Securities and Exchange Commission on November 8, 2001, the substance of which was confirmed in a subsequent report by a special independent committee of the company's board of directors dated February 1, 2002, filed with the federal court overseeing Enron's bankruptcy proceeding. Press Release, "Enron Provides Additional Information About Related Party and Off-Balance Sheet Transactions; Company to Restate Earnings of 1997-2001," November 8, 2001; Enron, Report on Form 8-K filed with the Securities and Exchange Commission, November 8, 2001; "Report of Investigation by the Special Investigative Committee of the Board of Directors of Enron Corp." (William C. Powers, Chairman; Raymond S. Troubh; and Herbert S. Winokur, Jr.), February 1, 2002.

3. Queena Sook Kim, "Rent-Way Details Improper Bookkeeping," *The Wall Street Journal*, June 8, 2001.
4. Chris Gaither "Critical Path Suspends 2 Executives and Starts Financial Inquiry," *The New York Times*, February 3, 2001; Chris Gaither, "Critical Path Says Problems Were Limited to One Quarter," *The New York Times*, March 5, 2001; Critical Path 1st Quarter 2001 Conference Call (May 14, 2001), http://biz.yahoo.com/cc/0/6560.html (listened to on June 8, 2001).
5. James Bandler and Mark Maremont, "Seeing Red: How Ex-Accountant Added up to Trouble For Humbled Xerox," *The Wall Street Journal*, June 28, 2001.
6. Some others are dissected and some lessons drawn in my book, *How To Think Like Benjamin Graham and Invest Like Warren Buffett* (McGraw-Hill, 2001), 153–168.
7. For example, consult *American Heritage Dictionary* (Houghton Mifflin, 2d ed. 1985), 30–33 (debate: "Resolved: The prevailing usage of its speakers should be the chief determinant of acceptability in language," with dueling essays by Dwight Bolinger (for the affirmative) and William F. Buckley, Jr. (for the negative)).
8. Mark Bradshaw, Matthew Moberg, and Richard G. Sloan, "GAAP versus the Street: An Empirical Assessment of Two Alternative Definitions of Earnings," *Accounting Scholarship Network Working Paper* (www.ssrn.com).
9. Jonathan Weil, "What's the P/E Ratio? Well, Depends on What Is Meant by Earnings" *The Wall Street Journal*, August 21, 2001.
10. Lynn E Turner, "Accounting Irregularities II: What's an Audit Committee To Do?" (Speech, Atlanta, Georgia February 21, 2001) (available at www.sec.gov).
11. Leopold A. Bernstein and John J. Wild, *Analysis of Financial Statements* (5th ed. McGraw-Hill, 2000), 155–62.
12. Laura Johannes, "No Accounting for the Net," *The Wall Street Journal*, May 19, 2000.
13. *In re Staples, Inc. Shareholders Litigation*, 2001 Del. Ch. LEXIS 79.
14. Joseph T. Halinan, "Devine Guidance," *The Wall Street Journal*, August 8, 2001. The Conseco shareholder was financier Irwin L. Jacobs.
15. Floyd Norris, "Conseco's Performance Isn't the Stuff of Sonnets," *The New York Times*, August 8, 2001; Conseco 2nd Quarter 2001 Conference Call (August 7, 2001), available from http://www.corporate-ir.net/ireye/ir_site.zhtml?ticker=CNC&script=2400 (listened to on August 7, 2001).
16. Bradshaw, Moberg and Sloan.
17. Alex Berenson, "More Than One Way of Looking at Software Maker's Earnings," *The New York Times*, May 23, 2001.
18. Conference call archived as Webcast, available through the Corporate Associates's Web site http://ca.com/invest/disclaimer.htm (May 22, 2001, Replay of the Webcast – FY2001 Earnings Announcement (RealVideo 83min. 31 sec.) listened to June 8, 2001).
19. Steve Liesman "Heard on the Street: Nascaq Companies' Losses Erase 5 Years of Profit," *The Wall Street Journal* (August 16, 2001).
20. Securities and Exchange Commission, "'Pro Forma' Financial Information: Tips for Investors," December 4, 2001.

21. Securities and Exchange Commission, Release Nos. 33-8039, 34-45124, FR-59, "Cautionary Advice Regarding the Use of '*Pro Forma*' Financial Information in Earnings Releases," December 4, 2001.
22. David Henry, "Cover Story: The Numbers Game," *Business Week*, May 14, 2001; Jonathan Weil, "What's the P/E Ratio? Well, Depends on What Is Meant by Earnings," *The Wall Street Journal*, August 21, 2001.
23. This material is mainly taken and adapted from *Rite Aid Corp. Securities Litigation*, 139 Federal Supplement 2d 649 (E.D. Pa. April 17, 2001), with some facts drawn from Mark Maremont, "Lawsuit Details Rite Aid's Accounting Woes," *The Wall Street Journal*, February 8, 2001.
24. Abraham J. Briloff, "Garbage In, Garbage Out: A Critique of the COSO Report and the SEC AAERs" (2000) (quoting from testimony of Briloff before a Senate Committee chaired by Sam Nunn).
25. Robert A. Prentice, "The Case of the Irrational Auditor: A Behavioral Insight into Securities Fraud Litigation," *Northwestern University Law Review*, vol. 95 (2000).
26. Karl Schoenberger, "When the Numbers Just Don't Add Up," *The New York Times*, August 19, 2001 (reporting studies prepared by Arthur Andersen and PricewaterhouseCoopers).

Notes to Chapter 9, Mind Games, Pages 165–179

1. The discussion of John Bennett and New Era draws on *United States v. Bennett*, 161 Federal Reporter 3d 171 (3d Circuit 1998); Evelyn Brody, "The Limits of Charity Fiduciary Law," *Maryland Law Review*, vol. 57 (1998); and Joseph Slobodzian, *National Law Journal*, March 17, 1997.
2. Roger Lowenstein, "Why Gurus Weren't Wise to New Era's Wiles," *The Wall Street Journal*, May 25, 1995.
3. The discussion of boiler room draws on Securities and Exchange Commission, "Investor Alert: Cold Calling—Unsolicited Calls From Brokers," September 28, 2000.
4. The discussion of Gartner is adapted from the facts set forth in *Securities and Exchange Commission v. InterLink Data Network of Los Angeles, Inc.*, Federal Securities Law Reporter, *Commerce Clearing House*, 98,049 (Central Federal District Court of California, 1993).
5. James S. Granelli, "O.C. Man Who Sold Bogus Securities Must Pay $8 Million," *The Los Angeles Times*, June 4, 1997.
6. The discussion of prime bank fraud draws on Securities and Exchange Commission, "Investor Alert: How Prime Bank Fraud Works," September 15, 2000.
7. The discussion of affinity fraud draws on Securities and Exchange Commission, "Investor Alert: Affinity Fraud—How to Avoid Investment Scams that Target Groups," March 15, 2001.
8. Judith Burns, "Swindlers Prey on the Devoted, Regulators Say," *The Wall Street Journal*, August 13, 2001.

9. *Ibid.*

10. Brenton R. Schlender, "Religion and Loyal Investors Play Big Role in Alleged Trading Fraud," *The Wall Street Journal*, September 20, 1985.

11. "Antifraud: Religious Group Members Vulnerable to 'Affinity Fraud,'" *Bureau of National Affairs Securities Law Daily*, September 2, 1999.

12. Earl C. Gottschalk, Jr., "Churchgoers Are the Prey as Scams Rise," *The Wall Street Journal*, August 7, 1989.

13. Randall Smith, "Loss-Plagued Baptist Foundation of Arizona Undergoes Investigation by Regulators in State," *The Wall Street Journal*, September 1, 1999.

14. Riva D. Atlas, "Why Juan Won't Use Banks to Save; Financial Services Industry Fails to Reach Many Hispanics," *The New York Times*, June 20, 2001; Paulette Thomas, "Investing Survey Shows Race Plays a Part," *The Wall Street Journal*, June 6, 2001.

15. The discussion of advance fee fraud draws on U.S. Secret Service, "Public Awareness Advisory Regarding '4-1-9' or 'Advance Fee Fraud' Schemes" (undated).

16. Douglas Cruickshank, "I Crave Your Distinguished Indulgence (and All Your Cash)," *Salon.com*, August 7, 2001.

On February 5, 2002, the author of this book received the following e-mail (with the punctuation and syntax as indicated):

Date: Tue, 5 Feb 2002 07:01:22 -0800 (PST)
From: "Frank Odion" <franodion@yahoo.com> |
Block Address | Add to Address Book
Subject: STRICTLY CONFIDENTIAL AND URGENT
To: franodion@yahoo.com
FRANK ODION
FOREIGN LIAISON OFFICER
NIGERIAN NATIONAL PETROLEUM CORPORATION
AMSTERDAM, THE NETHERLANDS
STRICTLY CONFIDENTIAL AND URGENT
ATTN: THE PRESIDENT/CEO

I am an executive accountant with the Nigerian National Petroleum Corporation (NNPC) and I am also a member of the Federal Government of Nigeria Contract Award and Monitoring Committee in the Nigerian National Petroleum Corporation. I am on a special diplomatic duty in the Nigeria Foreign Office in Amsterdam the Netherlands.

It is a pleasure involving you in this project. Sometime ago, a contract was awarded to a foreign firm in NNPC by my committee. This contract was over invoiced to the tune of US$21.5M. This was done deliberately. The over invoicing was a Deal by my committee to benefit from the project. We now desire to transfer this money which is in a Suspense Account with NNPC in any Oversea Account which we expect you to provide for us. For providing the account where we shall remit the money, you will be entitled to 30% of the money, 5% for incidental expenses incurred both locally and internationally to secure the funds successfully into your nominated account while the remaining 65% will be for my partners and me.

I would require the following:

1. Banker's Name and Address
2. Telephone and Fax Number of Bankers
3. Sort/ABA/Routing Number of Bankers
4. Account Number
5. Name of Beneficiary/Company Name/Address
6. Telephone and Fax Numbers of Beneficiary

The above information would be used to make formal application as a matter of procedure for the Release of the money and onward transfer to your account. It does not matter whether or not your Company does contract projects of this nature described here, the assumption is that your company Won the major contract and subcontracted it out to other companies. More often than not, big Trading companies or firms of unrelated fields win major contracts and subcontract to more specialized firms for execution of such contracts.

We have strong and reliable connections and contacts at the Apex Bank and Federal Ministry of Finance and we have no doubt that all this Money will be released and transferred if we get the necessary foreign partner to assist us in this Deal. Therefore, when the business is successfully concluded we shall through our connections withdraw all documents used from all the concerned Government Ministries for 100% Security. We are civil servants and we will not want to miss this opportunity.

Please contact me immediately through my E-mail address, whether or not you are interested in this deal. If you are not, it will enable me to scout for another foreign partner to carry out this deal. But where you are interested, send the required documents aforementioned Herein without delay as time is of the essence in this business.

I await in anticipation of your fullest co-operation.

Yours faithfully,

FRANK ODION

17. Homer, *The Odyssey* (T.E. Shaw trans., Woodsworth Editions Ltd., 1992), 170.

Notes to Chapter 10, Living With Emotions, pages 181–200

1. Benjamin Franklin, *Writings* (1st ed. 1772; rev. ed. 1987). Here is Franklin's decision-making advice written in a letter to his friend Joseph Priestly:

Dear Sir,

In the affair of so much importance to you, wherein you ask my advice, I cannot, for want of sufficient premises, advise you what to determine, but if you please, I will tell you how.

When these difficult cases occur, they are difficult chiefly because while we have them under consideration, all the reasons pro and con are not present to the mind at the same time; but sometimes some set present themselves, and at other times another, the first being out of sight. Hence the various purposes or inclinations that alternatively prevail, and the uncertainty that perplexes us.

To get over this, my way is to divide half a sheet of paper by a line into two columns; writing over the one pro, and over the other con. Then during three or four days, consideration, I put down under the different heads short hints of the different motives that at different times occur to me, for or against the measure.

When I have thus got them all together in one view, I endeavor to estimate their respective weights; and where I find two, one on each side, that seem equal, I strike them both out. If I find a reason pro equal to two reasons con, I strike out the three. If I judge some two reasons con, equal to some three reasons pro, I strike out the five; and thus proceeding I find at length where the balance lies; and if, after a day or two of further consideration, nothing new that is of importance occurs on either side, I come to a determination accordingly.

And, though the weight of reasons cannot be taken with the precision of algebraic quantities, yet when each is thus considered, separately and comparatively, and the whole lies before me, I think I can judge better, and am less liable to make a rash step, and in fact I have found great advantage from this kind of equation, in what may be called moral or prudential algebra.

Wishing sincerely that you may determine for the best, I am ever, my dear friend, yours most affectionately.

B. Franklin

2. Modern decision experts refer to this as preparing a consequences table. John S. Hammond, Ralph L. Keeney, and Howard Raiffa, *Smart Choices: A Practical Guide to Making Better Decisions* (Harvard Business School Press, 1999), 69–90.
3. David Leonhardt, "If Richer Isn't Happier, What Is?," *The New York Times*, May 19, 2001.
4. Herbert A. Simon, "Rational Choice and the Structure of the Environment," *Psychological Review*, vol. 63 (1956).
5. Irving Fisher, *The Theory of Interest* (McMillan, 1930).
6. Several of these examples are mentioned in Charles T. Munger, "Lecture," *Outstanding Investor Digest* (December 29, 1997), 24–25.
7. Warren Buffett, "Track Record is Everything," *Across the Board* (October 1991), 58.
8. Lela Lopes, "Between Hope and Fear: The Psychology of Risk," *Advances in Experimental Social Psychology* (1987).
9. Hammond, Keeney, and Raiffa, *Smart Choices*, 38–39.
10. Joachim Goldberg and Rüdiger Nitzsch, *Behavioral Finance* (German ed. 1999; Eng. trans. John Wiley & Sons, 2001), 167.

11. Robert Shiller, *Irrational Exuberance* (Princeton University Press, 2000), 52–55; Benjamin Graham, *The Intelligent Investor* (1st ed. 1949; 4 th rev. ed. Harper & Row, 1973), 122.
12. Daniel Kahneman and Mark W. Riepe, "Aspects of Investor Psychology," *The Journal of Portfolio Management*, vol. 24 (1998).
13. *Ibid.*
14. Amos Tversky and Daniel Kahneman, "Evidential Impact of Base Rates," in Daniel Kahneman, et al., eds., *Judgment Under Uncertainty: Heuristics and Biases* (Cambridge University Press, 1982), 151, 156–58.
15. Respectively: Shiller, *Irrational Exuberance*, 144; Amos Tversky and Daniel Kahneman, "Judgments of and by Representativeness," in *Judgment Under Uncertainty*, 84, 92–93.
16. These Web sites contain worksheets seeking the information elicited in brokerage forms:

financeware.com	quicken.com	decisioneering.com
troweprice.com	bankofamerica.com	fidelity.com
scudder.com	vankampen.com	csbsmarketwatch.com
vanguard.com	thestreet.com	

17. All these aspects of valuation are discussed at length in my book, *How To Think Like Benjamin Graham and Invest Like Warren Buffett* (McGraw-Hill, 2001).
18. Bernhard Borges, et al., "Can Ignorance Beat the Stock Market?," in Gerd Gigerenzer and Peter M. Todd, *Simple Heuristics That Make Us Smart* (Oxford University Press, 1999).

Notes to Chapter 11, Investor Evolution, Pages 201–220

1. Charles Darwin, *The Autobiography of Charles Darwin, 1809–1882* (1st ed. 1887; rev. ed. N. Barlow, 1969).
2. Joachim Goldberg and Rüdiger Nitzsch, *Behavioral Finance* (German ed. 1999; Eng. trans. John Wiley & Sons, 2001), 125–150.
3. Keith E. Stanovich and Richard F. West, "Individual Differences in Reasoning: Implications for the Rationality Debate?," *Brain and Behavioral Sciences*, vol. 22 (2000).
4. For a book he edited, British business-book purveyor Philip Jenks asked me to furnish a list of the top-10 investment lessons I could glean from the long-term value tradition epitomized by Benjamin Graham and Warren Buffett, and this is substantially what I came up with. Philip Jenks and Stephen Eckett (eds.), *The Global-Investor Book of Investing Rules: Invaluable Advice From 150 Master Investors* (Harriman House, 2001), 95–96.
5. Shlomo Benzarti and Richard H. Thaler, "Myopic Loss Aversion and the Equity Risk Premium Puzzle," *Quarterly Journal of Economics*, vol. 110 (1995).
6. Werner DeBondt and Richard H. Thaler, "Does the Stock Market Overreact?," *Journal of Finance*, vol. 40 (1985).
7. Daniel Kahneman and Mark W. Riepe, "Aspects of Investor Psychology," *The Journal of Portfolio Management*, vol. 24 (1998).

8. Charles T. Munger, "Lecture," *Outstanding Investor Digest* (March 13, 1998), 58.

9. Jason Zweig, "Do You Sabotage Yourself?," *Money* (May, 2001)

10. Edward E. Joyce and Gary C. Biddle, "Anchoring and Adjustment in Probabilistic Inference in Auditing," *Journal of Accounting Research*, vol. 19 (1981).

11. *Ibid.* Baruch Fischhoff, "Hindsight is Not Equal to Foresight: The Effect of Outcome Knowledge on Judgment Under Uncertainty," *Journal of Experimental Psychology*, vol. 1 (1975).

12. Kahneman and Liepe, "Aspects of Investor Psychology."

13. Jonathan Fuerbringer, "Investors Jolted as Stocks Tumble Sharply After 3 Days," *The New York Times*, March 30, 2001.

14. "Be A Better Investor," *Money* (May, 2001) (reporting study by Paul Andreassen).

15. I give the following example in my book, *How To Think Like Benjamin Graham and Invest Like Warren Buffett* (McGraw-Hill, 2001), 74–75:

    Suppose you invest $200 per month in Procter & Gamble during 3 months when its stock price on the purchase dates was $80, $120, and $100, respectively. The average price during that period was $100 (80 + 120 +100 divided by 3). But your average cost would have been $97 (you would have acquired 2.5 shares at $80; 1.66 shares at $120; and 2 shares at $100, so you have invested $600 and acquired 6.16 shares).

16. Jonathan Clements, "Getting Going: 'Sector Funds' Need a Warning Label," *The Wall Street Journal*, August 14, 2001.

17. The discussion of the Beardstown Ladies saga is taken from a California judge's opinion in one of two class action lawsuits brought by buyers of the books. *Keimer v. Buena Vista Books, Inc.*, 75 Cal. App. 4th 1220, 89 Cal. Rptr. 2d 781 (1999). The other lawsuit was brought in New York *Lacoff v. Buena Vista Publishing, Inc.*,183 Misc. 2d 600; 705 N.Y.S.2d 183 (N.Y. Sup. 2000).

18. NAIC Online Beardstown Ladies and Club Accounting (March 25, 1998) summarizes rate of return calculations developed for investment clubs by the NAIC with EasyWare Software Inc., available at http://www.better-investing.org/clubs/lacies.html.

19. Thomas E. O'Hara and Kenneth S. Janke, Sr., *Starting and Running a Profitable Investment Club: The Official Guide from the National Association of Investors Corporation* (Times Business, 1998), 237.

20. *Ibid.*, 7–9.

21. *Ibid.*, 161.

22. This discussion draws on Stephen Bainbridge, "Why A Board?," *Social Science Research Network* (Working Paper, 2001).

23. Thomas Gilovich, *How We Know What Isn't So: The Fallibility of Human Reason In Everyday Life* (The Free Press, 1991), 58. Linus Pauling (1901–1994) is the only person to win two undivided Nobel Prizes–Chemistry in 1954 and Peace in 1962 (Marie S. Curie won for Chemistry in 1911 and shared the Prize in Physics for 1903). http://www.nobel.se.

24. Marjorie E. Shaw, "Comparison of Individuals and Small Groups in the Rational Solution of Complex Problems," *American Journal of Psychiatry*, vol. 44 (1932).

25. Alan S. Blinder and John Morgan, "Are Two Heads Better than One? An Experimental Analysis of Group Versus Individual Decision Making," *National Bureau of Economic Affairs Working Paper No. 7909* (September, 2000).
26. Gayle W. Hill, "Group Versus Individual Performance: Are N + 1 Heads Better than One?," *Psychology Bulletin*, vol. 91 (1982).
27. Frederick C. Miner, Jr., "Group Versus Individual Decision Making: An Investigation of Performance Measures, Decision Strategies, and Process Losses/Gains," *Organizational Behavior and Human Performance*, vol. 33 (1984); Starr Roxanne Hiltz et al., "Experiments in Group Decision Making: Communication Process and Outcome in Face-to-Face Versus Computerized Conferences," *Human Communication Research*, vol. 13 (1986).
28. Ernest Hall et al., "Group Problem Solving Effectiveness Under Conditions of Pooling Versus Interaction," *Journal of Social Psychology*, vol. 59 (1963).
29. D. Kravitz and B. Martin, "Ringelmann Rediscovered: The Original Article," *Journal of Personality and Social Psychology*, vol. 50 (1986).
30. *Ibid.*, 163.
31. Lynn Cowan and Cheryl Winokur Munk, "Investment Clubs Shift to More Cautious Strategy," *The Wall Street Journal*, June 11, 2001.
32. The founder of modern security analysis and renowned investment theorist Benjamin Graham said that if forced to distill the key to investment success into three words they would be "margin of safety." Benjamin Graham, The Intelligent Investor (1st ed. 1949; 4th rev. ed. Harper & Row, 1973), 277. Generations of his students, most notably Warren Buffett, concur. Warren E. Buffett and Lawrence A. Cunningham, *The Essays of Warren Buffett: Lessons for Corporate America* (1st ed. 1997; rev. ed. The Cunningham Group, 2001), 105, 88. Note also Subrata N. Chakravarty, "Three Little Words," *Forbes*, April 6, 1998.

Notes to Chapter 12, The Opposite of Cool, Pages 221–238

1. Edward Chancellor, *Devil Take the Hindmost: A History of Financial Speculation* (Plume, 1999), 136.
2. Warren E. Buffett and Lawrence A. Cunningham, *The Essays of Warren Buffett: Lessons for Corporate America* (1st ed. 1997, rev. ed. The Cunningham Group, 2001), 205.
3. The discussion of Desmond draws on these sources: Alan Oscroft, "Fool's Eye View: Wise Lessons," *The Motley Fool UK*, January 24, 2000; Interview, "Online Brokers on the Hot Seat," *TechTV* (2001); "Who's On Call?," *Financial Planning Interactive*, January 26, 2000.
4. Gretchen Morgenson, "Buying on Margin Becomes a Habit," *The New York Times*, March 24, 2000.
5. Dow Jones Newswires, "Minus a Big Rebound, Today Could Bring Some Margin Calls," *The Wall Street Journal*, September 18, 2001.
6. Cassell Bryan-Low, "Inside Track: Margin Calls Hit Some Tech Executives," *The Wall Street Journal*, February 7, 2001.

7. Dow Jones Newswires, September 18, 2001.

8. Aaron Elstein and Stacy Forster, "NYSE Hits Day Traders With Tighter Margin Rule," *The Wall Street Journal*, August 27, 2001.

9. Susanne Craig, "Regulators Zap Day-Trading Guru Houtkin And All-Tech," *The Wall Street Journal*, June 14, 2001.

10. United States Senate, "Day Trading: An Overview," Hearing Before the Permanent Subcommittee on Governmental Affairs, 106th Congress, 1st Session, September 16, 1999.

11. Nelson D. Schwartz, "Can't Keep a Good Day Trader Down," *Fortune*, February 19, 2001.

12. Daniel Kahneman and Mark W. Riepe, "Aspects of Investor Psychology," *The Journal of Portfolio Management*, vol. 24 (1998); Shlomo Benartzi and Richard H. Thaler, "Myopic Loss Aversion and the Equity Risk Premium Puzzle," *Quarterly Journal of Economics*, vol. 110 (1995).

13. Charles D. Ellis and James R. Vertin, *Wall Street People* (John Wiley & Sons, 2001), 31–41

14. Andrew Meinck, "George Doriot and the Birth of Venture Capital," *The Financial Times*, July 2, 2001 (citing study by George W. Fenn, Nellie Liang, and David Prowse, "The Private Equity Industry: An Overview").

15. Monica McGlinchey and John Taylor, "Investors Continue to Show Interest in Early Stage Funds," *Thomson Financial Securities Data*, April 15, 2001.

16. Michael C. Ferkins and Celia Nunez, "Why Market Insiders Don't Feel Your Pain," *The Washington Post*, March 15, 2001.

17. Robert Cialdini, *Influence: Science and Practice* (3d ed. Harper Collins, 1993).

18. Ian Springsteel, "VC for Everyman: Firms Lure a New Class of Investors, But Will They Get Burned?," *Investment Dealers Digest*, August 7, 2000.

19. John T. Noonan, Jr., *The Scholastic Analysis of Usury* (Harvard University Press, 1957).

20. Thomas E. O'Hara and Kenneth S. Janke, Sr., *Starting and Running a Profitable Investment Club: The Official Guide from the National Association of Investors Corporation* (Times Business, 1998), 232.

Notes to Conclusion, Pages 239–244

1. George A. Akerlof, "The Market for Lemons," *Quarterly Journal of Economics*, vol. 84 (1970). Akerlof was a forerunner of the discipline that later emerged under the name behavioral economics. Along with Joseph Stiglitz and Michael Spence, he won the Nobel Prize in Economics in 2001.

2. Partners in this mission range from governmental agencies, such as the Departments of Labor and Justice, the Federal Trade Commission, and the Social Security Administration, to trade groups, such as the Securities Industry Association, the American Association of Retired Persons (AARP) and the National Association of Securities Dealers, and quasipublic bodies, such as the New York Stock Exchange. See www.investoreducation.org.

3. Savings Are Vital to Everyone's Retirement Act of 1997, 29 U.S.C. §§ 1146-47 (Supp 1997) (SAVER Act).

4. Letter from the U.S. Department of Labor to the House Subcommittee on Employer-Employee Relations of the House Committee on Education and the Workforce, "Opportunities to Improve DOL's SAVER Act Campaign," *Federal Document Clearing House, Inc.*, June 6, 2001.
5. SAVER Act, § 1146(c)(2)(E)-(F).
6. Lawrence A. Cunningham, *How To Think Like Benjamin Graham and Invest Like Warren Buffett* (McGraw-Hill, 2001), 75–77.
7. "A Screaming Buy?," *The Wall Street Journal*, July 27, 2001. The firm was Legg Mason of Baltimore. On further reflection, the firm thought better of it and opted instead for an investor silhouetted before a row of colorful computer modules, all screaming muted.
8. Ronald Alsop, "Survey Rates Companies' Reputations, and Many Are Found Wanting," *The Wall Street Journal*, February 7, 2001.

Index

Note: Boldface numbers indicate illustrations.

About the Author

Lawrence A. Cunningham is a professor at New York's Cardozo Law School, director of the school's Samuel and Ronnie Heyman Center on Corporate Governance, and professor of law and business at Boston College. The author of bestsellers including *The Essays of Warren Buffett* and *How to Think Like Benjamin Graham and Invest Like Warren Buffett*, Cunningham has been featured in *Forbes* and *Money*, as well as on CNBC, CNN, and PBS's *The News Hour* with Jim Lehrer.